Hugo Canedo
George Trombley

Spanish From Zero! Update 1.1

Proven Methods to Learn Spanish with Integrated Workbook

PREFACE

Spanish From Zero! is a Spanish language book series built on Spanish grammar that makes sense! Each book is crafted page by page and lesson by lesson to have relevant (and sometimes fun) Spanish conversation and sentence structure patterns that enhance the Spanish learner's ability to speak Spanish faster, and understand the small nuances of gender, plurality, and everyday Spanish speech.

DEDICATION

This book series is dedicated and made for:

Spanish culture lovers, Spanish language learners, Spanish soap opera watchers, Spanish beginners, latin music fans, people of Spanish heritage connecting to their history, and anyone planning travel to Spain, Mexico, or other Spanish speaking country!

For the last 27 years I've been writing language textbooks. But it wasn't until co-author Hugo Canedo strongly suggested we do a Spanish book that I finally relented and began this project. Going in I thought it would be easy since my entire life I had heard that Spanish was easy. But I learned the hard way that Spanish has a lot more intricacies than I initially thought. I'm so fortunate to have worked with a great co-author Hugo Canedo who was able to artfully, and sometimes while I yelled at him, calmly teach me how Spanish works.

All of us on the Spanish From Zero! team wish you success on your road to Spanish fluency and hope this book is a solid first step!

COPYRIGHT / TRADEMARKS

Printed in USA / England / Australia (and other territories) ISBN-13: 978-1959949091

1st edition - May 2026
Update 1.1 - minor corrections - June 2026

DISTRIBUTION

Distributed in the USA & Canada by:
From Zero LLC (publisher)
10624 S. Eastern Ave. #A769
Henderson, NV 89052, USA
sales@fromzero.com

Distributed in the UK & Europe by:
Bay Language Books Ltd.
Unit 4, Kingsmead, Park Farm,
Folkestone, Kent. CT19 5EU, Great Britain
sales@baylanguagebooks.co.uk

Spanish From Zero! ®
Book 1

– CONTENTS –

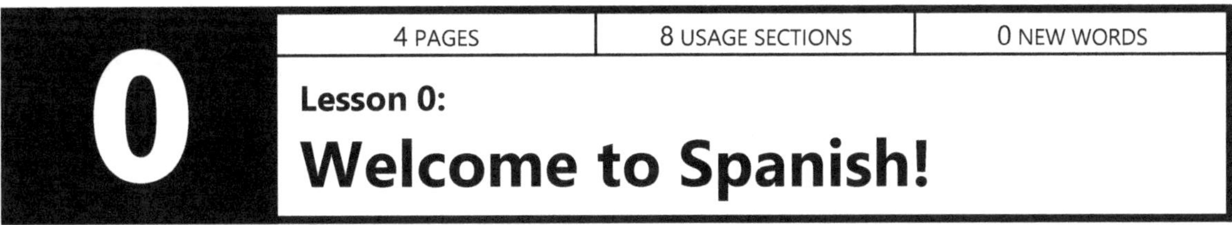

0 Getting Started *Empezando*

● 0-1. Lesson order

This book is designed to be read in order. It's okay to skip around after you've been through it, but if you skip around, you might end up with questions and misunderstandings you wouldn't have if you had followed the order we crafted.

● 0-2. About how we created the book

Usage of AI

No AI was used to write any content in this book. Every word was personally crafted by Hugo and me (George). Each grammar was debated, refined, and built from our human brains. Additionally, multiple reviews were done by living Spanish teachers and not AI.

The one usage of AI in this book is the music for a verb conjugation song that we personally wrote lyrics for. There was significant debate if we should keep it in the book, but I thought the song was helpful so I decided it was worth any anti-AI backlash.

The book art

The Spanish character on the cover was drawn and designed by our staff artist Silt. The internal art in the book is a mix of staff artist Haruna, Silt or crafted by us using licensed clipart. We never use art created by AI even from the sites we license.

Typos and errors

Since, as we mentioned, this book is completely human-created, occasionally you might see typos or other unintentional errors despite our best efforts to eliminate them. We would love to hear about them so we can fix them. In the event that you do find any issues, please let us know here: **https://learnfz.com/SFZ1errors**

● 0-3. Our method

This book assumes that you haven't learned any Spanish prior to this book. We actually assume you haven't studied ANY language. It's designed to walk you through the basics of Spanish while building off of the prior lessons and only using words and concepts taught in those preceding lessons.

0 Welcome *Bienvenido*

0-4. Welcome to Spanish!

The good news about Spanish is that because it's closely related to English, it will most likely be easier than other languages such as Japanese or Chinese. However, that being said, it's not as easy as many English speakers think.

If you live in America, you will fortunately have access to many native Spanish speakers to practice your Spanish with. Of course with the internet, everyone has access to Spanish speaking media which will help you build your listening skills.

Once you can understand Spanish an entire new world will open up for you. Imagine traveling to Mexico, Spain, Argentina, or other Spanish speaking countries and enjoying their rich culture without an English filter. Traveling to a country when you can speak its language is a much more enjoyable experience!

Okay! Enough dream building... let's get to work!

0-5. A world of Spanish

Spanish is the 2nd most commonly spoken language when counting just native speakers. It's the official, or most commonly spoken language in 20 countries and the United States territory, Puerto Rico. Just like English has regional differences in the United States or the United Kingdom, Spanish also has slight variations depending on where it's spoke. Normally this is limited to words unique to that area's culture and or history.

While there are minor differences in Spanish depending on the country, this book will focus on a "general" Spanish understood in all Spanish speaking countries. Even with regional differences in Spanish, most foreign language movies and TV shows (from America, Japan etc.) are dubbed in Mexican Spanish, which is considered the standard.

At times there may be a slight lean towards Mexican Spanish, as it's the most popular variant and the co-author of the book is from Mexico. From time to time we will point out key differences in other Spanish variants.

Here you can see just how many people and how many countries speak Spanish.

Country	Population	Spanish Variant Spoken	Location
Mexico	130,207,371	Mexican Spanish	North America
Colombia	50,355,650	Colombian Spanish	South America
Spain	47,260,584	Peninsular Spanish	Southern Europe

Argentina	45,864,941	Rioplatense Spanish	South America
Peru	32,201,224	Peruvian Ribereño Spanish	South America
Venezuela	29,069,153	Venezuelan Spanish	South America
Chile	18,307,925	Chilean Spanish	South America
Guatemala	17,422,821	Guatemalan Spanish	Central America
Ecuador	17,093,159	Ecuadorian Spanish	South America
Bolivia	11,758,869	Bolivian Spanish	South America
Cuba	11,032,343	Cuban Spanish	The Caribbean *
Dominican Republic	10,597,348	Dominican Spanish	The Caribbean
Honduras	9,346,277	Honduran Spanish	Central America
Paraguay	7,272,639	Paraguayan Spanish	South America
El Salvador	6,528,135	Salvadoran Spanish	Central America
Nicaragua	6,243,931	Nicaraguan Spanish	Central America
Costa Rica	5,151,140	Costa Rican Spanish	Central America
Panama	3,928,646	Panamanian Spanish	Central America
Puerto Rico	3,142,779	Uruguayan Spanish	The Caribbean
Uruguay	3,398,239	Puerto Rican Spanish	South America
Equatorial Guinea	1,468,777	Equatoguinean Spanish	Central Africa
Total	467,651,951		
Source: https://en.wikipedia.org/wiki/List_of_countries_where_Spanish_is_an_official_language			

0-6. Common misconceptions

Latin America is a term for countries in North, Central, and South America where the majority of the spoken languages are Latin based such as Spanish and Portuguese.

And since the majority of Spanish spoken is concentrated in Latin America, let's take a moment to dispel some common misconceptions about Latin America.

MYTH #1 **Spain has the largest population of Spanish speakers**

As you can see in the chart above, the country with the largest Spanish-speaking population is Mexico, followed by Colombia, and not Spain as some might think.

MYTH #2 **Mexico is in South America**

It's easy to think of everything below the United States as South America, but Mexico is considered part of North America. Below Mexico is Central America, and Colombia is at the top of South America and is the second most populous Spanish speaking country.

MYTH #3 **Brazil is a Spanish speaking country**

It's a common misconception that because Brazil is in South America, it's a Spanish speaking country. However, Brazil was a colony of Portugal and as a result its official language is Portuguese, with over 205 million speakers. After you learn Spanish, Portuguese is a great next language since there are many similarites.

0-7. A bit about Spanish spelling

In English speaking countries it's common to have spelling bees in school. This is because English has words that are not easy to spell. However, a spelling bee in a Spanish speaking country is unheard of. The reason why is because Spanish spelling is consistent with its pronunciation, so it wouldn't present much of a challenge to the contestants.

Of course, that doesn't mean you will immediately know how to spell every Spanish word, because, after all, you are new to Spanish. Also, the pronunciation of many commonly used Spanish words in the United States is inaccurate. For example, "Los Angeles" is Spanish for "The Angels." However, in the United States it's commonly read as "Las Angeles" with an "ah" sound. It should actually be read with an "oh" sound and the G would be read as an H sound.

The good news is that once you get a few Spanish spellings in your head, the rest should be pretty easy. Then you can focus on the parts of Spanish that are sometimes considered challenging for English only speakers.

0-8. Spanish is easy!?

Hugo Canedo, a native Spanish speaker, began writing this book years before it was finally published. I, George Trombley, a native English speaker, joined after much of version 1 was written with a very limited understanding of Spanish. In fact, I learned most of the Spanish I know during our rewriting of Hugo's original work over the last three years.

I was already fluent in Japanese and Korean, and studied Chinese, which are all considered difficult languages for English speakers. It was my assumption for a long time that Spanish would be easy because of its similarity to English. However, I was wrong. While it's true there are parts of Spanish that are VERY easy because of similarities to English, other parts are SO different that it makes my brain bend in ways it's never bent with Asian languages.

I will say that Spanish is ABSOLUTELY the easiest language for an English speaker to learn, but be ready for parts that will challenge your English brain. The good news is once you get past these basics and the initial hurdles, Spanish is indeed easy. So let's get started!

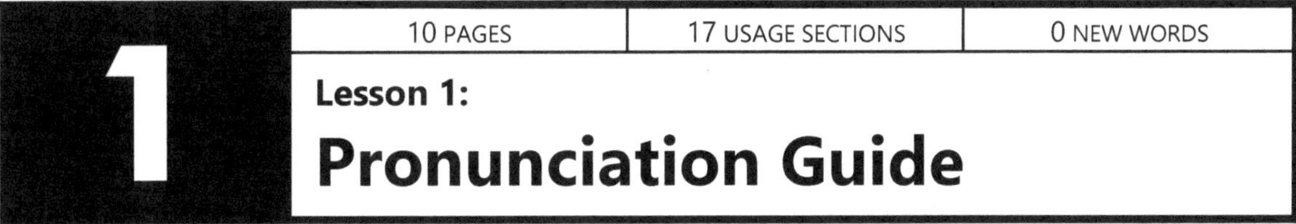

1 Spanish Pronunciation *Pronunciación del español*

NOTE: When this book refers to English, we mean English spoken in the United States.

● 1-1. Spanish vowels

Spanish vowels have consistent sounds. Meaning that, unlike English, each vowel has just one sound regardless of usage.

Vowel	Always Sounds Like	Example
a	ah as in f**a**ther	**a**la (wing)
e	eh as in m**e**n	**e**co (echo)
i	ee as in s**ee**	**i**nicio (start)
o	oh as in b**oa**t	**o**la (wave)
u	oo as in b**oo**k	**u**no (one)

Keep these sounds in mind when you read any Spanish word.

● 1-2. The Spanish alphabet

In the rest of this chapter we will be talking a lot about the Spanish alphabet. Luckily it's the same as the English alphabet, except for one additional letter between ***n*** and ***o*** called ***eñe*** (enyay) which will be explained in the next section.

The letters are named differently from English. You don't need to learn the names now, but it might be helpful to know them when interacting with Spanish speakers.

The Spanish Alphabet and Names								
A a	**B** be	**C** ce	**D** de	**E** e	**F** efe	**G** ge	**H** hache	**I** i
J jota	**K** ka	**L** ele	**M** eme	**N** ene	**Ñ** eñe	**O** o	**P** pe	**Q** cu
R erre	**S** ese	**T** te	**U** u	**V** uve	**W** doble u	**X** equis	**Y** i griega/ye	**Z** zeta

NOTE: Here is a great Spanish alphabet song: **https://learnfz.com/esABC**

1-3. The letter Ñ

Ñ (enye) is a unique independent letter with a permanent ~ on top. In fact, it even has its own key on the keyboard. Sometimes in handwriting the ~ is written as a straight line.

The pronunciation of ***ñ*** is similar to "ny" in the English word, "ca**ny**on".

SPANISH	PRONUNCIATION	ENGLISH
montaña	montanya	mountain
año	anyo	year

You can combine the letter ***ñ*** with any vowel using the same sound as in ca**ny**on.

Spanish	Pronunciation	Meaning
araña	aranya	spider
muñeca	munyeca	doll
dañino	danyino	harmful
niño	ninyo	boy
pañuelo	panyuelo	tissue

FUN FACT! The word canyon is an *englishification* of the Spanish word ***cañón*** used to refer to a deep valley, just like The Grand Canyon.

1-4. Spanish consonants

Any letter that isn't a vowel is a consonant, including ***ñ*** (enye). Some Spanish consonants have special rules or sounds that we will discuss in the following sections.

IMPORTANT! You don't need to learn all the rules in this lesson at once. We'll remind you of the rules as needed. You can also revisit this lesson to refresh your memory at any time.

1-5. Spanish H

In Spanish, ***h*** is silent in the same way "h" is silent in the English words "honest" or "hour".

SPANISH	PRONUNCIATION	ENGLISH
habilidad	abilidad	ability
helado	elado	ice cream

1-6. Spanish G

In Spanish, ***g*** can be pronounced like an English "h" and other times like a typical hard "g" sound. **NOTE:** In Spanish, ***g*** is never pronounced as "j" in the way English can.

G Rule #1 Before **a**, **o**, **u** and **consonants** it sounds like the "g" in the English word "go".

SPANISH	PRONUNCIATION	ENGLISH
gato	gato	cat
gol	gol	goal (soccer, etc.)
gusano	gusano	worm
grande	grande	big

G Rule #2 When ***g*** is directly in front of ***e*** or ***i***, it's pronounced like an English "h".

SPANISH	PRONUNCIATION	ENGLISH
gelatina	helatina	jello
ligero	lihero	light
original	orihinal	original
congelador	conhelador	freezer
digital	dihital	digital
gigante	higante	giant

The second ***g*** is standard ***g*** sound because it's used before an ***a***.

1-7. Spanish J

In Spanish, ***j*** is pronounced like an English "h".

SPANISH	PRONUNCIATION	ENGLISH
jugo	hugo	juice
juego	huego	game

 *Más Detalles* **More Details** 

Harsh J sound in Spain

You may hear some Spanish speaking people pronounce ***j*** and ***g*** with a very harsh throat sound, like they are clearing their throat, however this would sound strange in most Spanish speaking areas. Around only 7% of the Spanish speaking population use this sound, so just be aware of its existence and don't get confused if you happen to hear it.

1-8. Spanish R

You may have heard that Spanish ***r*** is a "rolling r". However, it doesn't always "roll". ***R*** actually has two different sounds in Spanish. Let's start with the "rolling" one first.

There are three situations where the rolling ***r*** sound is used:

Rolling R Rule #1 When there are two ***rr*** together, they will have a "rolling r" sound.

SPANISH	PRONUNCIATION	ENGLISH
perro	pe**rr**o	dog
carril	ca**rr**il	lane

Rolling R Rule #2 When ***r*** is the first letter of a word then the "rolling r" sound is used.

SPANISH	PRONUNCIATION	ENGLISH
risa	**r**isa	laughter
Rusia	**R**usia	Russia

Rolling R Rule #3 If there is an ***n*** in front of ***r***, like ***nr***.

SPANISH	PRONUNCIATION	ENGLISH
enredado	en**r**edado	tangled
honra	on**r**a	honor

Remember ***h*** is silent.

All other r's don't roll, but are pronounced stronger than English "r". There are two ways to think about how these r's sound.

1. It's like a "mini roll" or "single roll" ***r***. It rolls but stops after the first tongue drop.

2. Think of how "tt" in "gotta" sounds. It sounds more like a "lazy d" than a "t". The sound is made by flicking your tongue on the ridge on top of your mouth behind your front teeth.

SPANISH	PRONUNCIATION	ENGLISH
pero	petto, pero	but
libro	libtto, libro	book

If you can't pronounce the ***r*** sounds at first, don't worry, you can use the English "r" sound and still be understood. Practice by listening to the sounds on *FromZero.com*, or ask a Spanish speaking friend to help you practice until you get comfortable with it.

1-9. Spanish LL

When two ***L*** are together as in ***LL***, they are pronounced similarly to an English "J".

SPANISH	PRONUNCIATION	ENGLISH
lluvia	juvia	rain
cuchillo	cuchijo	knife

NOTE: ***LL*** will never sound like an individual ***L***.

Even though ***LL*** officially sounds similar to the English "J", when read in Spanish, it's often also pronounced like an English "Y" by native speakers. There are no rules as to when and why it becomes a "Y" sound, it's a personal choice that varies from person to person.

That being said, the previous set of examples can be pronounced with either sound.

LL sounding as an English "Y" or "J"

SPANISH	PRONUNCIATION	ENGLISH
lluvia	**y**uvia / **j**uvia	rain
cuchillo	cuchi**y**o / cuchi**j**o	knife

1-10. Spanish Y

Spanish words with ***y*** can be pronounced like you would expect, similar to English.

SPANISH	PRONUNCIATION	ENGLISH
yogur	**y**ogur	yogurt
hoyo	o**y**o (Remember, "h" is silent.)	hole

In the same way that Spanish ***LL*** (double L) can sound like "J" or "Y", Spanish ***Y*** is also on the same sound spectrum. Essentially you can treat ***LL*** and ***Y*** as the same thing.

Spanish ***Y*** sound can be pronounced similar to English J, Y or something in between.

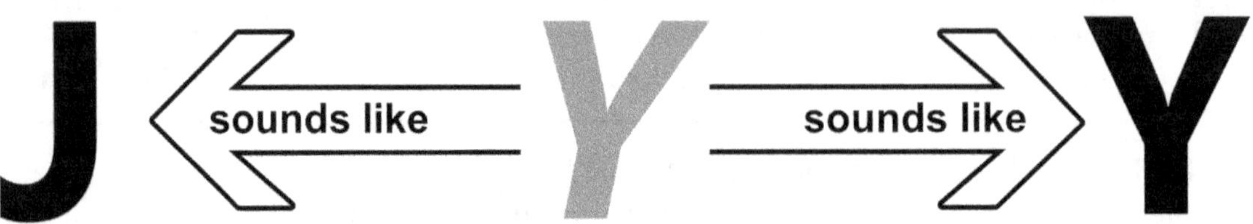

That means that the previous set of examples can be pronounced with either sound.

Y **sounding as an English "J" or "Y"**

SPANISH	PRONUNCIATION	ENGLISH
yogur	jogur / yogur	yogurt
hoyo	ojo / oyo	hole

The sound used will depend on the region and maybe even the speaker. Don't worry, even if you mix it up, you won't accidentally say an unintended word.

1-11. The CH Combination

Ch shares the English pronunciation.

SPANISH	PRONUNCIATION	ENGLISH
chocolate	chocolate ('late' is pronounced like 'latte'.)	chocolate
chile	chile	hot pepper

NOTE: In English, ***ch*** can be "k" sound such as in *ache*, but in Spanish ***ch*** is never "k" sound.

Más Detalles More Details

A bit of history on CH

Prior to its removal in 2010, ***ch*** was a single character called, "che".

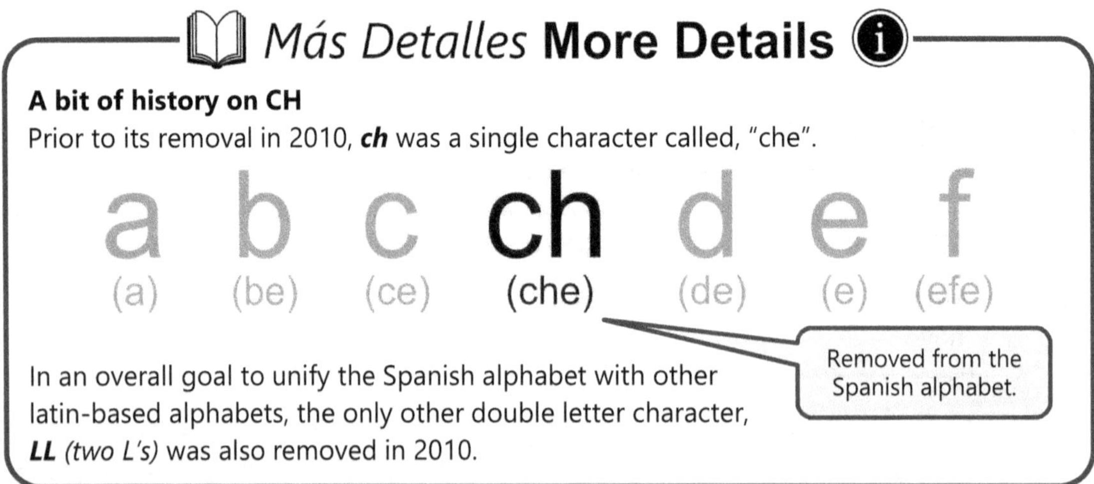

In an overall goal to unify the Spanish alphabet with other latin-based alphabets, the only other double letter character, ***LL*** *(two L's)* was also removed in 2010.

● 1-12. Spanish C

The letter ***c*** follows ALMOST all the same English rules, first let's look where it's the same:

C Rule #1 Before **a**, **o**, **u** and **consonants** it sounds like a "k".

SPANISH	PRONUNCIATION	ENGLISH
carro	karro	car
cortina	kortina	curtain
cucaracha	kukaracha	cockroach
cristal	kristal	crystal

C Rule #2 Before ***e*** and ***i*** it sounds like an "s".

SPANISH	PRONUNCIATION	ENGLISH
cena	sena	dinner
cine	sine	movie theater
oficial	ofisial	official

NOTE: In Spanish, ***c*** is never pronounced as "sh" such as in English like, special.

C Rule #3 Just like English, "k" and "s" versions of ***c*** can be in a word at the same time.

SPANISH	PRONUNCIATION	ENGLISH
cerca	serka	fence
credencial	kredensial (This is not "SH" sound.)	credential

● 1-13. Spanish B and V

Officially the letters ***b*** and ***v*** follow the same rules of pronunciation as English. However, some native Spanish speakers flip the pronunciation of ***b*** and ***v***.

SPANISH	PRONUNCIATION	ENGLISH
bueno	bueno / vueno	good
viento	viento / biento	wind
cambio	cambio / camvio	change
favorito	favorito / faborito	favorite

1-14. Spanish Z

Spanish **z** is pronounced like an "s". The English "z" sound doesn't exist in Spanish.

SPANISH	PRONUNCIATION	ENGLISH
fuerza	fuersa	strength
zorro	sorro	fox

 *Más Detalles* **More Details** 

The TH *lisp* of Spain

We learned that C and Z can both be an S sound. However, in Spain when C and Z are S sound they are said as a "lisp" that sounds similar to English "TH".

SPANISH	PRONUNCIATION	ENGLISH
fuerza	fuertha	strength
zorro	thorro	fox
cena	thena	dinner
oficial	ofithial	official

NOTE: S itself doesn't change to TH, and when C is read as K it doesn't become TH.

casa	kasa	house
sábados	sábados	Saturday

It's okay if you don't use TH sound, as speakers in Spain are used to other Spanish speakers not using it. Just be aware of its existence as you may hear it.

1-15. Spanish X

In most cases, ***x*** sounds just like it does in English.

SPANISH	PRONUNCIATION	ENGLISH
experto	experto	expert
extra	extra	extra

When the conquistadors arrived, they used ***x*** to represent the non-silent "h", and "sh" sounds of the existing native languages. This is especially common in place names.

SPANISH	PRONUNCIATION	ENGLISH
México	mehico	Mexico
Texas	tehas	Texas
Xalapa	halapa	(City in Mexico)

X also sounds like "h" or "sh" for things unique to the Americas when the conquistadors arrived, such as new plants, animals, or traditional items.

SPANISH	PRONUNCIATION	MEANING
xolo	sholo	Mexican hairless dog
axiote	ashiote	Mexican cuisine spice
mixiote	mishiote	pit-barbecued meat dish
axolote	aholote	Mexican salamander
xoconostle	shoconostle	sour prickly cactus pear

Remember that Spanish ***e*** is pronounced "eh", so the "nostle" part is "nost leh"

xolo
(**sho**-lo)

xoconostle
(**sho**-ko-nost-le)

a**xo**lote
(a-**ho**-lo-te)

1-16. Spanish GUE and GUI

Gue and ***gui*** are pronounced like the gue in guest and the gui and guitar.

SPANISH	PRONUNCIATION	ENGLISH
guitarra	gita**rr**a	guitar
guerrero	ge**rr**ero	warrior

For double ***rr***'s *...keep rolling, rolling, rolling...*

When two small dots ¨ are over ***u*** in ***güi*** and ***güe*** the ***u*** is read like a W sound.

SPANISH	PRONUNCIATION	ENGLISH
pingüino	pingwino	penguin
bilingüe	bilingwe	bilingual

Más Detalles More Details

Common misspellings

When texting, Spanish speakers often type ***güi*** and ***güe*** as ***gui*** or ***gue*** so they aren't slowed down by long holding ***u*** to get ***ü*** while typing.

What are the two dots called?

The dots above the ***u*** in Spanish are called ***diéresis***. Technically, they are not the same as the *umlaut* dots used in German.

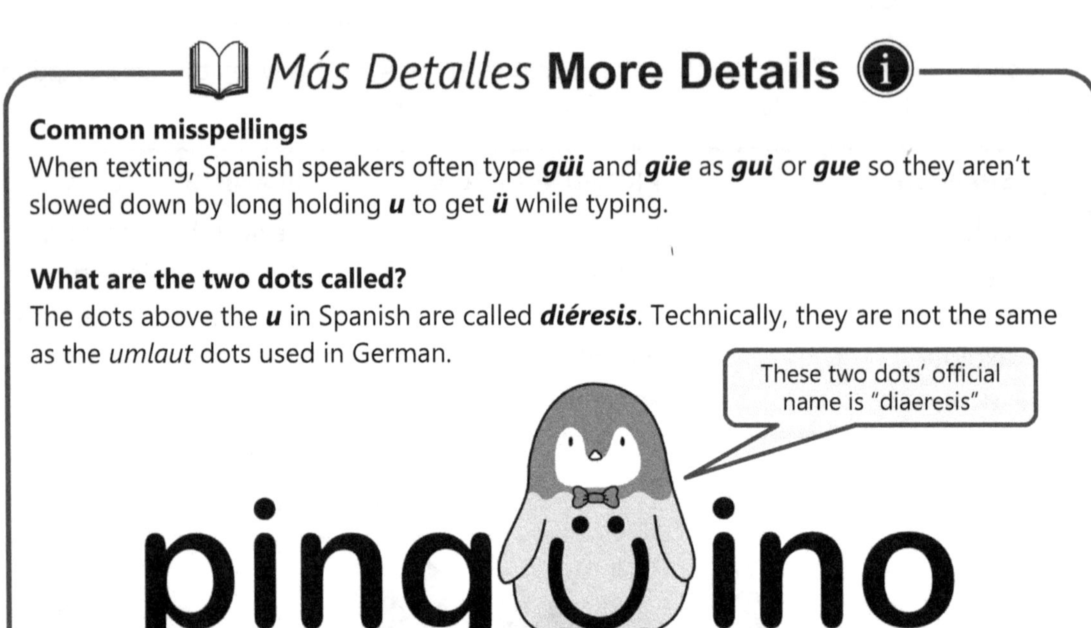

A ***pingüino*** always needs two little dots.

1-17. Spanish Q

Spanish ***Q*** is almost always combined with ***u*** and the resulting ***QU*** is pronounced like "k".

SPANISH	PRONUNCIATION	ENGLISH
queso	keso	cheese
paquete	pakete	package
quieto	kieto	quiet; still
queja	keha	complain
parque	parke	park

Remember, ***j*** is pronounced as "h".

Remember, ***e*** is pronounced as "eh".

EXCEPTION NOTE

With some non-Spanish words ***Q*** isn't combined with ***U*** such as, ***Dinastía Qing*** (Qing Dynasty), or ***Teclado Qwerty*** (Qwerty Keyboard). But the ***Q*** is still pronounced as ***K***.

1 Workbook 1: Lesson Activities

1 Spanish 101

1. Test your Spanish knowledge

Answer the following questions about Spanish.

1. **How many letters are in the Spanish alphabet?**
   A. 25
   B. 26
   C. 27

2. **Which letter is NEVER silent in Spanish?**
   A. H
   B. Ñ
   C. U

3. **Which of the following rules explain when to fully roll an "R" in Spanish?**
   A. When there are two R's in row such as in *perro* (dog)
   B. When R is after N such as in *sonrisa* (smile)
   C. When R is the first letter in a word as in *ropa* (clothes)
   D. All of the above are true

4. **In Spanish, which letters have more than one possible sound?**
   A. B, V, and P
   B. B, LL, and C
   C. J, Y, and D
   D. Both A and B are correct

5. **Which English sound DOES NOT exist in Spanish?**
   A. The "x" sound as in "extra"
   B. The "sh" sound as in "flash"
   C. The "z" sound as in "zone"
   D. Both A and C are correct

6. **In which of the following words is "u" NOT silent?**
   A. guerrero
   B. pingüino
   C. paquete

7. When is "H" silent in Spanish?

A. Never
B. Always
C. Only when it's the first letter of a word
D. Only when it's in the middle of a word

8. Which of these letters in Spanish can be pronounced like the English "s"?

A. Z
B. C
C. S
D. All of the above.

9. In which of the following is "u" silent in both groupings?

A. *gua* and *gue*
B. *gue* and *gui*
C. *gui* and *guo*

10. Which of the following can sound like "th" in some situations?

A. QU
B. Z
C. CH
D. LL

11. When is the letter "g" pronounced as an English "h"?

A. When it's in front of *e* or *i*
B. When it's in front of *a* or *i*
C. When it's in front of *a* or *u*
D. G is always pronounced like H

12. X can sound like SH depending on the word.

A. TRUE
B. FALSE

13. Which letter can never be pronounced as the English H?

A. J
B. H
C. X
D. G

1 Answer Key *Clave de Respuestas*

1. Test your Spanish knowledge (answers)

1. C
2. B
3. D
4. B
5. C
6. B
7. B
8. D
9. B
10. B
11. A
12. A
13. B

5 PAGES	5 USAGE SECTIONS	0 NEW WORDS

2 Lesson 2: Accent Marks etc.

2 Speaking Naturally *Hablando de Forma Natural*

● 2-1. Spanish syllables

Understanding Spanish syllables helps in understanding Spanish stressing. A syllable is a single unit of *sound* in a word. A word can have one or more syllables. Here are some rules for how Spanish words count their syllables. This is important later on.

1. Every syllable must have at least one vowel. (syllables are separated with a hyphen)

1 syllable	**2 syllables**	**3 syllables**	**4 syllables**
yo (I)	ga-to (cat)	a-ho-ra (now)	lu-cha-do-res (wrestlers)
sal (salt)	pe-rro (dog)	mi-nu-to (minute)	la-pi-ce-ro (pen)

2. Sometimes two or more vowels in a row are considered one syllable.

1 syllable	**2 syllables**	**2 syllables**	**3 syllables**
cien (hundred)	pue-blo (town)	quie-to (quiet)	rui-do-so (noisy)
bien (good)	true-no (thunder)	cier-vo (deer)	cua-der-no (notebook)

3. An accent mark on one of two vowels in a row creates a new syllable.

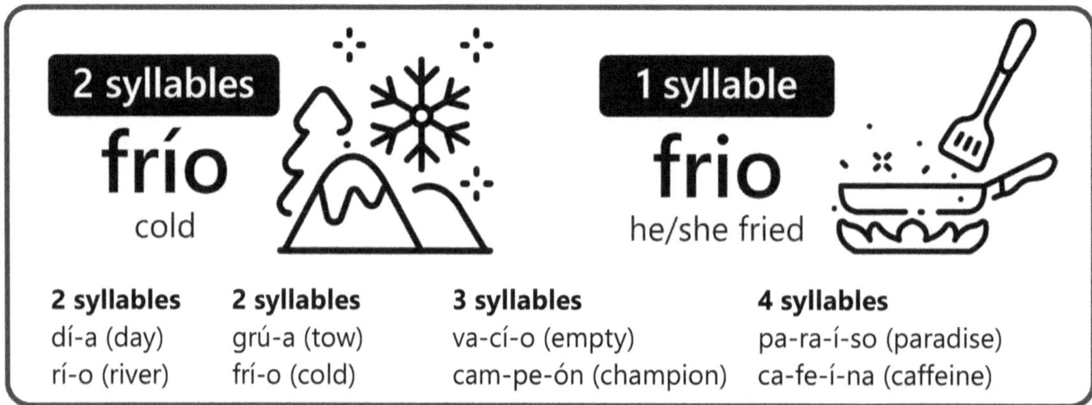

2 syllables	**2 syllables**	**3 syllables**	**4 syllables**
dí-a (day)	grú-a (tow)	va-cí-o (empty)	pa-ra-í-so (paradise)
rí-o (river)	frí-o (cold)	cam-pe-ón (champion)	ca-fe-í-na (caffeine)

● 2-2. Natural stress rules (words without stress marks)

For words without accent marks there are two natural rules for which syllable to stress.

1. For words ending in a **vowel**, ***n***, or ***s***, ALWAYS stress the <u>second to the last syllable</u>.

ends in vowel	ends in 'n'	ends in 's'
re-GA-lo	**JO-ven**	**lu-cha-DO-res**
regalo (gift)	joven (young)	luchadores (wrestlers)

2. For words ending with **all other letter** ALWAYS stress the <u>last syllable</u>.

ends in 'r'	ends in 'd'	ends in 'z'
co-me-DOR	**ver-DAD**	**a-RROZ**
comedor (dining room)	verdad (truth)	arroz (rice)

● 2-3. Forced stress with Spanish accent marks

The small diagonal line sometimes placed on top of a vowel is called an *accent mark*. Accent marks are used when a word **<u>doesn't follow</u>** the natural stress rules.

á é í ó ú

Before Spanish, let's look at English. The words below are read differently depending on their meaning, but there are no indications of how they should be pronounced.

record (music album / medical ~ etc.)	**record** (to record)
present (for a birthday; a gift)	**present** (to present)
produce (fruits / vegetables)	**produce** (to make)

If these words had accent marks, they would look like this.

récord (music album / medical ~ etc.)	**recórd** (to record)
présent (for a birthday; a gift)	**presént** (to present)
próduce (fruits / vegetables)	**prodúce** (to make)

Where the stress is on a word, can change the meaning of the word.

EXAMPLES

Spanish	**Stress**
circulo (I circulate)	cir-CU-lo (natural stress rules)
circuló (he circulated)	cir-cu-LO (stress on last syllable)
círculo (a circle)	CIR-cu-lo (stress on first syllable)
publico (I publish)	pu-BLI-co (natural stress rules)
publicó (he published)	pu-bli-CO (stress on last syllable)
público (public)	PU-bli-co (stress on first syllable)
mascara (mascara (makeup))	mas-CA-ra (natural stress rules)
máscara (mask; mascara (makeup))	MAS-ca-ra (stress on first syllable)
mascará (He/she will chew)	mas-ca-RA (stress on last syllable)

máscara

máscara
Official for mascara for eyelashes.

mascara
Used in Latin America sometimes.

mascará

NOTE: ***Rímel*** is also used to say 'mascara'.

Accent marks are sometimes used to simply differentiate words with the same spelling.

EXAMPLES

más (more)
mas (but)

él (him)
el (the)

mi (my)
mí (me)

Single syllable words, with and without an accent mark, are pronounced the same.

● 2-4. Putting it all together

Now that you've learned the Spanish alphabet, its pronunciation, and how stressing works, you should be able to read any Spanish text out loud whether you understand it or not.

Look closely at the sentences below. What differences can you spot?

> 1. Tu papá tiene treinta años.
> 2. Tu papa tiene treinta anos.

They may look similar, but there are two *visually* subtle, yet drastic differences:

---

1. The first sentence has an accent mark on ***papá***, and an ***ñ*** (enye) in ***años***.
2. The second sentence has no accent mark on ***papa***, and an ***n*** in ***anos***.

These differences are visually small, but they hugely change the meaning.

> 1. Tu papá tiene treinta años.
> Your dad is thirty years old.

> 2. Tu papa tiene treinta anos.
> Your potato has thirty anuses.

Hopefully you see the importance of accent marks and not mixing up ***n*** and ***ñ*** (enye).

● 2-5. Question and exclamation marks

Spanish uses an upside-down question mark "**¿**" at the beginning of a question. Questions in Spanish are always enclosed by two question marks "**¿?**".

Here focus only on the question marks usage. You'll learn these phrases in a future lesson.

EXAMPLE QUESTIONS

Spanish	**English**
¿Qué hora es**?**	What time is it**?**
Hola, **¿**cómo estás**?**	Hello, how are you**?**

The same thing is done with exclamation marks.

EXAMPLE EXCLAMATIVE SENTENCES

Spanish	**English**
¡Buenos días**!**	Good morning**!**
Nos vemos luego, **¡**gracias**!**	See you later, thank you**!**

2 Workbook 2: Lesson Activities

2 Spanish 101

1. Test your Spanish knowledge

1. **Which of the following explains when the second to last syllable is stressed.**
   A. Words ending in a vowel.
   B. Words ending in a consonant other than ***n*** or ***s***.
   C. Words ending in ***n***, ***s***, or a vowel.

2. **Which of the following explains when the LAST SYLLABLE is stressed.**
   A. Words ending in a vowel.
   B. Words ending in any letter other than ***n***, ***s***, or a vowel.
   C. Words ending in ***n***, ***s***, or a vowel.

3. **Underline stressed vowel of the following words.**
   A. ***perro*** (dog)
   B. ***yogur*** (yogurt)
   C. ***manzana*** (apple)
   D. ***refrigerador*** (refrigerator)
   E. ***cuchillo*** (knife)
   F. ***fresa*** (strawberry)
   G. ***oficial*** (oficial)
   H. ***naranja*** (orange)
   I. ***habilidad*** (ability)
   J. ***cocina*** (kitchen)
   K. ***aguacate*** (avocado)
   L. ***tomate*** (tomato)

2 Answer Key *Clave de Respuestas*

1. Test your Spanish knowledge (answers)

1. C
2. B
3. A. ***perro*** (dog)
   B. ***yogur*** (yogurt)
   C. ***manzana*** (apple)
   D. ***refrigerador*** (refrigerator)
   E. ***cuchillo*** (knife)
   F. ***fresa*** (strawberry)
   G. ***oficial*** (oficial)
   H. ***naranja*** (orange)
   I. ***habilidad*** (ability)
   J. ***cocina*** (kitchen)
   K. ***aguacate*** (avocado)
   L. ***tomate*** (tomato)

3	7 PAGES	10 USAGE SECTIONS	MANY NEW NUMBERS!

Lesson 3: Basic Counting

3 Counting in Spanish *Contando en español*

3-1. Counting 1-10

Basic counting in Spanish is easy! Even though this is Spanish From Zero! you probably already know a few of these numbers.

Counting 1-10			
1	uno	**6**	seis
2	dos	**7**	siete
3	tres	**8**	ocho
4	cuatro	**9**	nueve
5	cinco	**10**	diez

NOTE: Zero in Spanish is ***cero***. Rememer that in this case ***c*** is read as an **s** (sero)

3-2. The teens (part 1) 11-15

The numbers from 11 to 15 are named uniquely, please take time to memorize them.

Counting 11-15		
#	**Spanish**	**Pronunciation Help**
11	once	on-se
12	doce	doh-se
13	trece	tre-se
14	catorce	ca-tor-se
15	quince	keen-se

3-3. The teens (part 2) 16-19

In Spanish "and" is ***y***, but pronounced as the English letter "e". We will use ***y*** in numbers in this section, but ***y*** is also used in between other words as "and".

To form numbers 16 to 19, we use the pattern below.

diez + y + single number

For example 16 is made by saying "10 and 6":

diez (ten) + y (and) + seis (six)
diez y seis

16-19 is made with the pattern above. However, in modern Spanish they are written as a single word with the same pronunciation.

Counting 11-15		
#	Previously (remember with this)	Modern Spanish (use this)
16	diez y seis	dieciséis ★
17	diez y siete	diecisiete
18	diez y ocho	dieciocho
19	diez y nueve	diecinueve

★ Notice ***dieciséis*** has an accent mark.

3-4. The tens

To count to 100, we need a few more unique numbers.

The tens 20-90			
20	veinte	**60**	sesenta
30	treinta	**70**	setenta
40	cuarenta	**80**	ochenta
50	cincuenta	**90**	noventa

● 3-5. The twenties

To create a number from 21 to 29, just take the slightly modified version of 20 : ***veinti~*** and add the single number you need.

veinti~ + single number

The twenties 20-29			
20	veinte	**25**	veinticinco
21	veintiuno	**26**	veintiséis ★
22	veintidós ★	**27**	veintisiete
23	veintitrés ★	**28**	veintiocho
24	veinticuatro	**29**	veintinueve

★ Notice that ***veintidós***, ***veintitrés*** and ***veintiséis*** have accent marks.

● 3-6. Combining tens and singles

From 30 and up the numbers are simple. Just add a ten number to a single.
For example ***30 + y + 1***, is 31 in Spanish.

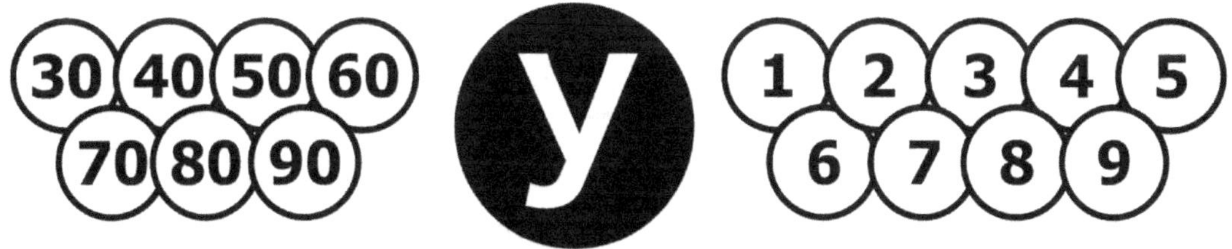

EXAMPLES

cuarenta y cuatro	44	setenta y siete	77
cincuenta y cinco	55	ochenta y ocho	88
sesenta y seis	66	noventa y nueve	99
cuarenta y dos	42	setenta y cinco	75
cincuenta y tres	53	ochenta y seis	86
sesenta y cuatro	64	noventa y siete	97

3-7. The hundreds 200-900

Hundreds are made by adding ***cientos*** (hundred) to a single number. Since "one hundred" has multiple versions, we'll start with the easier, 200-900.

single number + cientos

EXAMPLES

1. dos cientos — two hundred (200)
2. tres cientos — three hundred (300)
3. cuatro cientos — four hundred (400)

The hundreds 200-900			
#	Made this way	Written this way	★ NOTES
200	dos + cientos	doscientos	
300	tres + cientos	trescientos	
400	cuatro + cientos	cuatrocientos	
500	quin +ientos ★ (the c is dropped)	quinientos	Never "cinco cientos"
600	seis + cientos	seiscientos	
700	sete + cientos ★	setecientos	Never "siete cientos"
800	ocho + cientos	ochocientos	
900	nove + cientos ★	novecientos	Never "nueve cientos

3-8. Four ways to say 100 in Spanish

In Spanish counting, "hundred" in numbers can be ***cien***, ***ciento***, ***cientos***, and even ***ientos***.

cien, ciento By itself "hundred" is ***cien***. For numbers 101-199 "hundred" is ***ciento***.

EXAMPLES

cien — (100) one hundred
ciento uno — (101) one hundred and one
ciento once — (111) one hundred and eleven
ciento veintidós — (122) one hundred and twenty two
ciento treinta y tres — (133) one hundred and thirty three

cientos, ientos For 200-900 "hundred" is ***cientos***, except 500 where it is ***ientos***.

EXAMPLES (HUNDREDS)	
(200) doscientos	(600) seiscientos
(300) trescientos	(700) setecientos
(400) cuatrocientos	(800) ochocientos
(500) quinientos	(900) novecientos

3-9. Thousands

In English, slang for 'million' is sometimes "mil". But don't let that confuse you since in Spanish ***mil*** means "thousand".

For the thousands take any number from 1 to 999 and add ***mil*** (thousand).

5,000	50,000	500,000
cinco mil	cincuenta mil	quinientos mil

EXAMPLES (THOUSANDS)	
(1,000) mil	(11,000) once mil
(2,000) dos mil	(15,000) quince mil
(10,000) diez mil	(110,000) ciento diez mil
(26,000) veintiséis mil	(700,000) setecientos mil
(38,000) treinta y ocho mil	(950,000) novecientos cincuenta mil

When counting in thousands and above, ***uno*** changes to ***un***.

31,000
✗ ~~treinta y **uno** mil~~
✓ treinta y **un** mil

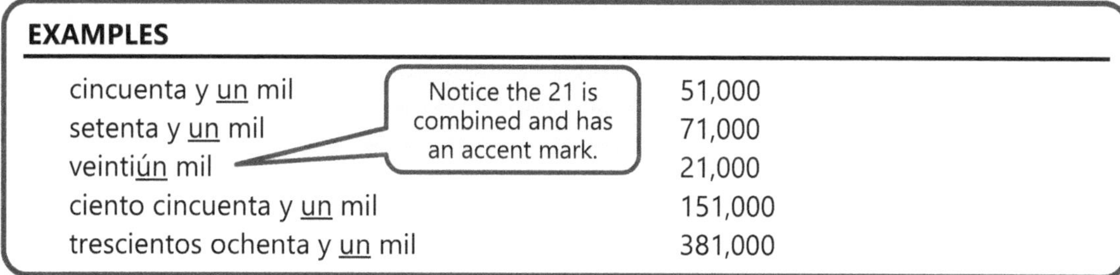

EXAMPLES

cincuenta y un mil	51,000
setenta y un mil	71,000
veintiún mil	21,000
ciento cincuenta y un mil	151,000
trescientos ochenta y un mil	381,000

Notice the 21 is combined and has an accent mark.

With the "hundred-thousands" you just add ***mil*** to the hundreds.

EXAMPLES

cien mil	(100,000) one hundred **thousand**
doscientos mil	(200,000) two hundred **thousand**
trescientos mil	(300,000) three hundred **thousand**
cuatrocientos mil	(400,000) four hundred **thousand**
quinientos mil	(500,000) five hundred **thousand**
seiscientos mil	(600,000) six hundred **thousand**
setecientos mil	(700,000) seven hundred **thousand**
ochocientos mil	(800,000) eight hundred **thousand**
novecientos mil	(900,000) nine hundred **thousand**

3-10. Putting all the numbers together

So as not to overwhelm you, we will handle millions later on. With all that we know now you should be able to count from 1 to 999,999 in Spanish.

The first few examples below will use repeating numbers to help you get used to putting the numbers together.

EXAMPLES

444	cuatrocientos cuarenta y cuatro
888	ochocientos ochenta y ocho
222	doscientos veintidós
555	quinientos cincuenta y cinco
4,444	cuatro mil cuatrocientos cuarenta y cuatro
7,777	siete mil setecientos setenta y siete

Now let's mix up the numbers. Make sure you understand the numbers with variations and keep track of the accent marks.

EXAMPLES

639	seiscientos treinta y nueve
360	trescientos sesenta
2,512	dos mil quinientos doce
8,096	ochomil noventa y seis
9,853	nueve mil ochocientos cincuenta y tres
10,626	diez mil seiscientos veintiséis

Now let's go HARD CORE! Just to get our bearings let's again start with repeating numbers.

NUMBERS EXERCISE #1

How do you say 444,444 in Spanish?

First ask, HOW MANY **mil** (thousands) are there?

There are 444 of them, so we have 444,000 which is ***cuatrocientos cuarenta y cuatro mil***. Then we just need to add 444 which is ***cuatrocientos cuarenta y cuatro.***

444 mil

400 ⇨ cuatrocientos
40 and ⇨ cuarenta y
4 ⇨ cuatro

Answer: cuatrocientos cuarenta y cuatro mil cuatrocientos cuarenta y cuatro.

NUMBERS EXERCISE #2

How do you say 654,321 in Spanish?

First ask, HOW MANY **mil** (thousands) are there?

There are 654 of them, so we have 654,000 which is ***seiscientos cincuenta y cuatro mil***. Then we just need to add 321 which is ***trescientos veintiuno.***

654 mil

600 ⇨ seiscientos
50 and ⇨ cincuenta y
4 ⇨ cuatro

Answer: seiscientos cincuenta y cuatro mil trescientos veintiuno.

3 Practice and Review *Práctica y Repaso*

Practice saying your phone number, pin, and other numbers you use every day in Spanish. Learn them forwards and backwards.

When you are riding in a car, practice reading the numbers on other cars' license plates.

3 Workbook 3: Lesson Activities

3 Usage Activities *Actividades de Uso*

1. Number conversion

Write out the following numbers in Spanish.

1) 34 ______________________
2) 59 ______________________
3) 29 ______________________
4) 78 ______________________
5) 120 ______________________
6) 392 ______________________
7) 57 ______________________
8) 3,004 ______________________
9) 1,203 ______________________
10) 789 ______________________
11) 99 ______________________
12) 4,675 ______________________
13) 932 ______________________
14) 8,773 ______________________

2. Everyday usage

Write the required number.

1. Write your phone number in Spanish.

____

2. Write your work phone number or a friend's number in Spanish.

____

3. Write your postal code number in Spanish.

____

3 Answer Key *Clave de Respuestas*

1. Number conversion (answers)

1. treinta y cuatro
2. cincuenta y nueve
3. veintinueve
4. setenta y ocho
5. ciento veinte
6. trescientos noventa y dos
7. cincuenta y siete
8. tres mil cuatro
9. mil doscientos tres
10. setecientos ochenta y nueve
11. noventa y nueve
12. cuatro mil seiscientos setenta y cinco
13. novecientos treinta y dos
14. ochomil setecientos setenta y tres

2. Everyday usage (answers)

1. (answer will vary)
2. (answer will vary)
3. (answer will vary)

4 PAGES	6 USAGE SECTIONS	0 NEW WORDS

4 Lesson 4: First Meetings

From the teacher...

Before we get into any grammar, it's good to know how to introduce yourself. Try not to focus on the structure or logic of the phrases taught here, so as to not stress yourself out. These should be memorized for now.

4 Culture Clip *Clip Cultural*

4-1. Greeting with a kiss

Spanish speaking countries are known for the custom of cheek kissing. You don't have to kiss random strangers, however kisses are expected for people you know, people introduced to you by a friend, or someone you've planned to meet even for the first time.

There are two types of kisses. An "air kiss" where right cheeks are pressed together while kissing into the air, is the most standard greeting. A "cheek kiss", a direct kiss to the cheek, is common for close friends, family, and couples. Handshakes are common among men, while women most often do an "air kiss" with both men and women.

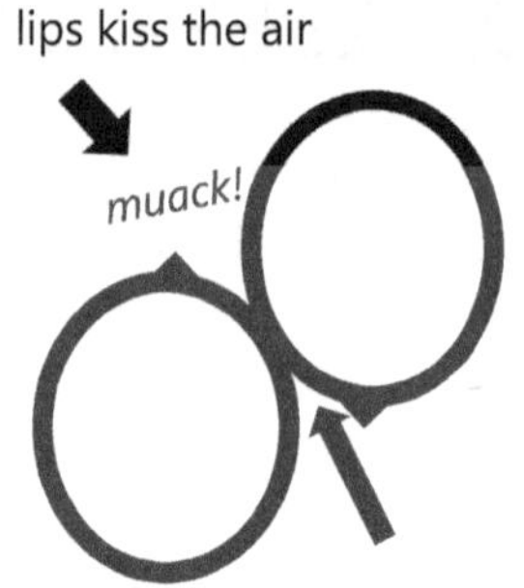

You might ask, "Can I refuse a kiss?" The short answer is yes, you can extend your hand for a shake instead. However, if you aren't fast enough, they might move in for the kiss. Refusing it by backing up etc, can be considered rude.

Note: In Spain, people may even do two kisses, one on each side, starting on the right.

4-2. The versatile *hola*

Hola, pronounced ***ola*** since "h" is silent in Spanish. It's a general greeting like "hi" in English. It's used in polite and informal situations. So it can replace "hello" and even "hey".

4 New Expressions *Expresiones Nuevas*

4-3. Phrases when meeting someone for the first time

1. **Hola, ¿Qué tal?** — **Hello, how is it going?**
   This is a polite thing said between people who just met, or that aren't close.
2. **Mucho gusto.** — **Nice to meet you.**
3. **Mi nombre es __(name)__.** — **My name is __(name)__.**
   In Spanish, just like English, there are a few ways to introduce yourself. You can also say, "***Me llamo (name)***" – *I'm called (name),* or the simplest form "***Soy (name)***" – *I'm (name).*
4. **Igualmente.** — **Likewise.**
   This is said in the spot where in English you would say, "Nice to meet you too." In Spanish, it sounds awkward to say similar phrases close to each other, so people say ***igualmente*** to avoid saying ***mucho gusto*** again.
5. **El placer es mío. / El gusto es mío.** — **My pleasure.**
   Some people say this instead of "***igualmente***."

Conversation 1: First meeting

Conversation between people meeting for the first time.

Ms. Carla: Hola, ¿Qué tal? Mi nombre es Carla.
Mr. Enrique: Hola, mi nombre es Enrique.
Ms. Carla: Mucho gusto
Mr. Enrique: Igualmente.

Ms. Carla: Hello, How is it going? My name is Carla.
Mr. Enrique: Hi, my name is Enrique.
Ms. Carla: Nice to meet you.
Mr. Enrique: Likewise.

4-4. Asking someone their age

You can use these age related phrases when appropriate.

1. **¿Qué edad tienes?** — **What is your age?**
2. **¿Cuantos años tienes?** — **How old are you?**
   Literally, how many years do you have? This question is a more casual and common way to ask someone their age than ***¿Qué edad tienes?***
3. **Tengo __(number)__ años de edad.** — **I'm __(number)__ years old.**
   The phrase ***años de edad*** means, "years old." It comes after the number representing your age.

EXAMPLES

Remember ñ is pronounced '**ny**'

3 years old	tres años de edad
16 years old	deciséis años de edad

Conversation 2: How old are you?	
Sammy:	¿Qué edad tienes?
Daniela:	Tengo veinte años de edad.
Sammy:	How old are you?
Daniela:	I am 20 years old.

● 4-5. Saying your age

To say your age, you say number + ***años de edad*** (years old). Find your age on the chart below or make it based on the pattern.

años de edad **(years old)**					
1	un *año de edad* *	14	catorce *años de edad*	27	veintisiete *años de edad*
2	dos *años de edad*	15	quince *años de edad*	28	veintiocho *años de edad*
3	tres *años de edad*	16	diez y seis *años de edad*	29	veintinueve *años de edad*
4	cuatro *años de edad*	17	diez y siete *años de edad*	30	treinta *años de edad*
5	cinco *años de edad*	18	diez y ocho *años de edad*	31	treinta y un *años de edad* *
6	seis *años de edad*	19	diez y nueve *años de edad*	40	cuarenta *años de edad*
7	siete *años de edad*	20	veinte *años de edad*	50	cincuenta *años de edad*
8	ocho *años de edad*	21	veintiún *años de edad* *	60	sesenta *años de edad*
9	nueve *años de edad*	22	veintidós *años de edad*	70	setenta *años de edad*
10	diez *años de edad*	23	veintitrés *años de edad*	80	ochenta *años de edad*
11	once *años de edad*	24	veinticuatro *años de edad*	90	noventa *años de edad*
12	doce *años de edad*	25	veinticinco *años de edad*	100	cien *años de edad*
13	trece *años de edad*	26	veintiséis *años de edad*	*	***uno*** changes to ***un***

NOTE: You can also omit ***años de edad***, but it's clearer if you include it.

4-6. How old do I look?

When first meeting someone, the following question makes for fun conversation with your new Spanish speaking friends when you are asked your age.

1. **¿De qué edad me veo?** — **How old do I look?**
   This is a common answer to ***¿Cuántos años tienes?*** (How old are you?). Be kind with your answer!

2. **Te ves de __(years)__ años de edad.** — **You look __(years)__ years old.**

Conversation 3-A: How old do I look?		
Sammy:	¿Qué edad tienes?	How old are you?
Daniela:	¿De qué edad me veo?	How old do I look?
Sammy:	Te ves de treinta y siete años de edad.	You look 37 years old.
Daniela:	¡Tengo diecinueve años de edad!	I'm 19 years old!

Conversation 3-B: How old do I look? (Shorter Version)		
Sammy:	¿Qué edad tienes?	How old are you?
Daniela:	¿De qué edad me veo?	How old do I look?
Sammy:	Te ves de veintiséis.	You look 26.
Daniela:	Tengo treinta y ocho.	I'm 38.

Notice ***años de edad*** is omitted.

4 Workbook 4: Lesson Activities

4 Usage Activities *Actividades de Uso*

1. Spanish ages

Translate the following into English.

1. Setenta y cinco años

____

2. Cuarenta y siete años

____

3. Ochenta y dos años

____

4. Ciento siete años

____

5. Treinta y cuatro años

____

6. Dieciséis años

____

7. Cincuenta y un años

____

8. Veinte años

____

9. Setecientos años

____

10. Un año

____

2. Question and answer 1

Answer the following questions in Spanish.

1. ¿Qué edad tienes?

____

2. ¿Cuál es tu nombre?

____

3. Question and answer 2

For each of the pictures below answer the question as if the person asked you.

¿De qué edad me veo?

1.

Answer: ______________________

2.

Answer: ______________________

3.

Answer: ______________________

4.

Answer: ______________________

5.

Answer: ______________________

6.

Answer: ______________________

4 Answer Key *Clave de Respuestas*

1. Spanish ages (answers)

1. 75 years old
2. 47 years old
3. 82 years old
4. 107 years old
5. 34 years old
6. 16 years old
7. 51 years old
8. 20 years old
9. 700 years old
10. 1-year-old

2. Question and answer 1 (answers)

1. How old are you? ____años de edad.
2. What is your name? Soy ____. / Mi nombre es____.

3. Question and answer 2 (example answers)

How old do I look?

1. Te ves de diez años de edad.
2. Te ves de dieciséis años de edad.
3. Te ves de sesenta años de edad.
4. Te ves de veinticinco años de edad.
5. Te ves de cincuenta años de edad.
6. Te ves de dos años de edad.

4 PAGES	2 USAGE SECTIONS	0 NEW WORDS

5 Lesson 5: Coming and Going

5 New Expressions *Expresiones Nuevas*

Don't worry about the grammar here. Just learn the phrases for communication.

● 5-1. Daily Greetings

Try to use the new phrases everyday with your friends and family. It will help you memorize them so that when you need them, you won't struggle to remember.

1. **Hola.** **Hello.**
   You can use this any time of the day when you meet someone.

2. **Adiós.** **Good Bye.**
   You can use this any time of the day you leave someone.

---

3. **Hasta luego.** **Until next time. (a bit formal)**
   This is similar to "See you later." It's more used in semi-formal situations.

4. **Nos vemos.** **See you. (casual)**
   This is the casual version of ***hasta luego***. Use it with friends and family since it's casual.

---

5. **Buenos Días.** **Good Morning.**
   Use this when meeting someone after midnight up until before noon.

6. **Buenas Tardes.** **Good Afternoon.**
   Use this when meeting someone after noon up until it gets dark.

7. **Buenas Noches.** **Good Evening / Good Night / Rest Well**
   Use this phrase after dark until before midnight.

midnight → noon	noon → dark→	dark→ → midnight
buenos días	**buenas tardes**	**buenas noches**

In the following conversations, notice the greeting changes according to the time.

Conversation 1: Good Evening	
It's 10:00 at night and Carlos is going to the convenience store.	
Carlos:	Hola, Buenas Noches.
Shop Clerk:	Buenas Noches.
Carlos:	Hello, Good Evening.
Shop Clerk:	Good Evening.

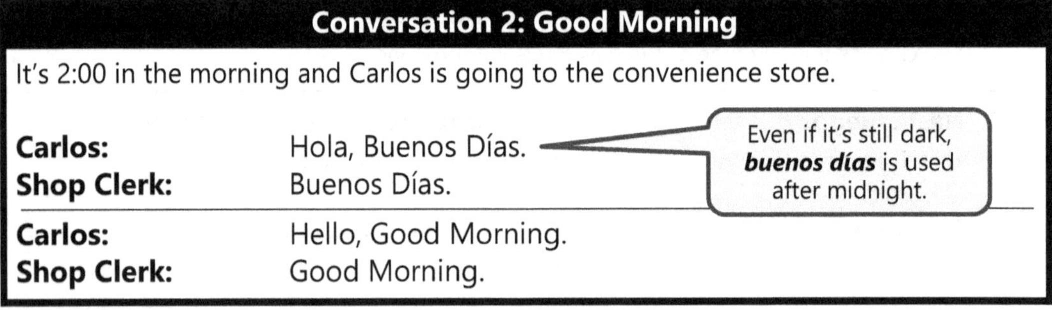

Conversation 2: Good Morning	
It's 2:00 in the morning and Carlos is going to the convenience store.	
Carlos:	Hola, Buenos Días.
Shop Clerk:	Buenos Días.
Carlos:	Hello, Good Morning.
Shop Clerk:	Good Morning.

Even if it's still dark, ***buenos días*** is used after midnight.

5-2. Everyday Manners

Regardless of the situation, in Spanish speaking countries, simple things such as saying ***por favor*** (please) and ***gracias*** (thank you) are very important; it's considered rude to not use these words. Make sure to say these phrases to give a good impression.

1. **Por Favor.** — **Please.**
2. **Gracias.** — **Thank you.**
3. **De nada.** — **You are welcome.**

   Even though in English sometimes people reply "sure" or "no problem" to a "thank you", if someone says ***gracias*** it's expected that you reply with **de nada**; other answers may be considered impolite.

4. Salud. **Bless you.**

When someone sneezes, stranger or not, it's common to say ***salud*** (bless you) to them. The response to ***salud*** is ***gracias*** (thank you). However, in this case you aren't expected to respond with ***de nada*** (you're welcome) unlike other times.

Conversation 3: Samuel Rides the Bus

Samuel sneezes on the bus. Liliana, a stranger, politely acknowledges it.

Samuel: *sneezes*
Liliana: Salud.

Samuel: Gracias.
Liliana: *does nothing*

Normally you reply ***de nada*** to ***gracias***, but here you don't need to.

Conversation 4: At a Street Taco Cart

At night Samuel eats at a taco cart and then talks with the ***taquero*** (taco cook).

Samuel: Gracias, buenas noches, ¡hasta luego!
Taquero: De nada, buenas noches.

Samuel: Thank you, good night, see you!
Taquero: You are welcome, good night.

5. Con Permiso. **With your permission. / Excuse me.**

Some uses of this phrase are not common in the English world.

When *con permiso* means, "excuse me"

- When kindly notifying someone you would like to pass in a crowd.

When *con permiso* means, "with your permission"

- Before entering or leaving someone's house, office, room, or personal space.
- Once when passing a public area with people, such as a waiting room or office. If there is time in between, say it when you enter and when you leave.

6. **Propio.** **Go ahead.**
   This is the response to ***con permiso*** when it's used after entering a place. Although not exactly the translation, a good way to think of its meaning is as, "make yourself welcome" or "go ahead".

Conversation 5: Walking Through a Room	
Samuel enters Raul's house and goes to Raul's room, passing by his mother, who's reading a book in the living room.	
Samuel:	Buenas tardes, con permiso.
Raul's Mom:	Hola, Samuel, propio.
Samuel:	Good afternoon, with your permission.
Raul's Mom	Hello, Samuel, go ahead.

Samuel walked through a room occupied by Raul's mom; even though he didn't get in her way at all, it was expected he asked for permission to walk across that room.

Conversation 2: Exiting a Room	
Sofía got her regular check-up done; she's heading out of the dentist's office.	
Sofía:	Gracias, con permiso.
Dentist:	De nada, propio, hasta luego.
Sofía:	Thank you, with your permission.
Dentist:	You are welcome, go ahead, see you later.

Sofía was exiting the dentist´s office, so it's expected that she says ***con permiso***.

5 Workbook 5: Lesson Activities

5 Usage Activities *Actividades de Uso*

1. Spanish Translation

Translate the following conversation into English.

1. Liliana is leaving a restaurant and says goodbye to the staff.	
Liliana:	Gracias, adiós.
Waiter:	Hasta luego.
Liliana:	
Waiter:	

2. Carlos leaves Abel's house at night and walks by Abel's family in the living room.	
Carlos:	Buenas noches, con permiso.
Abel's Mom:	Propio, nos vemos.
Carlos:	
Abel's Mom:	

5 Answer Key *Clave de Respuestas*

1. Spanish Translation (answers)

1. Liliana: Thank you, bye.
   Waiter: See you later.

2. Carlos: Good night, with your permission.
   Abel's Mom: Go ahead, see you.

2 PAGES	3 USAGE SECTIONS	0 NEW WORDS

6 Lesson 6: Typing in Spanish

6 Typing in Spanish *Tecleando en Español*

6-1. Adding a Spanish Keyboard

STEP 1: Find Keyboard Settings

As long as you can find the keyboard settings, or input settings, or whatever name it has on your device, you will be able to type in Spanish.

STEP 2: Choose a Spanish

There will be a long list of Spanish languages with the name of the country they are more specific to in parenthesis; we recommend you choose *Spanish (Latin America)*, but they all work almost the same, and they all allow you to input all the Spanish special characters: á é í ó ú ü ñ ¿ ¡

6-2. Adding a Spanish Keyboard

iOS: In iOS devices there is a world icon on the bottom left of the keyboard; tapping that will open a list of currently installed keyboards. You can select Spanish and start typing.

Windows: Click the start button and type "language" to find the "Language Settings". Click "Add a language". You can switch to Spanish by clicking the language icon near the clock.

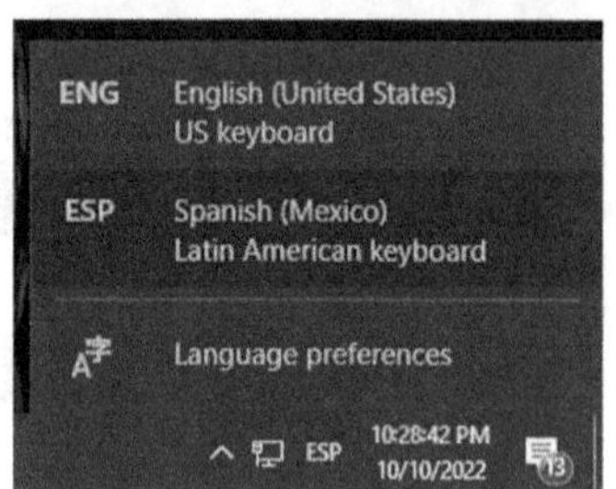

Mac: Mac's language option is on the right side of the top bar, among other options; the changing to Spanish one is available in this menu.

Android: Devices have a variety of keyboard selection methods; one of the most common ones is swiping the space key on the keyboard right or left.

Keep in mind that changing your keyboard to Spanish on a computer will change the location of all the Special characters and how they are inputted.

6-3. Inputting Special Characters

Mobile Devices

Accent marks: Tap and hold the vowel that needs an accent mark. The accent mark will show in the pop up, then slide and select.

ñ (enye): Tap and hold the n key until an ñ key pops up. slide and select.

Upside-down question and exclamation marks: These appear in the special characters area similar to English keyboards. Some devices might require you to tap and hold the standard ! or ? characters for the upside-down versions to show up. Then slide and select.

Windows

Accent marks: With the ESP (Spanish) keyboard selected, you can input an accent mark on a vowel by first clicking the key to the right of "P" and then pressing the desired vowel.

Upside-down question mark: When using the ESP (Spanish) keyboard, tap the key to left of the back space for an upside-down question mark ¿

Upside-down exclamation mark: When using the ESP (Spanish) keyboard, while pressing the shift key, press the key to the left of the back space (the += key). This will output an upside-down exclamation mark ¡

ñ (enye): The letter ***ñ*** has its own spot in a Spanish keyboard. If you are in the ESP (Spanish) keyboard, you just press the key on the right side of the L key (the colon : ; key). When pressed with no modifier keys, ***ñ*** will output.

Vocabulary Builder 1:
Group A

During your studies you will soon realize that grammar points aren't so easily forgotten. But you need more than grammar to speak effectively – you need a lot of vocabulary too!

Throughout this book, we will introduce groups of words that are important to everyday Spanish speaking. You don't have to try to memorize them all at once. Just familiarize yourself with each group since they will be showing up in subsequent lessons.

Group A Body Parts

la cabeza	head	**el estómago**	stomach
el ojo	eye	**la mano**	hand
la oreja	ear	**el dedo**	finger
la nariz	nose	**la pierna**	leg
la boca	mouth	**el pie**	foot

3 PAGES	4 USAGE SECTIONS	10 NEW WORDS

7 Lesson 7: Grammatical Gender

From the teacher...

Gender is important in Spanish. To avoid confusion between *actual* and *grammatical* gender, we will focus on *grammatical* gender in this lesson and *physical* gender in the next.

You don't have to immediately memorize every word introduced in the book, as sometimes words are used just to show a spelling or pronunciation rule. HOWEVER, we recommend you memorize the words in the "New Words" section as best as you can.

7 New Words *Palabras Nuevas*

Nouns etc.

el vestido dress
el árbol tree
el melón melon; cantaloupe
la montaña mountain
la flor flower
el número number
el refrigerador refrigerator
la edad age
la ciudad city

7 Speaking Naturally *Hablando de Forma Natural*

● 7-1. Spelling vs pronunciation

Many Spanish and English words are spelled similar or the same. Even with similar or same spelling, you'll need to properly pronounce the words with Spanish pronunciation.

Spanish	English	Spanish	English
solo	solo	***altar***	altar
teléfono	telephone	***motor***	motor
odor	odor	***restaurante***	restaurant
refrigerador	refrigerator	***color***	color

NOTE: Even with the same spelling Spanish words will NEVER sound exactly like English.

7 Grammar and Usage *Gramática y Uso*

● 7-2. How "grammatical" gender works

Every Spanish noun, from a 'rock' to a 'computer' has "gender". Gender is also matched in Spanish sentences. So, if you say a *grammatically* feminine object is "heavy", then the Spanish word for heavy (***pesado***) must also be in its feminine form (***pesada***).

It's interesting that grammatical gender seems mostly arbitrary. Something you might consider "feminine" can be grammatically "masculine" and vice-versa. For example:

English	Spanish	Gender
dress	vestido	masculine
bicycle	bicicleta	feminine

Mostly women wear dresses, so ***vestido*** being "masculine" might seem strange. Of course, historically men in many societies, including Spain, wore dresses, but that isn't the point.

Some words might seem to have the "wrong" gender. Interestingly, languages such as French and Italian, might use a different gender than Spanish for the same word.

● 7-3. The importance of *El* and *La* in Spanish

Because of the importance of gender in Spanish, nouns are *always* introduced with their "gender companion word", ***el*** (for masculine) or ***la*** (for feminine). ***El*** and ***la*** mean "the".

EXAMPLES

el vestido	the dress (masculine)
la bicicleta	the bicycle (feminine)
el libro	the book (masculine)
la biblioteca	the library (feminine)

Book is "masculine" but library is "feminine". Funny right?

7-4. Trick to determine gender

Often, we can look at the final vowel of a word and determine its gender. Be aware "final vowel" doesn't mean "final letter", but just the last vowel (A, E, I, O, or U) in a word.

When ***el*** or ***la*** are included with a word, the gender is obvious. But at times ***el*** and ***la*** aren't used. For these times, we can make a guess of gender based on the word's final *vowel*.

Final vowel ***A*** *usually* means a word is feminine.

EXAMPLES (FINAL VOWEL 'A' FOR 'FEMININE')

la cabeza	the head	la actividad	the activity
la bicicleta	the bicycle	la edad	the age
la montaña	the mountain	la ciudad	the city

Final vowel ***O*** *usually* means a word is masculine.

EXAMPLES (FINAL VOWEL 'O' FOR 'MASCULINE')

el ojo	the eye	el árbol	the tree
el número	the number	el refrigerador	the refrigerator
el dedo	the finger	el melón	the melon

NOTE: This trick only works with O and A. Other vowels E, I, U don't relate to gender. And even with the O and A trick, there are quite a few exceptions. It's best to always learn the word with its *gender companion word* ***el*** or ***la***.

Vowels ***E, I, U*** can be either masculine or feminine and aren't good gender determiners.

EXAMPLES (CAN BE EITHER GENDER)

la noche (f.)	night	la nariz (f.)	nose	la tribu (f.)	tribe
el cine (m.)	movie theatre	el taxi (m.)	taxi	el menú (m.)	menu

7 Workbook 7: Lesson Activities

7 Spanish 101

1. Test your Spanish knowledge

Answer the following questions about Spanish.

1. **What are the grammatical genders in Spanish?**
   A. masculine / feminine
   B. girl / boy
   C. male / female

2. **Spanish words are spelled the same as English words.**
   A. Always
   B. Never
   C. Sometimes

3. **Spanish words spelled the same as English words are pronounced the same.**
   A. Always
   B. Never
   C. Sometimes

4. **When a Spanish word ends in "o" what gender is it normally?**
   A. Feminine
   B. Neutral
   C. Masculine

5. **Words ending in "a" can be masculine or feminine but are usually:**
   A. Feminine
   B. Neutral
   C. Masculine

6. **There are two gender companion words in Spanish. They are:**
   A. EL for feminine and LA for masculine
   B. LA for feminine and EL for masculine
   C. LA for feminine and AL for masculine
   D. None of the above are correct

7 Answer Key *Clave de Respuestas*

1. Test your Spanish knowledge (answers)

1. A
2. C
3. B
4. C
5. A
6. B

Vocabulary Builder 2:

Groups B and C

Group B Occupations

el abogado	lawyer	**el vendedor**	salesperson; seller
el doctor	doctor	**el taxista**	taxi driver
el ingeniero	engineer	**el repartidor**	delivery person
el chofer	driver (uber, bus etc.)	**el camionero**	truck driver

Group C Animals

el búho	owl	**el conejo**	rabbit
el cocodrilo	crocodile	**el pez**	fish
la jirafa	giraffe	**el hámster**	hamster
el cerdo	pig	**el tigre**	tiger
el oso	bear	**el canguro**	kangaroo

4 PAGES	8 USAGE SECTIONS	8 NEW WORDS

8 Lesson 8: Physical Gender

From the teacher...

Physical gender refers to humans' or animals' gender, being either female or male. *Grammatical gender* is only referring to the way a word is treated in Spanish.

8 New Words *Palabras Nuevas*

Nouns etc.

el niño	child; boy	**la niña**	girl
el maestro	teacher	**el trabajador**	worker
el gato	cat	**el perro**	dog
la criatura	creature	**el luchador**	wrestler

8 Culture Clip *Clip Cultural*

● 8-1. Babies are creatures

Spanish speakers often refer to babies as ***la criatura*** (the creature) in a fond or cute way. Note that ***la criatura*** is grammatically feminine and does not have a masculine version. So regardless of the baby's gender, ***la criatura*** is always feminine grammatically.

● 8-2. You don't live in "America"

The continent of America got its name originally from the man who first mapped it, an Italian explorer named Amerigo Vespucci. Then England set up colonies in the northern area, and eventually they became independent states. After the American Revolution, the "United States of America" was born. It's common for people of the USA to say, "I live in America", but in Spanish, "America" is always called "Estados Unidos" since "America" refers to the entirety of North, Central, and South America.

8 Spanish Spelling *Ortografía del español*

8-3. Don't forget about the *enye*

When pronouncing words with ***ñ***, (pronounced en-yay) it's like having "n" followed by "y". For example, ***el niño*** sounds like, "el ninyo" and ***la niña*** is said as, "la ninya".

8-4. Masculine and feminine pattern

As previously learned, it's a common pattern that masculine words end with ***o*** and feminine with ***a***. Remembering this will help in this lesson.

8 Grammar and Usage *Gramática y Uso*

8-5. Words that change gender

We learned that Spanish assigns gender to all nouns, including non-living ones, such as ***el libro***, which is masculine. In this lesson, words with actual physical gender are introduced.

El niño (the boy) and ***la niña*** (the girl) have *physical* gender. A boy is always boy, therefore its *grammatical* and *physical* gender always match.

Spanish	English	Physical Gender	Grammatical Gender
el niño	the boy	male	masculine
la niña	the girl	female	feminine

Gender for humans

In some cases, *grammatical* gender needs to be changed to match *physical* gender. A person's job title changes based on the person's gender. For example, with male teachers, ***el maestro*** (masculine) is used, for female teachers, ***la maestra***, (feminine) is used.

English	Male	Female
the lawyer	el abogado	la abogada
the cook	el cocinero	la cocinera
the nurse	el enfermero	la enfermera
the waiter	el mesero	la mesera
the cashier	el cajero	la cajera

Gender for Animals

The same thing applies to most animals. For example, if a dog is male, then use ***perro*** (masculine for "dog"). And if the dog is female, use ***perra*** (feminine for "dog").

English	Male	Female
the cat	el gato	la gata
the rabbit	el conejo	la coneja
the pig	el cerdo	la cerda

 *Más Detalles* **More Details** 

New Words with Gender

Recently, English words with gender such as *actor* and *actress* are being unified into "actor" etc. However, Spanish sometimes adds new grammatical gender words.

For example, ***presidente*** (president) was previously used for both *male* and *female* presidents. More and more "***presidenta***" is being used to refer to female presidents.

8-6. Patterns in gender

Many people related words end in ***or***, which is typical of masculine words. However, we can easily make them feminine by adding ***a*** after ***or*** to match the person's *physical* gender.

English	Masculine	Feminine
the wrestler	el luchador	la luchadora
the runner	el corredor	la corredora
the player	el jugador	la jugadora
the worker	el trabajador	la trabajadora

Even names commonly end in ***o*** or ***a*** following gender lines in Spanish.

Boy's Names	Girl's Names
Julio	Julia
Carlo	Carla
Alejandro	Alejandra
Emilio	Emilia
Mario	María

8-7. Words that can be BOTH masculine and feminine

Some people related words can be masculine or feminine by just changing ***el*** and ***la***. In these cases, the final vowel being ***o*** or ***a*** doesn't help determine gender.

Masculine	English	Feminine
el estudiante	student	la estudiante
el turista	tourist	la turista
el dentista	dentist	la dentista
el cliente	costumer	la cliente
el testigo	witness	la testigo

8-8. Looking up words in the dictionary

When looking up words in a Spanish dictionary, instead of ***el*** and ***la*** you will see the symbols ***m.*** for masculine and ***f.*** for feminine in front of every noun.

1. f. Órgano prominente del rostro humano, entre la frente y la boca, con dos orificios, que forma parte del aparato respiratorio. U. t. en pl. con el mismo significado que en sing.

If a word can be both masculine and feminine you will see both listed. In many cases the full word for both genders won't be shown, but just the changed part.

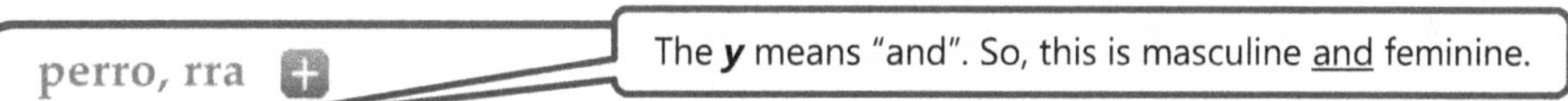

1. m. y f. Mamífero doméstico de la familia de los cánidos, de tamaño, forma y pelaje muy diversos, según las razas, que tiene olfato muy fino y es inteligente y muy leal a su dueño. U. en m. ref. a la especie.

The entries above are from the official Spanish-Spanish dictionary of Spain. (No English)

https://www.rae.es/

8 Workbook 8: Lesson Activities

8 Spanish 101

1. Test your Spanish knowledge

Answer the following questions about Spanish.

1. **Which of the following is true?**
   A. Physical gender is the same as grammatical gender.
   B. Living things have both physical and grammatical gender.
   C. Only non-living things have physical gender.

2. **Which group of words usually have a masculine and a feminine version?**
   A. Occupations
   B. Animals
   C. Insects
   D. A and B are true

3. **What does the word "America" refer to in Spanish?**
   A. The continent of North, Central and South America as a whole.
   B. The United States of America
   C. North America

4. **Which of the following words can be used only to refer to a female?**
   A. dentista
   B. estudiante
   C. criatura
   D. trabajadora

5. **The word *criatura* means "creature," but it is also used to refer to:**
   A. Babies
   B. Adults
   C. Butterflies

6. **Which of the following means "the male dentist"?**
   A. La dentista
   B. La dentisto
   C. El dentista
   D. El dentisto

8 Answer Key *Clave de Respuestas*

1. Test your Spanish knowledge (answers)

1. B
2. D
3. A
4. D
5. A
6. C

Vocabulary Builder 3:

Groups D and E

Group D Food and Drink

la fruta	fruit	**el agua**	water
la verdura	vegetable	**el jugo**	juice
la carne	meat	**el café**	coffee
la pizza	pizza	**el té**	tea
el frijol	bean	**la manzana**	apple
el plátano	banana	**el pan**	bread

Group E Countries

Remember the ***x*** is pronounced as "h".

México	Mexico	**Inglaterra**	England
España	Spain	**Canadá**	Canada
Estados Unidos	United States	**Japón**	Japan

9 PAGES	10 USAGE SECTIONS	19 NEW WORDS

9 Lesson 9: Introduction to Spanish Verbs

9 New Words *Palabras Nuevas*

Nouns etc.

sí yes
no no, not
la comida food, meal
la novela novel
el español Spanish (language)
el inglés English (language)
el libro book
el helado ice cream

Pronouns

yo I
tú you
él he
ella she

Verbs

estudiar to study
comer to eat
beber to drink
hablar to speak
vivir to live
escribir to write

Prepositions

en in

9 New Expressions *Expresiones Nuevas*

Don't worry about the grammar here. Just learn the phrases for communication.

1. **Por supuesto.** **Of course.**

9 Spanish Spelling *Ortografía del español*

● 9-1. Spanish capitalization

As you learn Spanish, you will see that Spanish doesn't capitalize words the same way as English. For example, languages and nationalities aren't capitalized, but countries are.

not capitalized	not capitalized	Capitalized
español Spanish language	español Spanish person	España Spain
inglés English language	inglés English person	Inglaterra England
japonés Japanese language	japonés Japanese person	Japón Japan

● 9-2. Getting the accent mark right

Accent marks are sometimes used just to distinguish similar words. ***El*** (the) and ***él*** (he) have the same pronunciation despite the accent mark. You can imagine the accent mark in ***él*** (he) is a mustache since "he" is male. Or just think, "he" has a mustache.

● 9-3. Basic Spanish plurals

Just like English, "s" and "es" are added to words to make them plural. You add "s" when the word ends with a vowel, and "es" when it ends with a consonant.

Singular		Plural	Singular		Plural
libro book	→	**libros** books	**novela** novel	→	**novelas** novels
frijol bean	→	**frijoles** beans	**flor** flower	→	**flores** flowers
fruta fruit	→	**frutas** fruits	**luchador** wrestler	→	**luchadores** wrestlers

9 Grammar and Usage *Gramática y Uso*

9-4. Pronouns with verbs

Depending on the pronoun used, English adds an "s" or "es" to the verb. For example, "He go<u>es</u> / She run<u>s</u> / Jeff talk<u>s</u>" end in "s" while "I go / we run / you talk" do not.

Spanish <u>also</u> makes changes to the verb based on the <u>pronoun</u> used and <u>verb type</u>. First, let's look at what changes with ***hablar*** (to speak).

English	Spanish
I speak.	Yo habl**o**.
You speak.	Tú habl**as**.
He speak**s**.	Él habl**a**.
She speak**s**.	Ella habl**a**.

Remember, the "h" is silent.

Because of double "LL" ***ella*** is pronounced "ehya."

EXAMPLE SENTENCES

1. Yo <u>hablo</u> español. — I <u>speak</u> Spanish.
2. Tú <u>hablas</u> español. — You <u>speak</u> Spanish.
3. Él <u>habla</u> español. — He <u>speaks</u> Spanish.
4. Ella <u>habla</u> español. — She <u>speaks</u> Spanish.

9-5. Spanish verb types

Every Spanish verb (in its "dictionary" or "base" form) ends with either -***ar***, -***er***, or -***ir***. Let's look at the six verbs in this lesson to see the differences.

Verb	English
estudi**ar**	to study
habl**ar**	to speak
com**er**	to eat
beb**er**	to drink
viv**ir**	to live
escrib**ir**	to write

Irregular verbs have unique conjugations that <u>must be memorized</u> for each verb. *Regular* verbs, like in this lesson, follow <u>standard conjugation rules</u> depending on if they end with ***ar***, ***er***, or ***ir***.

9-6. *Regular* Spanish verb conjugation rules

Step one to conjugate a regular verb is to remove the verb ending -***ar***, -***er***, or -***ir***. The result is called the "verb stem".

Dictionary Form		Remove Ending		Verb Stem
estudi**ar**	→	estudi~~ar~~	→	estudi~
com**er**	→	com~~er~~	→	com~
escrib**ir**	→	escrib~~ir~~	→	escrib~

Now we add a new ending based on the pronoun used and the verb's original ending.

Present Tense Conjugation for Regular Verb Types			
Pronoun	**~ar**	**~er**	**~ir**
yo (I)	~o	~o	~o
tú (you)	~as	~es	~es
él (he)	~a	~e	~e
ella (she)			

NOTE: ***él*** and ***ella*** conjugate the same way.

Let's try some! Look at the pronoun and verb type (***ar***, ***er***, ***ir***) and see if you can conjugate.

EXAMPLE SENTENCES

hablar (to speak) -***ar***

1. Yo hablo español. — I speak Spanish.
2. Tú hablas español. — You speak Spanish.
3. Él habla español. — He speaks Spanish.

comer (to eat) -***er***

1. Yo como pizza. — I eat pizza.
2. Tú comes pizza. — You eat pizza.
3. Ella come pizza. — She eats pizza.

escribir (to write) -***ir***

1. Yo escribo novelas. — I write novels.
2. Tú escribes novelas. — You write novels.
3. Hugo escribe novelas. — Hugo writes novels.

Hugo is a name. Names follow "he / she" rules.

9-7. Verb conjugations

Eventually you'll be able to conjugate regular verbs naturally using the *regular* conjugation rules. But until then, these charts will be handy. Here are the verbs in this lesson.

pronoun	estudiar	hablar	comer	beber	vivir	escribir
(I) **yo**	estudio	hablo	como	bebo	vivo	escribo
(you) **tú**	estudias	hablas	comes	bebes	vives	escribes
(he) **él**	estudia	habla	come	bebe	vive	escribe
(she) **ella**	estudia	habla	come	bebe	vive	escribe

Even better than memorizing conjugation charts and learning patterns is giving your brain a ton of examples that it can use to build its own verb understanding.

EXAMPLE SENTENCES

estudiar (to study) -ar

1. Yo estudio inglés.	I study English.
2. Tú estudias español.	You study Spanish.
3. Él estudia medicina.	He studies medicine.

hablar (to speak) -ar

4. Yo hablo español.	I speak Spanish.
5. Tú hablas inglés.	You speak English.
6. Ella habla francés.	She speaks French.

comer (to eat) -er

7. Yo como fruta.	I eat fruit.
8. Tú comes pizza.	You eat pizza.
9. Él come frijoles.	He eats beans.

beber (to drink) -er

10. Yo bebo té.	I drink tea.
11. Tú bebes café.	You drink coffee.
12. Ella bebe jugo.	She drinks juice.

vivir (to live) -ir

"In" is ***en*** in Spanish.

13. Yo vivo en México.	I live in Mexico.
14. Tú vives en la ciudad.	You live in the city.
15. Ella vive en Estados Unidos.	She lives in the United States.

escribir (to write) -ir

16. Yo escribo libros.	I write books.
17. Tu escribes novelas.	You write novels.
18. José escribe en inglés.	Jose writes in English.

9-8. Making questions in Spanish

Making questions in Spanish is super easy. The order of the sentence doesn't change like English. You just add question marks and BOOM you have a question.

Tú hablas español. **You speak Spanish.**	**¿Tú hablas español?** **Do you speak Spanish?**

Remember, Spanish uses the upside-down question mark: "**¿**" at the start of a question.

EXAMPLE Q&A

1. **¿Tú hablas español?**	**Do you speak Spanish?**
Sí, yo hablo español.	Yes, I speak Spanish.
No, yo hablo inglés.	No, I speak English.
2. **¿Tú comes carne?**	**Do you eat meat?**
Sí, yo como carne.	Yes, I eat meat.
No, yo como verduras.	No, I eat vegetables.
3. **¿Él habla inglés?**	**Does he speak English?**
Sí, él habla inglés.	Yes, he speaks English.
No, él habla español.	No, he speaks Spanish.

Yo **hablo** español.

Él **escribe** libros.

Yo **bebo** café.

9-9. Making verbs negative

We can make verbs negative by simply adding "***no***" before the verb.

EXAMPLE Q&A

1. **¿Ella habla español?**	**Does she speak Spanish?**
Sí, ella habla español.	Yes, she speaks Spanish.
No, ella <u>no</u> habla español.	No, she <u>doesn't</u> speak Spanish.
2. **¿Tú vives en México?**	**Do you live in Mexico?**
Sí, yo vivo en México.	Yes, I live in Mexico.
No, yo <u>no</u> vivo en México.	No, I <u>don't</u> live in Mexico.
No, yo vivo en Estados Unidos.	No, I live in the United States.

 *Más Detalles* **More Details** 

For the teetotallers

Some of you might not know, *teetotaller* means someone who doesn't drink alchohol. Using the Spanish we learned in this lesson you can let your Spanish speaking friends know that you "don't drink".

9 Memorization Techniques *Técnicas de Memorización*

9-10. Spanish S migration hint

As an English speaker, I used to mix up verb conjugations for ***Yo***, ***Tu***, and ***Él*** / ***Ella*** / ***Name***. Then I realized the "s" was just moving up one spot in the mental chart I had in my head. It doesn't help with every conjugation, but it at least fixes the "s" problem I was having.

I eat	[ ]	Yo como	[ ]
You eat	[ ]	Tú come	[s]
He eat	[s]	Él come	[ ]

EXAMPLE SENTENCES

1. Tú comes tacos.	You eat tacos.
2. Él come tacos.	He eats tacos.

9 Practice and Review *Práctica y Repaso*

1. Question and Answer (Spanish → English)

Each question has multiple answers. Cover up the right side and try to translate.

1. **¿Tú estudias francés?** — **Do you study French?**
   - Sí, yo estudio francés. — Yes, I study French.
   - No, yo no estudio francés. — No, I don't study French.
   - No, yo estudio español. — No, I study Spanish.

2. **¿Jorge escribe novelas?** — **Does Jorge write novels?**
   - Sí, él escribe novelas. — Yes, he writes novels.
   - No, Jorge no escribe. — No, Jorge doesn't write.

3. **¿Tú bebes jugo?** — **Do you drink juice?**
   - No, yo bebo agua. — No, I drink water.
   - Sí, yo bebo jugo. — Yes, I drink juice.

4. **¿Él vive en España?** — **Does he live in Spain?**
   - Sí, él vive en España. — Yes, he lives in Spain.
   - No, él vive en Estados Unidos. — No, he lives in the US.

5. **¿Ella habla español?** — **Does she speak Spanish?**
   - Sí, ella habla español — Yes, she speaks Spanish.
   - No, ella no habla español. — No, she doesn't speak Spanish.
   - No, ella habla inglés. — No, she speaks English.

2. Question and answer (English → Spanish)

Each question has multiple answers. Cover up the right side and try to translate.

1. **Do you study Spanish?** — **¿Tú estudias español?**
   - Yes, I study Spanish — Sí, yo estudio español.
   - No, I study English — No, yo estudio inglés.
   - No. — No.

2. **Do you eat ice cream?** — **¿Tú comes helado?**
   - Yes, I eat ice cream — Sí, yo como helado.
   - No, I don't eat ice cream. — No, yo no como helado.

3. **Does he drink coffee?** — **¿Él bebe café?**
   - Yes, he drinks coffee — Sí, él bebe café.
   - No, he doesn't drink coffee. — No, él no bebe café.
   - No. — No.

4. **Does she live in England?** — **¿Ella vive en Inglaterra?**
   - Yes, she lives in England. — Sí, ella vive en Inglaterra.
   - No, she lives in Mexico. — No, ella vive en México.
   - Yes. — Sí.

5. **Does Laura drink tea?** — **¿Laura bebe té?**
   - Yes, she drinks tea. — Sí, ella bebe té.
   - No, she drinks coffee. — No, ella bebe café.

9 Workbook 9: Lesson Activities

9 Vocabulary Drills *Ejercicios de Vocabulario*

● 1. Writing and Vocabulary

Write the Spanish for each of the pictures. Make sure to add accent marks when needed.

fruit, food, vegetables, coffee, tea, beans, meat, ice cream, book, juice

1.__________ 2.__________ 3.__________ 4.__________ 5.__________

6.__________ 7.__________ 8.__________ 9.__________ 10.__________

● 2. Gender Matching

From the words below write the Spanish above the matching English and circle the correct gender companion word.

ciudad, flor, fruta, jugo, melón, café, bicicleta, frijol, carne, refrigerador

1) el / la ____________________
(city)

2) el / la ____________________
(meat)

3) el / la ____________________
(fruit)

4) el / la ____________________
(coffee)

5) el / la ______________________
(cantaloupe)

6) el / la ______________________
(refrigerator)

7) el / la ______________________
(flower)

8) el / la ______________________
(juice)

9) el / la ______________________
(bicycle)

10) el / la ______________________
(bean)

9 Usage Activities *Actividades de Uso*

3. Reading Comprehension

Translate the following on a separate piece of paper or type in an electronic device.
New words: ***la cuenta*** "bill, check" (at a restaurant, etc)

Observations

We don't know enough to do coherent stories, but with your Spanish you can observe things.

Observations at school

Remember without a mustache ***el*** means "the".

❶ El maestro habla inglés.

❷ La maestra bebe café.

❸ Él estudia español.

❹ Ella estudia francés.

Observations at the restaurant

❺ El niño come pizza.

❻ Tú bebes jugo.

❼ Carlos come carne.

❽ La mesera escribe la cuenta.

4. Reading Comprehension Questions

Answer the following questions about the reading comprehension. Write full Spanish sentences. Note: The questions aren't in the same order as the observations.

1. What does the female teacher do?

   ____

2. What does the male teacher do?

   ____

3. What's she studying?

   ____

4. What are you drinking?

   ____

5. What is the boy eating?

   ____

6. What's the waitress doing?

   ____

7. Who is eating meat?

   ____

8. Does she study Spanish?

   ____

5. Spanish Translation

Translate the following conversations into English.

1.
A: ¿Tú estudias español? B: No, yo estudio inglés. A: ¿Tú escribes novelas? B: No, yo no escribo novelas.
A:
B:
A:
B:

6. English Translation

Translate the following conversations into Spanish.

1.
A: Do you eat meat? B: No, I don't eat meat. A: Do you eat vegetables? B: Yes, I eat vegetables.
A:
B:
A:
B:

7. Verb conjugation drills

Fill in the blanks with the proper verb conjugations.

1. Comer (to eat)

Pronouns	Present Tense
Yo	
Tú	
Él	
Ella	
Jorge	

2. Vivir (to live)

Pronouns	Present Tense
Yo	
Tú	
Él	
Ella	
Carlos	

3. Hablar (to speak)

Pronouns	Present Tense
Yo	
Tú	
Él	
Ella	
Daniela	

9 Answer Key *Clave de Respuestas*

1. Writing and Vocabulary (answers)

1. carne
meat

2. comida
food

3. café
coffee

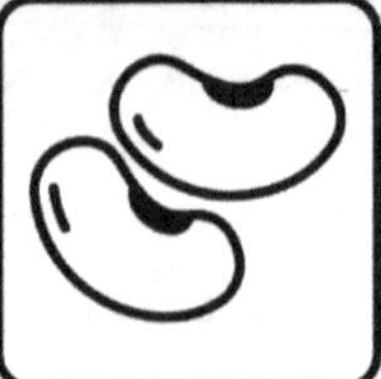
4. frijoles
beans

5. helado
ice cream

6. jugo
juice

7. frutas
fruits

8. verduras
vegetables

9. té
tea

10. libro
book

2. Gender Matching (answers)

1) la ciudad
2) la carne
3) la fruta
4) el café
5) el melón
6) el refrigerador
7) la flor
8) el jugo
9) la bicicleta
10) el té

3. Reading Comprehension Translation

At school.

① The teacher (male) speaks English.
② The teacher (female) drinks coffee.
③ He studies Spanish.
④ She studies French.

At the restaurant.

① The boy eats pizza.
② You drink juice.
③ Carlos eats meat.
④ The waitress writes the check.

4. Reading Comprehension Questions (answers)

1. What does the female teacher do? Ella bebe café.
2. What does the male teacher do? Él habla inglés.
3. What's she studying? Ella estudia francés.
4. What are you drinking? Yo bebo jugo.
5. What is the boy eating? El niño come pizza.
6. What's the waitress doing? La mesera escribe la cuenta.
7. Who is eating meat? Carlos come carne.
8. Does she study Spanish? No, ella estudia francés.

5. Spanish Translation (answers)

1. A: Do you study Spanish?
   B: No, I study English.
   A: Do you write novels?
   B: No, I don't write novels.

6. English Translation (answers)

1. A: ¿Tú comes carne?
   B: No, yo no como carne.
   A: ¿Tú comes verduras?
   B: Sí, yo como verduras.

7. Verb conjugation drills (answers)

1. Comer (to eat)	
Pronouns	Present Tense
Yo	como
Tú	comes
Él	come
Ella	come
Jorge	come

2. Vivir (to live)	
Pronouns	Present Tense
Yo	vivo
Tú	vives
Él	vive
Ella	vive
Carlos	vive

3. Hablar (to speak)	
Pronouns	Present Tense
Yo	hablo
Tú	hablas
Él	habla
Ella	habla
Daniela	habla

Vocabulary Builder 4:
Groups F and G

Group F Nationalities

español	Spanish	**chino**	Chinese
mexicano	Mexican	**argentino**	Argentinian
estadounidense	American	**chileno**	Chilean
inglés	English	**brasileño**	Brazilian
australiano	Australian	**colombiano**	Colombian
neozelandés	New Zealand	**italiano**	Italian
japonés	Japanese	**francés**	French
coreano	Korean	**alemán**	German

Group G More Countries

Argentina	Argentina	**Brasil**	Brazil
Australia	Australia	**Colombia**	Colombia
Nueva Zelanda	New Zealand	**Italia**	Italy
Corea	Korea	**Francia**	France
China	China	**Alemania**	Germany
Chile	Chile		

8 PAGES	9 USAGE SECTIONS	16 NEW WORDS

10 Lesson 10: Basic Spanish Sentences

10 New Words *Palabras Nuevas*

Nouns etc.

el tiempo	time	**el amigo**	friend
el dinero	money	**la mascota**	pet
el calor	heat	**el sueño**	sleepiness
el frío	coldness	**la sed**	thirst
el hambre	hunger	**el problema**	problem

Names

Juan	(boy's name)	**Luis**	(boy's name)
María	(girl's name)	**Sofía**	(girl' name)

Verbs

tener	to have	**ser**	to be (is, am, are)

10 Culture Clip *Clip Cultural*

In English we address people with the abbreviations Mr. (mister) and Mrs. (missus). Spanish also uses similar abbreviations ***Sr.*** for ***Señor*** (mister) and ***Sra.*** for ***Señora*** (missus).

In English we use Mr. and Mrs. for teachers, but in Spanish ***Maestro*** or ***Maestra*** is added in front of the teacher's name, or ***profesor*** or ***profesora*** for professors.

● 10-1. It might be difficult to be American

It might be difficult to be American since the word "American" in Spanish is so long! "American" in Spanish is ***estadounidense***. In reality for Spanish speakers, everyone born in South, Central, and North America are collectively called ***americanos***.

So, to say "I am an American" ***Yo soy americano*** just means you are from one of those regions. To truly be "American" in the English sense, you must say ***Yo soy estadounidense.***

10 Verb Usage *Uso de Verbos*

The verb usage area teaches the basics of the lesson's new verbs based on what we already know about Spanish. Additional new information will be in the *Grammar and Usage* section.

V-1

tener	to have	irregular
Yo ***tengo***.	I **have**.	
Tú ***tienes***.	You **have**.	
Él / Ella / Name ***tiene***.	He / She / Name **has**.	

It's an unfortunate fact of Spanish that some of the most COMMONLY used verbs such as ***tener*** are *irregular*, so their verb patterns are unique and must be memorized.

If ***tener*** was regular, it would conjugate as ***teno*** for ***yo*** and ***tenes*** for ***tú***. But it's irregular, so those conjugations are wrong. Instead, ***yo*** is ***tengo***, and ***tú*** is ***tienes***.

There probably won't be a day in your Spanish speaking life where you won't use ***tener***, so learning its irregular conjugations is important.

EXAMPLE SENTENCES

1. Yo no tengo dinero. — I don't have money.
2. ¿Tú tienes tiempo? — Do you have time?
3. Él no tiene amigos. — He doesn't have friends.
4. Ella tiene mascotas. — She has pets.

¡Yo no tengo tiempo!

10 Grammar and Usage *Gramática y Uso*

10-2. Single items vs multiple items

Just like English, you need to add "a, an" in front of the word. In Spanish, this is done with ***un*** for masculine words or ***una*** for feminine.

EXAMPLE SENTENCES

1. Yo tengo un gato. — I have a cat.
2. Ella tiene un libro. — She has a book.
3. Él tiene una manzana. — He has an apple.
4. Daniela tiene una mascota. — Daniela has a pet.
5. Juan tiene un problema. — Juan has a problem.

Problema ends with "a" but is masculine.

When someone has multiple items, then just like English, we can drop the ***un*** and ***una***.

EXAMPLE SENTENCES

1. Yo tengo gatos. — I have cats.
2. Ella tiene libros. — She has books.
3. Él tiene manzanas. — He has apples.
4. María tiene mascotas. — María has pets.
5. Juán tiene problemas. — Juan has problems.

The simple rule is, if there isn't an "a" or "an" in English then there won't be ***un*** or ***una***.

EXAMPLE SENTENCES

1. Yo tengo dinero. — I have money.
2. María no tiene tiempo. — María doesn't have time.
3. Juan no tiene problemas. — Juan doesn't have problems.

10-3. Specific amounts

Un perro means "a dog" and also "one dog". If we want to say more than one dog we can just put numbers in front of ***perros*** or ***perras*** for female dogs.

Masculine	Feminine	English
un perro ★	una perra	1 dog
dos perros	dos perras	2 dogs
tres perros	tres perras	3 dogs
cuatro perros	cuatro perras	4 dogs
cinco perros	cinco perras	5 dogs
seis perros	seis perras	6 dogs
siete perros	siete perras	7 dogs
ocho perros	ocho perras	8 dogs
nueve perros	nueve perras	9 dogs
diez perros	diez perras	10 dogs
veinte perros	veinte perras	20 dogs
veintiún perros ★	veintiuna perras	21 dogs
cien perros	cien perras	100 dogs
doscientos perros ★	doscientas perras	200 dogs
★ There are changes based on gender.		

EXAMPLE SENTENCES

1. Yo tengo tres gatos. — I have three cats.
2. Ella tiene siete libros. — She has seven books.
3. Él tiene una novela. — He has (a / one) novel.
4. María tiene vientiúna mascotas. — María has twenty one pets.

This is feminine because ***mascota*** is feminine.

10-4. Is / Am / Are in Spanish - *ser*

Ser means *is*, *am*, and *are*. Just like other verbs, it must conjugate based on the pronoun. ***Ser*** is irregular so you must memorize how it conjugates.

pronoun	**ser** (is, am, are)
(I) **yo**	soy
(you) **tú**	eres
(he) **él**	es
(she) **ella**	es
(name)	es

EXAMPLE SENTENCES

Yo soy estadounidense.	I am American.
Tú eres argentino.	You are Argentinian.
Él es mexicano.	He is Mexican.
Ella es coreana.	She is Korean.
Juan es chileno.	Juan is Chilean.

With identity, such as nationality or a job, English adds "a" or "an" in front of the word. For example, "a lawyer" or "an American." In Spanish for identity, ***un*** and ***una*** aren't used.

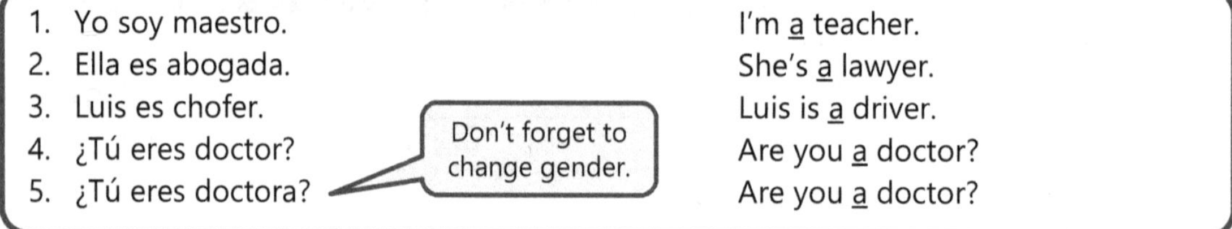

1. Yo soy maestro. — I'm a teacher.
2. Ella es abogada. — She's a lawyer.
3. Luis es chofer. — Luis is a driver.
4. ¿Tú eres doctor? — Are you a doctor?
5. ¿Tú eres doctora? — Are you a doctor?

10-5. Having hunger and cold - *tener*

Here is a part of Spanish that is quite different from English. In English, we can say, "I am hungry" or "I am cold," but in Spanish, "I have hunger" and "I have coldness" is used.

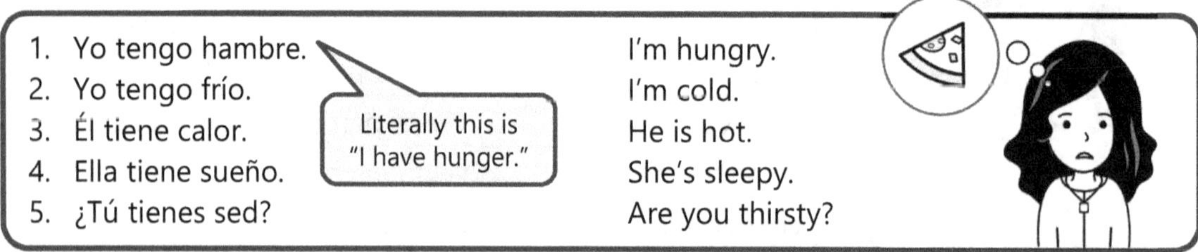

1. Yo tengo hambre. — I'm hungry.
2. Yo tengo frío. — I'm cold.
3. Él tiene calor. — He is hot.
4. Ella tiene sueño. — She's sleepy.
5. ¿Tú tienes sed? — Are you thirsty?

NOTE: In English we can say, "She's hot" to mean a person is "attractive" or "He's cold" to mean a person isn't kind, but in Spanish these phrases are only about temperature.

10-6. Having age in Spanish - *tener*

When you want to say how old someone is, you can't us ***ser*** *(is, am, are)*. Instead you use ***tener*** to say, "have years of age."

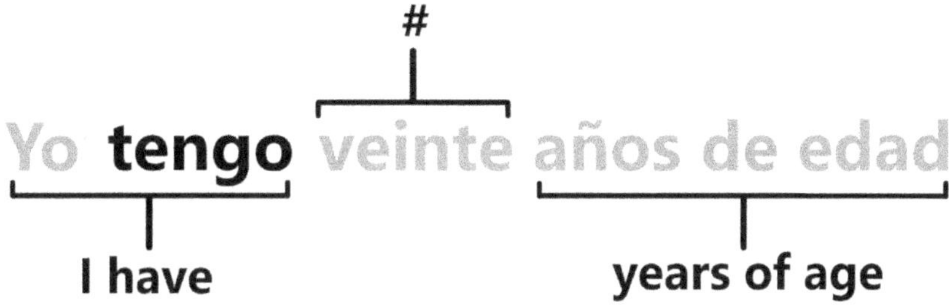

If needed, review lesson 3 (Basic Counting) to re-familiarize yourself with Spanish counting.

EXAMPLE SENTENCES	
1. Yo tengo veinticinco años de edad.	I'm 25 years old.
2. Ella tiene treinta y dos años de edad.	She's 32 years old.
3. Sofía tiene once años de edad.	Sofia is 11 years old.
4. ¿Tú tienes dieciocho años de edad?	Are you 18 years old?

NOTE: It's common that ***de edad*** (of age) is removed when speaking.

EXAMPLE SENTENCES	
1. Yo tengo dieciséis años.	I'm 16.
2. Él tiene cincuenta y nueve años.	He's 59.

10-7. Saying people's names with *ser*

You previously learned "***Soy (name)***" to say your name, but this phrase only works for YOUR name. To introduce other people, you'll need to properly conjugate the ***ser***.

EXAMPLE SENTENCES	
1. Yo soy Carlos.	I'm Carlos.
2. Ella es Sofía.	She is Sofia.
3. Él es Juan.	He is Juan.
4. ¿Tú eres María?	Are you María?

Carlos Maria

● 10-8. Sentence order with negative *ser*

For most negative verbs, the ***no*** translates to "don't" so the order is the same as English.

Yo **no** tengo. I **don't** have.
Yo **no** estudio. I **don't** study.
Yo **no** bebo. I **don't** drink.

The tricky part is with the verb ***ser*** (is, am, are) ***no*** translates to "not" and in English the "not" comes after (~am not, ~is not). HOWEVER, in Spanish the ***no*** must come before ***ser***.

Yo **no** soy mexicano. I am **not** Mexican.
Tú **no** eres mexicano. You are **not** Mexican.
Él **no** es mexicano. He is **not** Mexican.

If you remember that ***no*** always comes before the verb, your Spanish will always be correct (at least in this particular case). The rest of your Spanish might be horrible, but at least this part will be good. 😊

● 10-9. Gender in nationalities

For nationalities you must modify them to match the gender of the person.
There are patterns to make modifications.

If the final letter of the nationality is ***o***, then just change it to ***a***.

nationality	male	female
Mexican	mexicano	mexicana
Brazilian	brasileño	brasileña
Colombian	colombiano	colombiana

If the nationality ends in a consonant you add a to it to make it feminine.

nationality	male	female
Spanish	español	española
German	alemán	alemana
French	francés	francesa

For nationalities ending ending in ***e***, such as ***estadounidense*** (American), the word doesn't change based on gender.

10 Practice and Review *Práctica y Repaso*

1. Question and Answer (Spanish → English)

Each question has multiple answers. Cover up the right side and try to translate.

1. **¿Tú eres coreano?**	**Are you Korean?**
No, yo soy japonés.	No, I'm Japanese.
No, yo soy estadounidense.	No, I'm American.
No, yo no soy coreano.	No. I'm not Korean.
2. **¿Daniela es abogada?**	**Is Daniela a lawyer?**
Sí, Daniela es abogada.	Yes, Daniela is a lawyer.
No, Daniela es doctora.	No, Daniela is a doctor.
No, Daniela no es abogada.	No. Daniela is not a lawyer.
3. **¿Tú tienes hambre?**	**Are you hungry?**
Sí, tengo hambre.	Yes, I'm hungry.
No, no tengo hambre.	No, I'm not hungry.
No, yo tengo sed.	No. I'm thirsty.
4. **¿Luis tiene sueño?**	**Is Luis sleepy?**
No, él no tiene sueño.	No, he is not sleepy.
No, él tiene hambre.	No, I'm he is hungry.
Sí, el tiene sueño.	Yes, he is sleepy.
5. **¿Sofía tiene una mascota?**	**Does Sofía have a pet?**
Sí, ella tiene un perro.	Yes, she has a dog.
Sí, ella tiene cuatro gatos.	Yes, she has four cats.
No, Sofía no tiene una mascota.	No, Sofia doesn't have a pet.
6. **¿Tú tienes mascotas?**	**Do you have pets?**
Sí, yo tengo una gata.	Yes, I have a cat.
Sí, yo tengo dos búhos.	Yes, I have two owls.
No, yo no tengo mascotas.	No, I don't have pets.
7. **¿Juan tiene un problema?**	**Does Juan have a problem?**
Sí, él no tiene dinero.	Yes, he has no money.
Sí, él no tiene tiempo.	Yes, he doesn't have time.
No, él no tiene problemas.	No, he doesn't have problems.

2. Question and answer (English → Spanish)

Each question has multiple answers. Cover up the right side and try to translate.

1. **Are you English?** — **¿Tú eres Inglés?**
   - No, I'm American. — No, yo soy estadounidense.
   - No, I'm not English. — No, yo no soy inglés.
   - Yes, I'm English. — Sí, yo soy inglés.

2. **Is Juan Argentinian?** — **¿Juan es argentino?**
   - No, he is Mexican. — No, él es mexicano.
   - Yes, Juan is Argentinian. — Sí, Juan es argentino.
   - Yes. — Sí.

3. **Are you hot?** — **¿Tú tienes calor?**
   - Yes, I'm hot. — Sí, yo tengo calor.
   - No, I'm not hot. — No, yo no tengo calor.
   - No, I'm cold. — No, yo tengo frío.

4. **Does Carlos have cats?** — **¿Carlos tiene gatos?**
   - No, Carlos doesn't have cats. — No, Carlos no tiene gatos.
   - No, he doesn't have pets. — No, él no tiene mascotas.
   - Yes, he has cats. — Sí, él tiene gatos.

5. **Is Luis a driver?** — **¿Luis es chofer?**
   - No, he is a delivery person. — No, él es repartidor.
   - No, he is a teacher. — No, él es maestro.
   - Yes, he is a driver. — Sí, él es chofer.

6. **Do you have friends?** — **¿Tú tienes amigos?**
   - No, I don't have friends. — No, yo no tengo amigos.
   - Yes, I have one friend. — Sí, yo tengo una amiga / un amigo.
   - Yes, I have ten friends. — Sí, yo tengo diez amigos.

7. **Are you hungry?** — **¿Tú tienes hambre?**
   - No, I'm not hungry. — No, yo no tengo hambre.
   - Yes, I'm hungry. — Sí, yo tengo hambre.
   - Do you have food? — ¿Tú tienes comida?
   - No, I'm thirsty. — No, yo tengo sed.

10 Workbook 10: Lesson Activities

10 Vocabulary Drills *Ejercicios de Vocabulario*

1. Writing and vocabulary

Write the Spanish for each of the pictures. Make sure to add accent marks when needed.

sales person, lawyer (female), lawyer (male), doctor, delivery person, taxi driver, pig, fish, truck driver, United States

1.__________

2.__________

3.__________

4.__________

5.__________

6.__________

7.__________

8.__________

9.__________

10.__________

2. Gender Matching

From the words below, write the Spanish above the matching English and circle the correct gender companion word.

sueño, mascota, dinero, helado, comida, té, libro, árbol, frío, tiempo

1) el / la ____________________
(sleepiness)

2) el / la ____________________
(money)

3) el / la ____________________
(pet)

4) el / la ____________________
(tree)

5) el / la ______________________
(ice cream)

6) el / la ______________________
(food / meal)

7) el / la ______________________
(tea)

8) el / la ______________________
(book)

9) el / la ______________________
(coldness)

10) el / la ______________________
(time)

10 Usage Activities *Actividades de Uso*

● 3. Reading Comprehension

Translate the following on a separate piece of paper or type in an electronic device.

Talking About People

With your current Spanish, you can talk about people's nationalities, occupations and ages.

❶ Sofía es mexicana. Ella habla español.

❷ Juan es estadounidense. Él habla inglés.

❸ María es francesa. Ella habla francés.

❹ Jimin es coreano. Él habla coreano.

❺ Laura es abogada. Ella tiene treinta y cinco años.

❻ Daniela es maestra. Ella tiene veintisiete años.

❼ Carlos es estudiante. Él tiene diecisiete años.

❽ Felipe es chofer. Él tiene cuarenta y un años.

4. Reading Comprehension Questions

Answer the following questions about the observations made in the reading comprehension. Write full sentences with pronouns and verbs.

1. Who is Mexican?

____

2. Who speaks English?

____

3. Who is American?

____

4. Who speaks Korean?

____

5. How old is the driver?

____

6. What occupation is the 35-year-old person?

____

7. Who is a teacher?

____

8. Who is 17 years old?

____

● 5. Spanish Translation

Translate the following conversations into English.

1.
A: ¿Tú tienes sed? B: No, no tengo sed. A: ¿Tú tienes hambre? B: Sí, tengo hambre.
A:
B:
A:
B:

● 6. English Translation

Translate the following conversations into Spanish.

1.
A: How old are you? B: I'm 22 years old. A: Are you a student? B: No, I'm not a teacher.
A:
B:
A:
B:

7. Verb conjugation drills

Fill in the blanks with the proper verb conjugations.

1. Ser (to be)	
Pronouns	**Present Tense**
Yo	
Tú	
Él	
Ella	
Jorge	

2. Tener (to have)	
Pronouns	**Present Tense**
Yo	
Tú	
Él	
Ella	
Carlos	

10 Answer Key *Clave de Respuestas*

1. Writing and Vocabulary (answers)

1. doctor
doctor

2. pez
fish

3. abogada
lawyer (female)

4. camionero
truck driver

5. cerdo
pig

6. estados unidos
United States

7. vendedor
sales person

8. abogado
lawyer (male)

9. taxista
taxi driver

10. repartidor
delivery person

2. Gender Matching (answers)

1) el sueño
2) el dinero
3) la mascota
4) el árbol
5) el helado
6) la comida
7) el té
8) el libro
9) el frío
10) el tiempo

3. Reading Comprehension Translation

① Sofia is Mexican. She speaks Spanish.
② Juan is American. He speaks English.
③ María is French. He speaks French.
④ Jimin is Korean. He speaks Korean.

① Laura is a lawyer. She is 35 years old.
② Daniela is a teacher. She is 27 years old.
③ Carlos is a student. He is 17 years old.
④ Felipe is a driver. He is 41 years old.

4. Reading Comprehension Questions (answers)

1. Who is Mexican? — Sofía es mexicana.
2. Who speaks English? — Juan habla inglés.
3. Who is American? — Juan es estadounidense.
4. Who speaks Korean? — Jimin habla coreano.
5. How old is the driver? — El chofer / Felipe tiene 41 años de edad.
6. What occupation is the 35-year-old person? — Laura es abogada.
7. Who is a teacher? — Daniela es maestra.
8. Who is 17 years old? — Carlos tiene 17 años.

5. Spanish Translation (answers)

1. A: Are you thirsty?
   B: No, I'm not thirsty.
   A: Are you hungry?
   B: Yes, I'm hungry.

6. English Translation (answers)

1. A: ¿Cuántos años tienes?
   B: Yo tengo 22 años.
   A: ¿Tú eres estudiante?
   B: No, yo soy maestro.

7. Verb conjugation drills (answers)

1. Ser (to be)	
Pronouns	Present Tense
Yo	soy
Tú	eres
Él	es
Ella	es
Jorge	es

2. Tener (to have)	
Pronouns	Present Tense
Yo	tengo
Tú	tienes
Él	tiene
Ella	tiene
Carlos	tiene

Vocabulary Builder 5: Groups H and I

Group H Family

el padre	father	**el hijo**	son
la madre	mother	**la hija**	daughter
el papá	dad	**el tío**	uncle
la mamá	mom	**la tía**	aunt
el hermano	brother	**el primo**	cousin (male)
la hermana	sister	**la prima**	cousin (female)

Group I Clothing

la camisa	shirt	**la falda**	skirt
la camiseta	t-shirt	**la calceta**	sock
el zapato	shoe	**el pantalón**	pant
el brasier	bra	**el calzón**	briefs; panties
la chaqueta	jacket		

17 PAGES	12 USAGE SECTIONS	0 NEW WORDS

11 Lesson 11: New Pronouns and Possession

From the teacher...

In this lesson we expand on Spanish plurals. To do this, we will introduce some words that might seem unnecessary at this level but help teach plurals.

11 New Words *Palabras Nuevas*

Nouns etc.

el interés	interest	**la luz**	light
el autobús	bus	**el dios**	god
la nuez	nut	**el volcán**	volcano
el día	day	**la mañana**	morning
todos	every~; all~	**el mañana**	tomorrow
la puerta	door	**la ventana**	window
el manga	Japanese comics	**la novia**	girlfriend; bride
la casa	house; home	**la ropa**	clothes
la tienda	store	**el trabajo**	work; job

Pronouns

usted	you (respectful)	**ustedes**	y'all; you guys
nosotras	we (feminine)	**nosotros**	we (masculine)
ellos	they (masculine)	**ellas**	they (feminine)
mi	my~	**tu**	your~
su	their~		

Verbs

cocinar	to cook	**leer**	to read
abrir	to open		

11 Word Usage *Uso de Palabras*

W-1	**mañana**	**morning; tomorrow**

It's interesting that in Spanish the same word has two meanings, the only difference is gender. "Morning" is feminine ***la mañana***, and "tomorrow" is masculine, ***el mañana***.

el mañana tomorrow	**la** mañana morning

Without more grammar we can't do much with these. More to come!

W-2	**todos**	**every~; all~**

We can use ***todos*** (every) in combination with ***el dia*** (day) and ***la mañana*** to say, "every day" and "every morning." For masculine words, use ***todos*** and for feminine ***todas***.

todos los dias every day	**todas** las mañanas every morning	**todos** los libros all the books

We learn more about ***los*** and ***las*** in this lesson, but in short, these are plural versions of ***el*** and ***la***. Essentially in Spanish we are saying, "every the days" and "every the mornings".

EXAMPLE SENTENCES

1. Yo como verduras todos los días.	I eat vegetables every day.
2. Él escribe todos los días.	He writes every day.
3. Ella estudia español todas las mañanas.	She studies Spanish every morning.
4. Carla bebe café todas las mañanas.	Carla drinks coffee every morning.
5. Yo tengo todos los libros.	I have all the books.
6. ¿Tú tienes todas las novelas?	Do you have all the novels?

See how ***todos*** is used to say "all".

Yo escribo libros todos los dias.

W-3

ropa	**clothes**

In English, "fish" can be plural as in "there are two fish," however, we can also say, "fishes" to mean "more than one species of fish." ***Ropa*** (clothes) is similar in Spanish as it is plural without having an "s" at the end. ***Ropas*** is used to mean "clothing types."

EXAMPLE Q&A

1. ¿Tú tienes ropa en el hotel?	**Do you have clothes at the hotel?**
No, yo no tengo.	No, I don't have (any).
Sí, yo tengo ropa en el hotel.	Yes, I have clothes at the hotel.
No, yo tengo ropa en mi auto.	No, I have clothes in my car.

 *Más Detalles* More Details 

Other plural mind benders

In English, "pants" is a plural word, but in Spanish ***el pantalón*** means "pants" all by itself. This can be mind bending because our English brain isn't prepared to say, "I have a pant" which is the direct translation of ***Yo tengo un pantalón***, but what it really means is "I have pants."

When you want more than one pair of pants you'll need to make the plural of pants, ***pantalones***, but the crazy part is ***pantalones*** can also be used for ONE pair.

1. Yo tengo un pantalón. (This is just 1 pair.) — I have (a) pants.
2. Yo tengo unos pantalones. (This can be ONE or MORE pairs.) — I have some pants.

Remember, when making plurals of nouns ending in ***s*** or ***n*** you add ***es*** and remove the accent mark. That's why ***pantalón*** becomes ***pantalones.***

But what about shoes and socks?

Because shoes and socks are actually two pieces they are used similar to English.

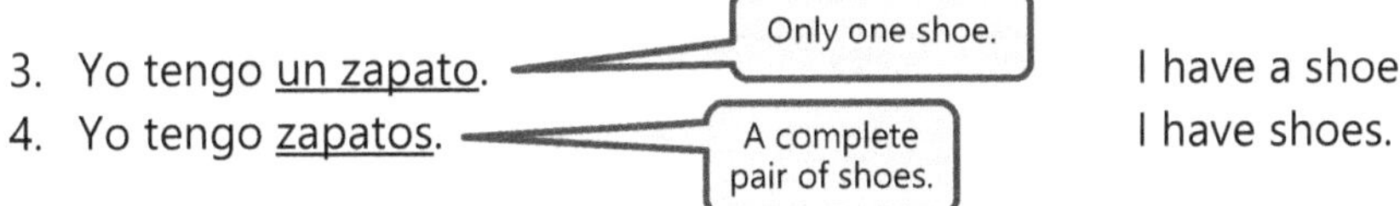

3. Yo tengo un zapato. — I have a shoe.
4. Yo tengo zapatos. — I have shoes.

But for ***el calzón*** (briefs; panties) the same pattern as ***pantalón*** (pants) is used.

5. Yo tengo un calzón. (Just one pair.) — I have (an) briefs / panties.

11 Verb Usage *Uso de Verbos*

V-1

cocinar	**to cook**	**regular**
Yo	***cocino*** (food).	I **cook** (food).
Tú	***cocinas*** (food).	You **cook** (food).
Él / Ella / Usted	***cocina*** (food).	He / She / You (polite) **cook(s)** (food).

The pronunciation of ***cocinar*** is co-si-nar.

EXAMPLE SENTENCES

1. Yo cocino carne. — I cook meat.
2. Él cocina verduras. — He cooks vegetables.

EXAMPLE Q&A

1. **¿Tú cocinas?** — **Do you cook?**
   Sí, yo cocino comida todos los días. — Yes, I cook food every day.
   No, yo no cocino. — No, I don't cook.

V-2

leer	**to read**	**regular**
Yo	***leo*** (item).	I **read** (item).
Tú	***lees*** (item).	You **read** (item).
Él / Ella / Usted	***lee*** (item).	He / She / You (polite) **read(s)** (item).

The pronunciation of ***leer*** is le-er. Make sure you say each "e" without combining them.

EXAMPLE SENTENCES

1. Yo leo libros. — I read books.
2. Ella lee novelas. — She reads novels.

EXAMPLE Q&A

1. **¿Tú lees manga?** — **Do you read manga?**
   Sí, yo leo manga todos los días. — Yes, I read manga every day.
   No, yo leo novelas. — No, I read novels.

V-3

abrir	to open	regular
Yo ***abro*** (item).	I **open** (item).	
Tú ***abres*** (item).	You **open** (item).	
Él / Ella / Usted ***abre*** (item).	He / She / You (polite) **open(s)** (food).	

EXAMPLE SENTENCES

1. Yo abro la ventana todas las mañanas. — I open the window every morning.
2. El perro abre la puerta. — The dog opens the door.

11 Culture Clip *Clip Cultural*

● 11-1. Family members

When talking about family in Spanish, we can repurpose some of the words in Group H from the Vocab Builder.

Spanish	Meaning 1	Meaning 2
padres	fathers	parents
papás	dads	parents
hermanos	brothers	siblings (brothers and sisters)
hijos	sons	children (sons and daughters)
tíos	uncles	uncles and aunts

Masculine words are used to describe groups containing both male and female. However, for only female groups ***hermanas*** (sisters), ***hijas*** (children), ***tias*** (aunts) are used.

11 Grammar and Usage *Gramática y Uso*

● 11-2. How to say "and" in Spanish

Spanish has two ways to say, "and". The first is ***y*** pronounced like "ee" in "meet".

EXAMPLES

1. gatos, perros y búhos	cats, dogs, and owls
2. tú, yo y ella	you, me, and her
3. un té, dos cafés y cuatro jugos.	one tea, two coffees, and four juices

EXAMPLE SENTENCES

1. Ella come carne y verduras.
   She eats meat and vegetables.
2. Jorge lee novelas y mangas.
   George reads novels and manga.

The second "and" is ***e*** (eh) only used when the next word starts with ***i***, or ***hi***.

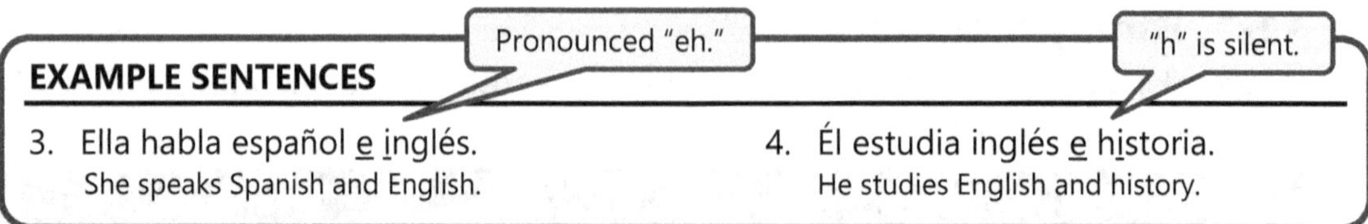

EXAMPLE SENTENCES

3. Ella habla español e inglés.
   She speaks Spanish and English.
4. Él estudia inglés e historia.
   He studies English and history.

This ***e*** (eh) version of "and" is used because Spanish doesn't like to repeat the same sound in a row. This is similar to how we don't say, "a apple" in English but instead say, "an apple." So to avoid the same sound, the ***e*** (eh) version is used when the next sound is the same.

Spanish Letter	Sounds Like
y, i, hi	"ee" in meet
e	"eh" in met

You must use e (eh) if the next word starts with "i" or "hi"

~ e inglés
~ e historia

Just like English, we can also connect sentences using ***y*** and ***e***.

EXAMPLE SENTENCES

1. Laura estudia inglés e Iván estudia español.
   Laura studies English and Ivan studies Spanish.
2. Tú bebes café y yo bebo té.
   You drink coffee and I drink tea.

● 11-3. Moving forward with new pronouns

Until now we've only taught how to use verbs with "I", "you", "he / she" and a name. For example, ***comer*** (to eat) is conjugated as follows:

comer (to eat) ***-er***

1. Yo como pizza. — I eat pizza.
2. Tú comes pizza. — You eat pizza.
3. Él come pizza. — He eats pizza.
4. Ella come pizza. — She eats pizza.
5. Jorge come pizza. — George eats pizza.

Now let's add pronouns, "we", "you all", "they", and "respectful you" to make your Spanish fully functional. Luckily, this only results in two more verb conjugations patterns.

Let's look at the new pronouns first.

Pronoun	English
nosotros (m.) ***nosotras*** (f.)	we
ustedes	you all, y'all, you guys
ellos (m.) ***ellas*** (f.)	they
usted	you (respectful)

Here are how the new pronouns conjugate for regular verbs.

Present Tense Conjugation of Regular Verbs			
Pronoun	**~ar**	**~er**	**~ir**
nosotros / ***nosotras*** (we)	~amos	~emos	~imos
ustedes (y'all)	~an	~en	~en
ellos / ***ellas*** (they)	~an	~en	~en
usted (you) [formal]	~a	~e	~e

Let's look at the new pronouns in action with verbs we already know.

EXAMPLE SENTENCES (ALL REGULAR VERBS)

hablar (to speak) ***-ar***

1. Nosotros hablamos español. — We speak Spanish.
2. Ustedes hablan inglés. — Ya'll speak English.
3. Ellos hablan chino. — They speak Chinese.

About a mixed gender group or just men.

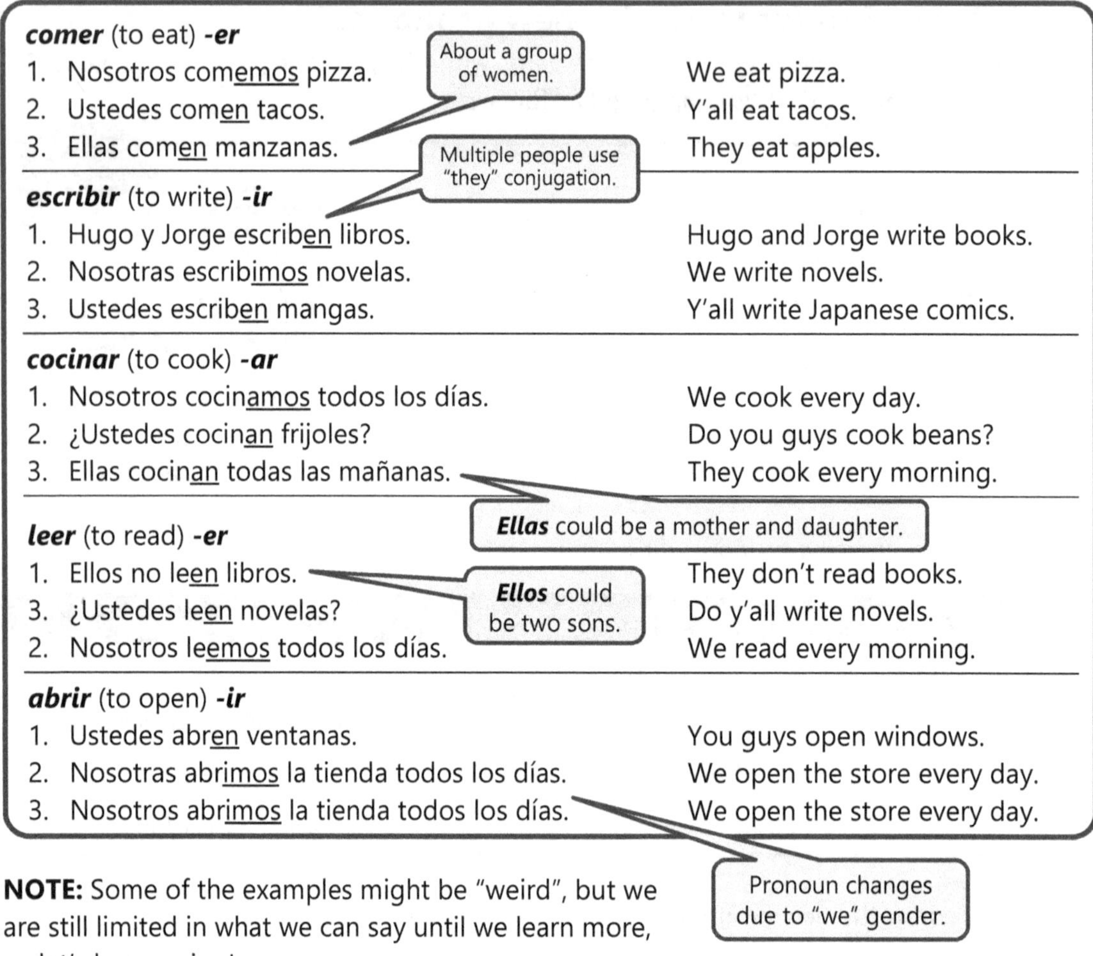

comer (to eat) ***-er***

1. Nosotros comemos pizza. — We eat pizza.
2. Ustedes comen tacos. — Y'all eat tacos.
3. Ellas comen manzanas. — They eat apples.

escribir (to write) ***-ir***

1. Hugo y Jorge escriben libros. — Hugo and Jorge write books.
2. Nosotras escribimos novelas. — We write novels.
3. Ustedes escriben mangas. — Y'all write Japanese comics.

cocinar (to cook) ***-ar***

1. Nosotros cocinamos todos los días. — We cook every day.
2. ¿Ustedes cocinan frijoles? — Do you guys cook beans?
3. Ellas cocinan todas las mañanas. — They cook every morning.

leer (to read) ***-er***

1. Ellos no leen libros. — They don't read books.
3. ¿Ustedes leen novelas? — Do y'all write novels.
2. Nosotros leemos todos los días. — We read every morning.

abrir (to open) ***-ir***

1. Ustedes abren ventanas. — You guys open windows.
2. Nosotras abrimos la tienda todos los días. — We open the store every day.
3. Nosotros abrimos la tienda todos los días. — We open the store every day.

NOTE: Some of the examples might be "weird", but we are still limited in what we can say until we learn more, so let's keep going!

● 11-4. Conjugations for *ser* (is, am, are) and *tener* (to have)

Both ***ser*** and ***tener*** are *irregular* so we just have to memorize their conjugations.

pronoun	**ser** (are)
(we) (m) **nosotros**	somos
(we) (f) **nosotras**	somos
(y'all) **ustedes**	son
(they) (m) **ellos**	son
(they) (f) **ellas**	son

EXAMPLE SENTENCES

1. Nosotros somos estadounidenses. — We are American.
2. Nosotras somos chinas. — We are Chinese.
3. Ustedes son chilenos. — Y'all are Chilean.
4. Ellos son mexicanos. — They are Mexican.
5. Ellas son coreanas. — They are Korean.

pronoun	**tener** (have)
(we) (m) **nosotros**	tenemos
(we) (f) **nosotras**	tenemos
(y'all) **ustedes**	tienen
(they) (m) **ellos**	tienen
(they) (f) **ellas**	tienen

EXAMPLE SENTENCES

1. Nosotros tenemos un perro.	We have a dog.
2. Nosotras tenemos gatos.	We have cats.
3. Ustedes tienen un pez.	Y'all have a fish.
4. Ellos tienen una hermana.	They have a sister.
5. Ellas tienen un hermano.	They have a brother.

11-5. The respectful "you" - *Usted*

Usted is a respectful / polite version of "you". However, it follows the same conjugation pattern as ***él*** (he) and ***ella*** (she) and not of the standard ***tú*** (you).

Spanish	English	Conjugated endings
tú	**you (standard)**	**~as, ~es**
usted	**you (respectful)**	**~a, ~e**

In some situations, in order to not sound rude you should use ***usted*** over ***tú***.

- **talking to a teacher, particularly at school.**
- **talking to your superiors and colleagues at work.**
- **talking to an obviously older stranger.**

EXAMPLE Q&A

1. ¿Usted tiene mascotas?	**Do you have pets? (respectful)**
Sí, yo tengo un perro.	Yes, I have a dog.
No, yo no tengo mascotas.	No, I don't have pets.
2. ¿Usted tiene hambre?	**Are you hungry? (respectful)**
Sí, yo tengo hambre.	Yes, I am hungry.
No, yo no tengo hambre, gracias.	No, I am not hungy, thank you.
3. ¿Usted es maestra?	**Are you a teacher? (respectful)**
No, yo soy abogada.	No, I'm a lawyer.
No, yo soy doctora.	No, I'm a doctor.
4. ¿Usted es australiano?	**Are you Australian?**
Sí, yo soy australiano.	Yes, I am Australian.
No, yo soy estadounidense.	No, I'm American.

11-6. Every rule for Spanish plurals

Regardless of gender, Spanish plurals are made with the following rules.

Rule #1 Words ending in vowels

Nouns ending in a **vowel** are made plural by adding ***~s***

perro dog	**perros** dogs
gato cat	**gatos** cats

Rule #2 Words ending in consonants

Nouns ending in a **consonant** (except z) are made plural by adding **~es.**

luchador wrestler	**luchadores** wrestlers	**ciudad** city	**ciudades** cities

Some singular words end in ***s***, but they aren't plural until you add ***es***.

mes month	**meses** months	**dios** god	**dioses** gods

Rule #3 Removing accent marks for *'s'* or *'n'* plurals

After making a noun ending with ***s*** or ***n*** plural, if there is an accent mark it is removed. The stress naturally stays on the second to last syllable, where the accent mark originally was.

invitación invitation	**invitaciones** invitations	**volcán** volcano	**volcanes** volcanoes
interés interest	**intereses** interests	**autobús** bus	**autobuses** buses

Rule #4 Words ending in with Z

For nouns ending in **~z**, change ***z*** to **~*ces***.

luz light	**luces** lights	**nariz** nose	**narices** noses
nuez nut	**nueces** nuts	**pez** fish	**peces** fishes

FUN TO KNOW

* When Spanish speakers say ***nuez*** (nut), they normally think "pecan".
* In English, "fish" is singular and plural, but in Spanish you say ***peces*** to mean more than one fish.

● 11-7. Plural Gender Companion Words

When a noun is plural, its gender companion word MUST also be made plural.
The masculine ***el*** becomes ***los*** and the feminine ***la*** becomes ***las***.

(masculine) **El** ⟶ **Los**
(feminine) **La** ⟶ **Las**

Singular	Plural
la flor the flower	**las flores** the flowers
el árbol the tree	**los árboles** the trees

Singular	Plural
la montaña the mountain	**las montañas** the mountains
el vaso the cup	**los vasos** the cups

Masculine Examples			
singular		plural	
el perro	the dog	**los perros**	the dogs
el gato	the cat	**los gatos**	the cats

Feminine Examples			
singular		plural	
la perra	the dog	**las perras**	the dogs
la gata	the cat	**las gatas**	the cats

EXAMPLE SENTENCES

1. Los perros tienen sueño.
   The dogs are sleepy.
2. Las gatas tienen calor.
   The cats are hot.
3. Las estudiantes tienen libros.
   The students have books.
4. Las pingüinas tienen frío.
   The penguins are cold.
5. Los tigres tienen hambre.
   The tigers are hungry.
6. Los niños tienen sed.
   The boys are thirsty.

11-8. Generic Masculine Rule

For groups of things that are of mixed or unknown gender, Spanish defaults to the masculine gender. This is known as the *generic masculine rule*.

Since there are only males, **los gatos** is used.

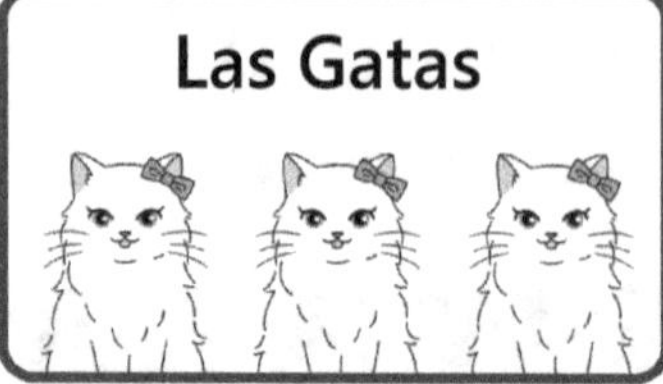

There are only females in this group, so **las gatas** is used.

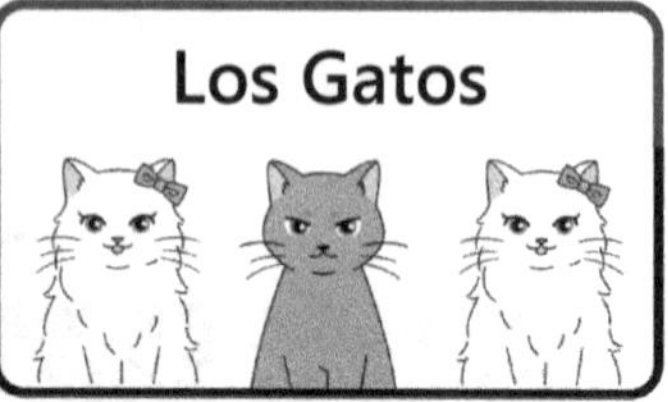

Since there are both genders in the group, **los gatos** is used.

When talking about a group of unseen cats, or of unknown gender, you should always default to masculine ***los gatos***. A single cat of unknown gender is also ***el gato***.
If you go to a wrestling show not knowing what wrestlers are there, you would say ***los luchadores***. If you then find out all the wrestlers are women, you say ***las luchadoras***.

unknown gender wrestlers	los luchadores
mixed gender wrestlers	los luchadores
all **male** wrestlers	los luchadores
all **female** wrestlers	las luchadoras

los luchadores
(the wrestlers)

EXAMPLE SENTENCES

1. Las maestras beben café.
   The teachers drink coffee. (all female)
2. Las gatas tienen sueño.
   The cats are sleepy. (all female)
3. Los maestros comen tacos.
   The teachers eat tacos. (all male or mixed)
4. Los perros tienen hambre.
   The dogs are hungry. (all male or mixed)

11-9. Talking about "some" things

We previously learned ***un*** and ***una*** to say "a" or "one". If we have more than one non-specific amount of something, in Spanish you use ***unos*** for masculine and ***unas*** for feminine groups.

EXAMPLES

1. unos búhos — some owls
2. unas amigas — some friends (all female)
3. unas manzanas — some apples
4. unos amigos — some friends (all male or mixed group)

EXAMPLE Q&A

1. **¿Tú tienes mascotas?**	**Do you have pets?**
Sí, yo tengo unos perros.	Yes, I have some dogs.
Sí, yo tengo unas perras.	Yes, I have some dogs.
Sí, yo tengo cinco gatos.	Yes, I have five cats.
No, yo no tengo mascotas.	No, I don't have pets.

11-10. Simple possession words (no gender)

Spanish possessive pronouns "my~" and "your~" come in singular and plural forms.

English	Singular	Plural
my~	***mi~***	***mis~***
your~	***tu~***	***tus~***

EXAMPLES

mi libro	my book	tu amigo	your friend
mis libros	my books	tus amigos	your friends

In English, we have gender-specific "his" and "her" possession words, which might make you think Spanish should as well, especially with its focus on gender. However Spanish uses a single word, ***su*** to say his~, her~, their~, its~, and even the polite version of "your~"

English	Singular	Plural
his~ / her~ / their~ / its~ / your~ (polite)	***su***	***sus***

EXAMPLES

Talking about a girl

su mano	her hand
sus ojos	her eyes

Talking about a boy

su gato	his cat
sus perros	his dogs

Talking about a soccer team

su nombre	their name
sus camisas	their shirts

Talking about some ballet dancers

su maestra	their teacher
sus faldas	their skirts

Talking about a building

su puerta	its door
sus ventanas	its windows

Talking about an animal

su cabeza	its head
sus orejas	its ears

EXAMPLE SENTENCES

1. Mis gatos beben café.
   My cats drink coffee.
2. Mi mamá estudia español.
   My mom studies Spanish.
3. Su novia es estadounidense.
   His girlfriend is American.
4. Sus puertas tienen luces.
   Its doors have lights.
5. Sus libros son novelas.
   His / her books are novels.
6. ¿Tus gatos beben café?
   Your cats drink coffee?

The majority of English speakers, at least those in ***Estados Unidos***, have probably heard the phrase, ***mi casa es su casa*** or some variation of it.

mi casa es **su** casa
my house is your house

 *Más Detalles* **More Details** 

Why use "su casa" instead of "tu casa"

We know ***tu*** means "your~" and that ***su*** also translates to a respectful "your~". So, in the phrase, ***mi casa es su casa***, to show respect, ***su*** is used and not ***tu***.

In reality, in the Spanish speaking world, the phrase is more commonly said as ***mi casa es tu casa***. But why? Shouldn't we show respect to a guest in our home? Of course we should, however, often a homeowner is older than their guests, and it's strange to use respectful words such as ***usted*** or, the polite "your~", ***su*** with a younger person.
So, this is why it's more common to say ***mi casa es tu casa***.

11-11. Not so simple possession (*nosotros*)

Unlike other possession words, "our" must pay attention to the *gender* of the owned item.

English	for masculine item(s)	for feminine item(s)
our~ (item)	***nuestro~***	***nuestra~***
our~ (items)	***nuestros~***	***nuestras~***

nuestro perro
our dog

nuestros perros
our dogs

nuestra perra
our dog

nuestras perras
our dogs

EXAMPLE SENTENCES

1. Nuestra maestra es mexicana.
   Our teacher is Mexican. (a female teacher)
2. Nuestros amigos son ingleses.
   Our friends are English. (males or mixed gender)
3. Nuestra casa tiene diez ventanas.
   Our house has ten windows.
4. Nuestros niños tienen sueño.
   Our children are sleepy. (all boys or mixed)
5. Nuestro día es mañana.
   Our day is tomorrow.
   día is masculine
6. Nosotros comemos nuestras verduras.
   We eat our vegetables.

11-12. BONUS: Verb conjugation song

Verb conjugation can be a challenge. We had some fun making a song that "might" help!

Scan the QR code to listen. We're not sure how effective the song is, so here is the main part of the lyrics just in case.

Yo rhymes with ***o***. ***Tú*** goes to ***s***.

For ***él***, ***ella*** and even a name, the verb always ends with ***a*** (ah) or ***e*** (eh)

If the pronoun ends in ***ros*** or ***ras***, put ***mos*** on the verb end.
For all other ***S*** pronouns, the verb always ends with ***N***.

11 Practice and Review *Práctica y Repaso*

1. Question and Answer (Spanish → English)

Each question has multiple answers. Cover up the right side and try to translate.

1. ¿Tú comes pizza todos los días?	**Do you eat pizza every day?**
Sí, yo como pizza todos los días.	Yes, I eat pizza every day.
No, yo como verduras todos los días.	No, I eat vegetables every day.
No, yo no como pizza.	No. I don't eat pizza.
2. ¿Usted tiene hijos?	**Do you have children?**
No, yo no tengo hijos.	No, I don't have children.
Sí, yo tengo un hijo y una hija.	Yes, I have a son and a daughter.
Sí, yo tengo tres hijos.	Yes, I have three children.

3. **¿Ellas tienen hermanos?** — **Do they have siblings?**
   - Sí, ellas tienen dos hermanas. — Yes, they have two sisters.
   - Sí, ellas tienen un hermano. — Yes, they have a brother.
   - No, ellas no tienen hermanos. — No, they don't have siblings.

4. **¿Ustedes tienen hambre?** — **Are you guys hungry?**
   - Sí, nosotros tenemos hambre. — Yes, we are hungry.
   - No, nosotros no tenemos hambre. — No, we are not hungry.
   - No, gracias. — No, thanks.

5. **¿Nosotros tenemos tiempo?** — **Do we have time?**
   - Sí, nosotros tenemos tiempo. — Yes, we have time.
   - No, nosotros no tenemos tiempo. — No, we don't have time.

6. **¿Ustedes cocinan todos los días?** — **Do you guys cook every day?**
   - Sí, nosotros cocinamos todos los días. — Yes, we cook every day.
   - No, nosotros no tenemos tiempo. — No, we don't have time.
   - No todos los días. — Not every day.

2. Question and answer (English → Spanish)

Each question has multiple answers. Cover up the right side and try to translate.

1. **Do you open the store every day?** — **¿Tú abres la tienda todos los días?**
   - Yes, I open the store every day. — Sí, yo abro la tienda todos los días.
   - Yes, I open the store every morning. — Sí yo abro la tienda todas las mañanas.
   - No, I don't open. — No, yo no abro.

2. **Do your brothers live in England?** — **¿Tus hermanos viven en Inglaterra?**
   - Yes, they live in England — Sí, ellos viven en Inglaterra.
   - No, they live in France. — No, ellos viven en Francia.
   - No, they live in Argentina. — No, ellos viven en Argentina.

3. **Are your parents teachers?** — **¿Tus padres son maestros?**
   - Yes, they are teachers. — Sí, ellos son maestros.
   - No, they are doctors. — No, ellos son doctores.
   - No, they are not teachers. — No, ellos no son maestros.

4. **Are your (polite) children students?** — **¿Sus hijos son estudiantes?**
   - Yes, my children are students. — Sí, mis hijos son estudiantes.
   - No, my children are not students. — No, mis hijos no son estudiantes.
   - No, they are teachers. — No, ellos son maestros.

5. **Is our dog sleepy?** — **¿Nuestro perro tiene sueño?**
   - Yes, our dog is sleepy. — Sí, nuestro perro tiene sueño.
   - No, our dog is not sleepy. — No, nuestro perro no tiene sueño.
   - No, our dog is hungry. — No, nuestro perro tiene hambre.

6. **Are y'all Spanish?** — **¿Ustedes son Españoles?**
   - Yes, we are Spanish. — Sí, nosotros somos españoles.
   - No, we are Argentinian. — No, nosotros somos argentinos.
   - No, we are Chilean. — No, nosotros somos chilenos.

Workbook 11: Lesson Activities

11 Vocabulary Drills *Ejercicios de Vocabulario*

1. Writing and Vocabulary

Write the Spanish for each of the pictures. Make sure to add accent marks when needed.

shirt, skirt, t-shirt, shoe, bra, window, socks, pants, panties (briefs), jacket

1.__________ 2.__________ 3.__________ 4.__________ 5.__________

6.__________ 7.__________ 8.__________ 9.__________ 10.__________

2. Gender Matching

Write the following words and circle the gender companion word for each one.

luz, interés, autobús, día, volcán, mañana, mañana, ventana, brasier, puerta

1) el / la ____________________
(interest)

2) el / la ____________________
(light)

3) el / la ____________________
(bus)

4) el / la ____________________
(day)

5) el / la ______________________ (volcano)

6) el / la ______________________ (door)

7) el / la ______________________ (morning)

8) el / la ______________________ (tomorrow)

9) el / la ______________________ (window)

10) el / la ______________________ (bra)

3. Vocab translation

Translate the following words into Spanish.

1) fathers ______________________

2) mothers ______________________

3) parents ______________________

4) moms ______________________

5) sisters ______________________

6) brothers ______________________

7) siblings ______________________

8) sons ______________________

9) daughters ______________________

10) children ______________________

4. Which one is "ours?"

In the following blanks write the correct version of "ours" for each item.

1) ________________ amigos

2) ________________ hermanas

3) ________________ familia

4) ________________ auto

5) ________________ padres

6) ________________ primo

7) ________________ mascota

8) ________________ ropa

11 Usage Activities *Actividades de Uso*

● 5. Reading Comprehension

Translate the following on a separate piece of paper or type in an electronic device.

Mi familia

Sofía wants to tell you about her family. What can you say about yours?

1. Mi nombre es Sofía. Yo soy estudiante.
2. Mi hermano es Carlos. Él es doctor.
3. Nuestro padre es Juan. Él es ingeniero.
4. Nuestra madre es Daniela. Ella es maestra.
5. Nosotros somos mexicanos.
6. Nosotros vivimos en México.
7. Mi hermano Carlos tiene un búho y mi mamá tiene un pez.
8. Yo tengo dos gatos y mi papá tiene un perro.

● 6. Reading comprehension questions

Answer the following questions about the reading comprehension in Spanish.

1. What nationality is Sofía's family?

____

2. How many children does Juan have?

____

3. How many pets does Sofía's family have?

____

4. Where does Carlos live?

____

5. Who is a student?

____

6. How many pets are in Sofía's family in total?

____

7. Who has a dog?

____

8. What is Juan's occupation?

____

7. Spanish Translation

Translate the following conversations into English.

1.
A: ¿Ustedes tienen sueño? B: No, nosotros no tenemos sueño. A: ¿Ustedes tienen hambre? B: Sí, nosotros tenemos hambre.
A:
B:
A:
B:

8. English Translation

Translate the following conversation into Spanish.

1.
A: Do you have brothers? B: Yes, I have two brothers. A: And, do you have sisters? B: No, I don't have sisters.
A:
B:
A:
B:

9. Plurals

Write the plural for the following words and their gender companion words.

1) la nariz ________________ 2) el brasier ________________

3) el calzón ________________ 4) la luz ________________

5) la mañana ________________ 6) el pantalón ________________

7) el maestro ________________ 8) la puerta ________________

9) la ventana ________________ 10) la nuez ________________

● 10. Verb conjugation drills

Fill in the blanks with the proper verb conjugations.

1. Leer (to read)	
Pronouns	**Present Tense**
yo	
tú	lees
él / ella / usted	
nosotros	
ustedes	
ellos / ellas	

2. Abrir (to open)	
Pronouns	**Present Tense**
yo	
tú	
él / ella / usted	
nosotros	abrimos
ustedes	
ellos / ellas	

3. Cocinar (to cook)	
Pronouns	**Present Tense**
yo	
tú	
él / ella / usted	
nosotros	
ustedes	cocinan
ellos / ellas	

11 Answer Key *Clave de Respuestas*

1. Verb conjugation drills (answers)

1. calcetas
socks

2. camiseta
t-shirt

3. ventana
window

4. pantalón
pants

5. zapato
shoe

6. chaqueta
jacket

7. brasier
bra

8. calzón
panties (briefs)

9. camisa
shirt

10. falda
skirt

2. Gender Matching (answers)

1) el interés
2) la luz
3) el autobús
4) el día
5) el volcán
6) la puerta
7) la mañana
8) el mañana
9) la ventana
10) el brasier

3. English Vocab translation (answers)

1) padres
2) madres
3) padres
4) mamás
5) hermanas
6) hermanos
7) hermanos
8) hijos
9) hijas
10) hijos

4. Which one is "ours?"

1) nuestros amigos
2) nuestras hermanas
3) nuestra familia
4) nuestro auto
5) nuestros padres
6) nuestro primo
7) neustra mascota
8) nuestra ropa

5. Reading Comprehension Translation

❶ My name is Sofía. I am a student.
❷ My brother is Carlos. He is a doctor.
❸ Our father is Juan. He is an engineer.
❹ Our mother is Daniela. She's a teacher.
❺ We are Mexican.

❻ We live in Mexico.
❼ My brother Carlos has an owl and my mom has a fish.
❽ I have two cats and my dad has a dog.

6. Reading Comprehension Questions (answers)

1. What nationality is Sofia's family? — Ellos son mexicanos.
2. How many children does Juan have? — Juan tiene dos hijos.
3. How many pets does Sofia have? — Sofía tiene dos mascotas.
4. Where does Carlos live? — Carlos vive en México.
5. Who is a student? — Sofía es estudiante.
6. How many pets does Sofía's family have? — Ellos tienen cinco mascotas.
7. Who has a dog? — Juan tiene un perro / Papá tiene un perro.
8. What is Juan's occupation? — Juan es ingeniero.

7. Spanish Translation (answers)

1. A: Are you guys sleepy?
   B: No, we are not sleepy.
   A: Are you guys hungry?
   B: Yes, we are hungry.

8. English Translation (answers)

1. A: ¿Tu tienes hermanos?
   B: Sí, yo tengo dos hermanos.
   A: Y, ¿tú tienes hermanas?
   B: No, yo no tengo hermanas.

9. Plurals (answers)

1) las narices
2) los brasieres
3) los calzones
4) las luces
5) las mañanas
6) los pantalones
7) los maestros
8) las puertas
9) las ventanas
10) las nueces

10. Verb conjugation drills (answers)

1. leer (to read)	
yo	leo
tú	lees
él / ella / usted	lee
nosotros	leemos
ustedes	leen
ellos / ellas	leen

2. abrir (to open)	
yo	abro
tú	abres
él / ella / usted	abre
nosotros	abrimos
ustedes	abren
ellos / ellas	abren

3. cocinar (to cook)	
yo	cocino
tú	cocinas
él / ella / usted	cocina
nosotros	cocinamos
ustedes	cocinan
ellos / ellas	cocinan

Vocabulary Builder 6: Groups J and K

Group J Rooms

la sala	living room	**el baño**	bathroom; restroom
la habitación	bedroom; room (hotel, etc.)	**el jardín**	garden; yard
el cuarto	room; bedroom	**la cocina**	kitchen
el comedor	dining room	**el garaje**	garage

Group K Places

la estación	station	**el parque**	park
la parada	stop (bus stop, etc)	**la cárcel**	jail
la iglesia	church	**la biblioteca**	library
el restaurante	restaurant	**la librería**	bookshop
el centro	downtown; city center	**la escuela**	school

 *Más Detalles* **More Details** 

Cuarto vs Habitación
Both ***cuarto*** and ***habitación*** are used to refer to a "bedroom", but also any "room" in general. While both are used in casual everyday Spanish, in formal situations such as in real estate listings, or booking a hotel room, ***habitación*** is used more commonly.

12 PAGES	7 USAGE SECTIONS	24 NEW WORDS

12 Lesson 12: Wants, Needs & Adjectives

12 New Words *Palabras Nuevas*

Nouns etc.

¿qué?	what?	**el juego**	game
el ahora	now	**nada**	nothing; anything
el dulce	candy (piece of)	**algo**	something; anything
el idioma	language	**la bebida**	drink; beverage
también	also; too	**el otro**	other; another

Adjectives

grande	big; great	**veloz**	fast
difícil	difficult; hard	**fácil**	easy
fuerte	strong	**débil**	weak
dulce	sweet	**inteligente**	smart; intelligent
interesante	interesting	**excelente**	excellent

Connectors

pero	but	**entonces**	well; well then

Verb

querer	to want	**necesitar**	to need

12 New Expressions *Expresiones Nuevas*

Don't worry about the grammar here. Just learn the phrases for communication.

1. **Disculpa / Disculpe / Disculpen** **Excuse me. / Sorry**
   This is both "sorry" and "excuse me". To say, "excuse me" to people your same age or younger use ***disculpa***. For an older person or someone you want to show respect to use ***disculpe***. Use ***disculpen*** anytime you're saying, "excuse me" to more than one person regardless of age or level of respect.

2. **Lo siento.** **Sorry.**
   Lo siento never means "excuse me" and is specifically used only for apologizing.

12 Memorization Techniques *Técnicas de memorización*

12-1. Remembering accented words

Do you immediately know ***el*** vs ***él*** and ***tu*** vs ***tú***? Previously we had the mustache guy trick to remember ***él*** is "he" and not "the." We can broaden that rule and say if ***tú*** has an accent mark, it's a person and not possession.

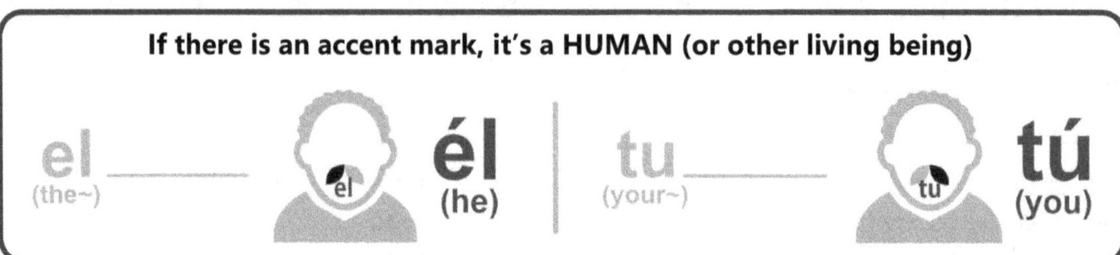

12 Word Usage *Uso de Palabras*

W-1	el ahora	now

El ahora is almost always said as just ***ahora***. Only in poetry or epic statements would someone say ***el ahora*** (the now).

EXAMPLE SENTENCES

1. Yo vivo en México ahora.	I live in Mexico now.
2. Ella tiene dos hijos ahora.	She has two children now.
3. ¿Tú bebes café ahora?	You drink coffee now?

W-2	pero	but

EXAMPLE SENTENCES

1. Yo no tengo dinero, pero yo tengo tiempo.
   I don't have money, but I have time.
2. Yo tengo sed, pero yo no tengo hambre.
   I'm thirsty, but I'm not hungry.
3. Él lee manga pero no lee libros.
   He reads manga but doesn't read books.

We can omit ***él*** in the connected sentences.

W-3

el otro — other; another

El otro (other; another) must match the gender and plurality of the word it's paired with.

EXAMPLE SENTENCES

1. ¿Tú tienes otra chaqueta?
   Do you have another jacket?
2. Mi otro auto es un Toyota.
   My other car is a Toyota.
3. Disculpa, otro café, por favor.
   Excuse me, another coffee, please.
4. Yo tengo otras mascotas.
   I have other pets.
5. Mis otros amigos viven en España.
   My other friends live in Spain.
6. Yo no hablo otros idiomas.
   I don't speak other languages.

W-4

también — also; too

También (also; too) is used similarly to English.

EXAMPLE SENTENCES

1. Mi papá también lee todos los días.
   My father also reads every day.
2. Yo tengo hambre, y yo también tengo sed.
   I'm hungry, and I'm also thirsty.
3. Mi otro amigo también vive en Japón.
   My other friend also lives in Japan.
4. ¿Tú también eres estadounidense?
   Are you American, too?

W-5

entonces — well; well then; then; so

Entonces is used at the beginning of a sentence after someone has said something and you want to ask a follow-up question.

1. Conversation at a small bakery.

Disculpa, ¿ustedes tienen café?	Excuse me, do you guys have coffee?
Lo siento, nosotros no tenemos.	Sorry, we don't have (any).
Entonces, ¿ustedes tienen té?	Well then, do you guys have tea?
¡Sí! Nosotros tenemos.	Yes! We have.

2. A Spanish conversation between a French person and an American.

Yo vivo en Canadá.	I live in Canada.
Entonces, ¿tú hablas francés?	Then, you speak French?
No, yo soy estadounidense.	No, I'm American.
Entonces, ¿tú no hablas otros idiomas?	So, you don't speak other languages?
No, lo siento.	No, I'm sorry.

W-6	el dulce	sweet; a piece of candy

Dulce is an *adjective* meaning "sweet" and also a *noun* meaning "candy". In English, "candy" is plural, but in Spanish, ***dulce*** is singular, so for plural you say ***dulces***.

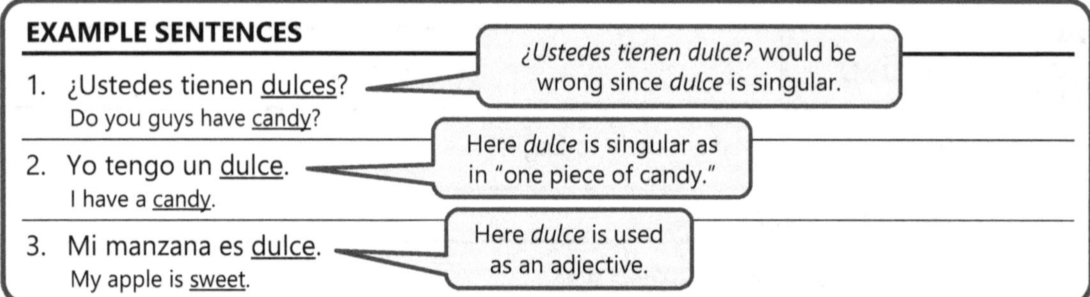

EXAMPLE SENTENCES

1. ¿Ustedes tienen dulces?
   Do you guys have candy?
2. Yo tengo un dulce.
   I have a candy.
3. Mi manzana es dulce.
   My apple is sweet.

12 Verb Usage *Uso de Verbos*

V-1	necesitar	to need	regular

Yo	**necesito** (something)	I **need** (something)
Tú	**necesitas** (something)	You **need** (something)
Él / Ella / Usted	**necesita** (something)	He / She / You (polite) **need(s)** (something)
Nosotros	**necesitamos** (something)	We **need** (something)
Ustedes	**necesitan** (something)	You guys **need** (something)

EXAMPLE SENTENCES

1. Yo necesito un auto.	I need a car.
2. Todos necesitan dinero.	Everyone needs money.
3. ¿Tú no necesitas un doctor?	Don't you need a doctor?
4. Nosotros necesitamos amigos.	We need friends.
5. ¿Ustedes necesitan agua?	Do you guys need water?

Todos can also mean "everyone."

V-2 **querer**	**to want**	irregular
Yo	**quiero** (something)	I **want** (something)
Tú	**quieres** (something)	You **want** (something)
Él / Ella / Usted	**quiere** (something)	He / She / You (polite) **want(s)** (something)
Nosotros	**queremos** (something)	We **want** (something)
Ustedes	**quieren** (something)	You guys **want** (something)

If ***querer*** was regular, it would conjugate as ***quero*** for ***yo*** and ***queres*** for ***tú***. But it's irregular, so those conjugations are wrong. Instead, ***yo*** is ***quiero***, and ***tú*** is ***quieres***.

EXAMPLE SENTENCES

1. Yo no quiero un perro.	I don't want a dog.
2. Ellos quieren helado.	They want ice cream
3. ¿Tú quieres unos tacos?	Do you want some tacos?
4. Nosotros queremos una casa.	We want a house.
5. ¿Ustedes quieren comida?	You guys want food?

12 Grammar and Usage *Gramática y Uso*

● 12-2. Plurality for adjectives

This rule might seem crazy for English speakers, but *adjectives* must match the *noun's* plurality. To make adjectives plural, you follow the same rules to make nouns plural.

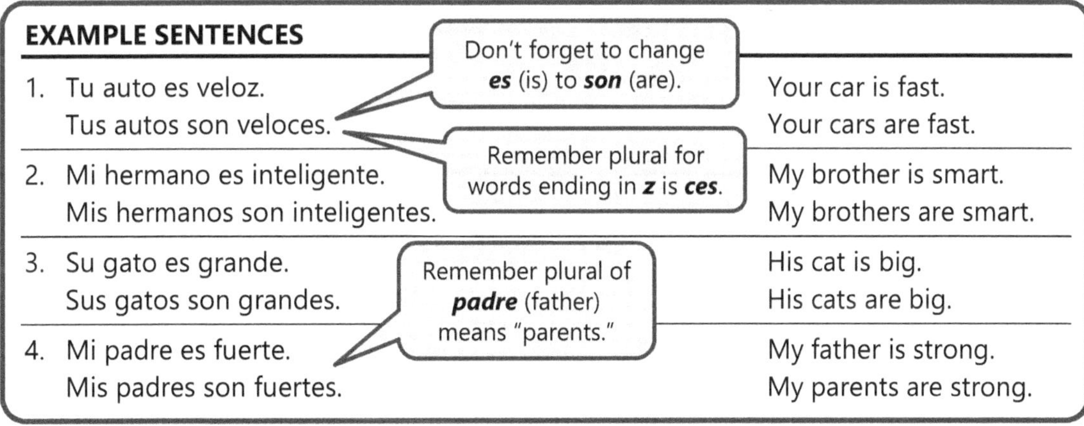

EXAMPLE SENTENCES

1. Tu auto es veloz. Tus autos son veloces.	Your car is fast. Your cars are fast.
2. Mi hermano es inteligente. Mis hermanos son inteligentes.	My brother is smart. My brothers are smart.
3. Su gato es grande. Sus gatos son grandes.	His cat is big. His cats are big.
4. Mi padre es fuerte. Mis padres son fuertes.	My father is strong. My parents are strong.

12-3. "General statement" rule

With general statements like "Bananas are sweet" or "Spanish is easy," Spanish keeps the gender companion word. However, in the English translation "the" isn't said.

EXAMPLE SENTENCES

1. Los plátanos son dulces.
   Bananas are sweet.
2. Los bebés son débiles.
   Babies are weak.
3. Los luchadores son fuertes.
   Wrestlers are strong.
4. Las gatas son fuertes y veloces.
   Cats are strong and fast.
5. El español es fácil, pero el japonés es difícil.
   Spanish is easy, but Japanese is hard.

12-4. Something, anything, and nothing

Algo translates to both "something", "anything" depending on the context.

EXAMPLE Q&A

1. ¿Tú necesitas algo?	**Do you need anything?**
Sí, yo necesito dinero.	Yes, I need money.
Sí, yo necesito tiempo.	Yes, I need time.
2. ¿Tú quieres algo?	**Do you want something?**
Sí, yo quiero dulces.	Yes, I want candy.
Sí, yo quiero una manzana.	Yes, I want an apple.

Nada means "nothing" or "anything."

EXAMPLE Q&A

3. ¿Tú necesitas algo?	**Do you need anything?**
No, nada.	No, nothing.
4. ¿Tú necesitas otro café?	**Do you need another coffee?**
Gracias, no necesito nada.	Thank you, I don't need anything.

Algo and ***nada*** both mean "anything," however, ***nada*** is used in negative sentences.

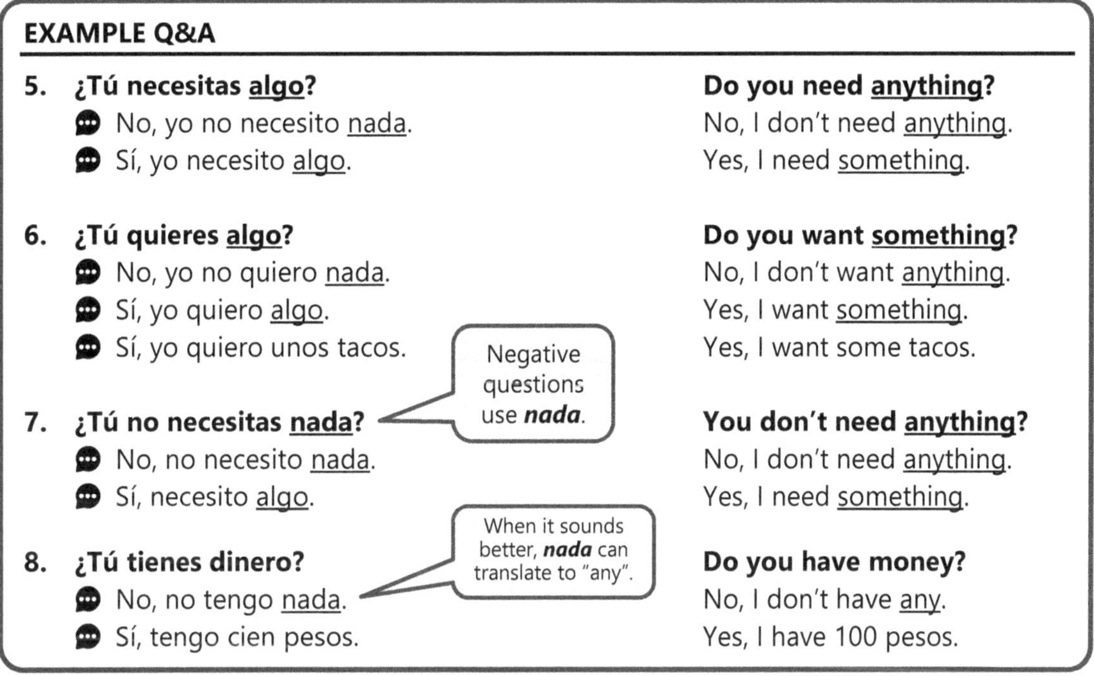

EXAMPLE Q&A

5. ¿Tú necesitas algo?	**Do you need anything?**
No, yo no necesito nada.	No, I don't need anything.
Sí, yo necesito algo.	Yes, I need something.
6. ¿Tú quieres algo?	**Do you want something?**
No, yo no quiero nada.	No, I don't want anything.
Sí, yo quiero algo.	Yes, I want something.
Sí, yo quiero unos tacos.	Yes, I want some tacos.
7. ¿Tú no necesitas nada?	**You don't need anything?**
No, no necesito nada.	No, I don't need anything.
Sí, necesito algo.	Yes, I need something.
8. ¿Tú tienes dinero?	**Do you have money?**
No, no tengo nada.	No, I don't have any.
Sí, tengo cien pesos.	Yes, I have 100 pesos.

12-5. S-V-O sentence order in Spanish

Spanish sentences, similar to English, are ordered Subject-**Verb**-*Object* or S-V-O for short. This is true if the sentence is a question, an answer, or a statement.

SENTENCE ORDER

You **need** *something*?	¿Tú **necesitas** *algo*?
I **need** *money*.	Yo **necesito** *dinero*.

The *subject* is the person doing the verb. The *object* is the thing the verb is acting upon. S-V-O order works with every Spanish verb. Just like English an *object* comes after the verb.

EXAMPLE SENTENCES (S-V-O ORDER)

1. ¿Tú **comes** *carne*?	Do you **eat** *meat*?
Sí, yo **como** *carne*.	Yes, I **eat** *meat*.
2. ¿Ella **habla** *español*?	Does she **speak** *Spanish*?
Sí, ella **habla** *español*.	Yes, she **speaks** *Spanish*.
3. ¿Ellos **necesitan** *comida*?	Do they **need** *food*?
Sí, ellos **necesitan** *comida*.	Yes, they **need** *food*.

 *Más Detalles* More Details 

How to say "Do you ______"

In this book we haven't learned the verb "to do" in Spanish. Spoiler alert, it's ***hacer***. Once ***hacer*** is learned, some students want to add it into phrases like "Do you have money?" or "Do you eat fish?". However, this is never done in Spanish. The "do" part is covered automatically with ***tienes***, ***comes*** or other verbs are in a question.

This means that ¿Tienes? by itself means, "Do you have?" and ¿Comes? by itself includes, "Do you eat?" So, while Spanish and English share many grammar constructions, using the verb "do" in this way is not one of them.

This applies for any time "do" is used in English with verbs.

EXAMPLE SENTENCES

1. ¿Tú tienes tiempo?	(Do) you have time?
2. ¿Ella trabaja los sabados?	(Does) she work on Saturdays?
3. ¿Ustedes hablan ingles?	(Do) you guys speak English?
4. ¿Nosotros no tenemos pan?	(Do) we not have bread?

12-6. Question words affect sentence order

The Spanish order changes when there is a *question word* such as ***qué*** in the sentence. Notice that the subject moves to the end of the sentence. This may take some getting used to since we don't do this in English.

EXAMPLE SENTENCES (QUESTION WORD ORDER)

1. ¿Qué **necesitas** tú?	What do you **need**?
2. ¿Qué **come** ella?	What does she **eat**?
3. ¿Qué **habla** tu padre?	What does your father **speak**?
4. ¿Qué **estudias** tú?	What do you **study**?
5. ¿Qué **queremos** nosotros?	What do we **want**?

Even when more things are added, if there is a *question word*, the order still stays as Question Word-Verb-Subject, with the subject at the end, which is weird for English.

EXAMPLE SENTENCES (QUESTION WORD ORDER)

1. ¿Qué **necesitas** tú ahora?	What do you **need** now?
2. ¿Qué comida **come** ella?	What food does she **eat**?
3. ¿Qué idiomas **habla** tu padre?	What languages does your father **speak**?
4. ¿Qué **estudias** tú en la escuela?	What do you **study** at school?
5. ¿Qué bebidas **queremos** nosotros?	What drinks do we **want**?

12-7. "The Mr" and "The Mrs"

There are occasions in English where we say, "The Mrs." For example, a sales call might ask, "May I speak to <u>the</u> Mrs.?" Spanish takes this to a whole new level. Anytime you are talking about a person that has a title such as Mr. or Dr., etc. then you must include the gender companion words ***el*** or ***la***.

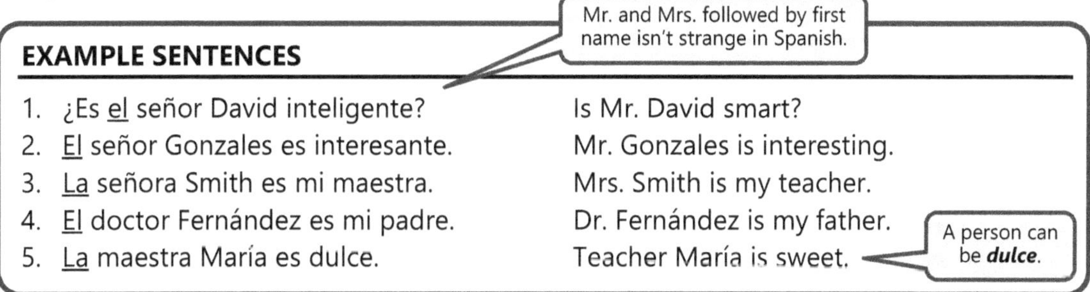

EXAMPLE SENTENCES

1.	¿Es <u>el</u> señor David inteligente?	Is Mr. David smart?
2.	<u>El</u> señor Gonzales es interesante.	Mr. Gonzales is interesting.
3.	<u>La</u> señora Smith es mi maestra.	Mrs. Smith is my teacher.
4.	<u>El</u> doctor Fernández es mi padre.	Dr. Fernández is my father.
5.	<u>La</u> maestra María es dulce.	Teacher María is sweet.

12-8. How to never forget a plural adjective

Since adjectives in English are <u>never</u> plural, it's easy to forget they <u>must</u> be plural in Spanish when the noun they describe is plural. It's easier to remember plural adjectives if you imagine adjectives as a <u>sticker</u> that you stick on each item. When you have multiple items, you need multiple stickers, which is why the adjective <u>must</u> be plural.

12-9. Using *el* for feminine words

We've learned that Spanish doesn't like to have the same vowel sounds back to back. For example with "and" you don't say ***y historia*** (and history), and instead use ***e historia***.

A similar thing happens with feminine words starting with ***a***, since ***la a~*** would be the same vowel sound back to back. This leads to ***agua***, which is feminine, becoming ***el agua*** and ***hambre***, which is also feminine, becoming ***el hambre***.

This only happens specifically when ***la*** is being used. This means even though ***el*** was used for "the" with ***el agua***, when saying "the waters" you use ***las aguas*** since there is no longer the same vowel sound being used back to back.

12 Practice and Review *Práctica y Repaso*

1. Question and Answer (Spanish → English)

Each question has multiple answers. Cover up the right side and try to translate.

1. **¿Qué quieres tú?** — **What do you want?**
   - Yo quiero un dulce. — I want a (piece of) candy.
   - Yo quiero otra bebida. — I want another drink.
   - Yo no quiero nada. — I don't want anything.

2. **¿Tú tienes hambre?** — **Are you hungry?**
   - Sí, yo tengo hambre. — Yes, I'm hungry.
   - Sí, yo quiero una pizza. — Yes, I want a pizza.
   - No, pero mi perro tiene hambre. — No, but my dog is hungry.

3. **¿Qué ropa quieres tú?** — **What clothing do you want?**
   - Yo quiero un pantalón. — I want pants.
   - Yo quiero unos calzones. — I want some briefs / panties.
   - Yo no quiero nada, pero necesito calcetas. — I don't want anything, but I need socks.

4. **¿Qué necesitas tú?** — **What do you need?**
   - Yo no necesito nada. — I don't need anything.
   - Yo necesito unas verduras. — I need some vegetables.
   - Yo necesito comida y también una bebida. — I need food and also a drink.

6. **¿Tus autos son veloces?** — **Are your cars fast?**
   - Uno es veloz. — One is fast.
   - Yo no tengo autos. — I don't have cars.
   - Sí, mis autos son veloces. — Yes, my cars are fast.

7. **¿Ustedes necesitan algo?** — **Do you guys need anything?**
   - Nosotros necesitamos otra pizza. — We need another pizza.
   - Nosotros no necesitamos nada. — We don't need anything.
   - Nosotros necesitamos unos dulces. — We need some candy.

8. **¿Tus hermanos son fuertes?** — **Are your brothers strong?**
   - Sí, ellos son fuertes y también veloces. — Yes, they are strong and fast, too.
   - No, mis hermanos son débiles. — No, my brothers are weak.
   - Yo no tengo hermanos. Yo tengo hermanas. — I don't have brothers. I have sisters.

2. Question and Answer (English → Spanish)

Each question has multiple answers. Cover up the right side and try to translate.

1. **What do you guys study at school?** — **¿Qué estudian ustedes en la escuela?**
   - We study Spanish. — Nosotros estudiamos español.
   - We study English. — Nosotros estudiamos inglés.
   - We don't study anything. — Nosotros no estudiamos nada.

2. **Is your school easy?** — **¿Tu escuela es fácil?**
   - Yes, my school is easy. — Sí, mi escuela es fácil.
   - No, my school is hard. — No, mi escuela es difícil.
   - No, it is hard but I'm smart — No, es difícil, pero yo soy inteligente.

3. **Do you eat meat?** — **¿Tú comes carne?**
   - No, I don't eat meat. — No, yo no como carne.
   - No, but my girlfriend eats meat. — No, pero mi novia come carne.
   - Yes, I eat meat every day. — Sí, yo como carne todos los días.

4. **What languages do you speak?** — **¿Qué idiomas hablas tú?**
   - I speak Japanese and also Chinese. — Yo hablo japonés y también chino.
   - I speak three languages. — Yo hablo tres idiomas.
   - Sorry, I don't speak English. — Lo siento, yo no hablo inglés.

5. **Excuse me, do you guys have tea?** — **Disculpa,¿Ustedes tienen té?**
   - Of course! Do you want a tea? — ¡Por supuesto! ¿Usted quiere un té?
   - Sorry, we don't have tea. — Disculpe, nosotros no tenemos té.
   - No, sorry, but we have coffee, juice, and other drinks. — No, disculpe, pero nosotros tenemos café, jugo y otras bebidas.

Costumers can use the standard form ***disculpa*** when addressing a clerk.

Clerks should use the respectful ***disculpe*** with a customer.

3. Spanish to English Conversation

Try translating the entire conversation before looking at the translation below.

1. Conversation between friends ordering a pizza online.

- ¿Qué pizza quieres tú? — What pizza do you want?
- Queso y pepperoni. — Cheese and pepperoni.
- Yo no quiero pepperoni. — I don't want pepperoni.
- Pero, el pepperoni es delicioso. — But pepperoni is delicious.
- Lo siento, pero, yo no quiero pepperoni en mi pizza. — I'm sorry, but I don't want pepperoni on my pizza.

2. Conversation between a mom and kid at the supermarket.

¿Qué fruta quieres tú?	What fruit do you want?
Yo quiero dulces. (This ***dulces*** means "candy".)	I want candy.
Los dulces no son fruta.	Candy isn't fruit.
Pero las frutas son dulces. (This ***dulces*** means "sweet".)	But fruit is sweet.

3. Conversation between friends on a long drive.

¿Tú tienes hambre?	Are you hungry?
No, yo tengo sueño. ¿Y tú?	No, I'm sleepy. And you?
Yo también tengo sueño. ¿Tú necesitas algo?	I'm also sleepy. Do you need anything?
Sí, yo quiero café.	Yes, I want coffee.

4. Conversation between friends ordering at a café.

¿Qué helado quieres?	What helado do you want?
Hmm, no quiero helado.	I don't want ice cream.
Entonces ¿qué quieres?	Well then, what do you want?
Quiero un café.	I want a coffee.
Ok, yo quiero café y también helado.	Ok, I want coffee and ice cream too.

5. Conversation between children on the playground.

Mi hermana habla francés.	My sister speaks French.
¿Y tu hermano?	And your brother?
No, él es tonto. Él no habla nada.	No, he's dumb. He doesn't speak anything.
Jajaja. ¿Y tú hablas francés?	Hahaha. And you speak French?
No, no hablo.	No, I don't speak.
...	...

4. English to Spanish conversation

Try translating the entire conversation before looking at the translation.

1. Conversation between friends in the drive thru.

Do you want some tacos.	¿Tú quieres unos tacos?
No, but I want an ice cream.	No, pero yo quiero un helado.
And do you want a drink?	¿Y tú quieres una bebida?
Yes, one juice please.	Sí, un jugo por favor.

2. Conversation between a human colonist and a Saraxian on a space station.

I need money now.	Yo necesito dinero ahora.
What?	¿Qué?
Do you have money?	¿Tú tienes dinero?
What?	¿Qué?
Do you speak Spanish?	¿Tú hablas español?
Yes, but I don't have money.	Sí, pero yo no tengo dinero.

3. Conversation between friends at a coffee shop.

Does your brother live in Australia?	¿Tu hermano vive en Australia?
No, he lives in Argentina now.	No, él vive en Argentina ahora.
Does he speak Spanish?	¿Él habla español?
No, but he studies Spanish now.	No, pero él estudia español ahora.

4. Conversation between a father, a son, and a clerk of a boardgame shop.

Son, do you want anything?	Hijo, ¿tú quieres algo?
Yes, I want a game!	Sí ¡Yo quiero un juego!
What game?	¿Qué juego?
I want a game in Spanish.	Yo quiero un juego en español.
Excuse me, do you guys have games in Spanish?	Disculpa, ¿ustedes tienen juegos en español?
Of course!	¡Por supuesto!

12 Workbook 12: Lesson Activities

12 Vocabulary Drills *Ejercicios de Vocabulario*

1. Writing and Vocabulary

Write the Spanish for each of the pictures. Make sure to add accent marks when needed.

park, kitchen, garden, bathroom, library, church, jail, school, living room, garage

1.__________ 2.__________ 3.__________ 4.__________ 5.__________

6.__________ 7.__________ 8.__________ 9.__________ 10.__________

2. Gender Matching

Write the following words and circle the gender companion word for each one.

parada, restaurante, habitación, comedor, cuarto, librería, dulce, bebida, idioma, plátano

1) la __________________
(room, femenine version)

2) el __________________
(room, masculine version)

3) el / la __________________
(bookstore)

4) el / la __________________
(dining room)

5) el / la ______________________ (banana)

6) el / la ______________________ (candy)

7) el / la ______________________ (restaurant)

8) el / la ______________________ (drink)

9) el / la ______________________ (language)

10) el / la ______________________ (stop [bus, etc.])

3. Adjective Translation

Translate the following adjectives into Spanish.

1) grande______________________

2) delicioso______________________

3) difícil______________________

4) dulce ______________________

5) fuerte______________________

6) inteligente______________________

7) veloz______________________

8) fácil ______________________

9) débil ______________________

10) interesante ______________________

12 Usage Activities *Actividades de Uso*

● 4. Reading comprehension

Translate the following on a separate piece of paper or type in an electronic device.

José y Laura

José isn't an interesting person. But he has some things to say. Let's listen in.

❶ Yo soy José.

❷ Yo tengo hambre, entonces necesito comida.

❸ Mi amiga es Laura.

❹ Laura tiene sed, entonces ella necesita una bebida.

❺ Yo quiero una manzana.

❻ Las manzanas son dulces.

❼ Laura quiere un café.

❽ El café es delicioso.

● 5. Reading Comprehension Questions

Answer the following reading comprehension questions in Spanish. Write full sentences.

1. ¿José tiene sueño?

____

2. ¿Qué necesita Laura?

____

3. ¿Qué necesita José?

____

4. ¿Laura tiene hambre?

____

5. ¿Qué quiere Laura?

____

6. ¿Qué quiere José?

____

6. Spanish Translation

Translate the following conversation into English.

1.
A: ¿Tú tienes tarea? B: Sí, yo tengo tarea. A: ¿Tu tarea es difícil? B: No, mi tarea es fácil. ¿Y tú? ¿Tú tienes tarea? A: No, yo no tengo tarea.
A:
B:
C:
D:

7. English Translation

Translate the following conversations into Spanish.

1.
A: Do you need something? (respectful you) B: Yes, I need a drink. A: Do you want coffee? B: No, I don't drink coffee. I want a juice.
A:
B:
A:
B:

8. Verb conjugation drills

Fill in the blanks with the proper verb conjugations.

1. Querer (to want)	
Pronouns	Present Tense
yo	
tú	
él / ella / usted	
nosotros	
ustedes	
ellos / ellas	

2. Necesitar (to need)	
Pronouns	Present Tense
yo	
tú	
él / ella / usted	
nosotros	
ustedes	
ellos / ellas	

3. Tener (to have)	
Pronouns	Present Tense
yo	
tú	
él / ella / usted	
nosotros	
ustedes	
ellos / ellas	

12 Answer Key *Clave de Respuestas*

1. Writing and Vocabulary (answers)

1. sala
living room

2. escuela
school

3. jardín
garden

4. cocina
kitchen

5. cárcel
jail

6. baño
bathroom / restroom

7. garaje
garage

8. biblioteca
library

9. parque
park

10. iglesia
church

2. Gender Matching (answers)

1) la habitación
2) el cuarto
3) la librería
4) el comedor
5) el plátano
6) el dulce
7) el restaurante
8) la bebida
9) el idioma
10) la parada

3. Adjective Translation (answers)

1) big
2) delicious
3) difficult
4) sweet
5) strong
6) smart/intelligent
7) fast
8) easy
9) weak
10) interesting

4. Reading Comprehension (answers)

❶ I'm José.
❷ I'm hungry, so I need food.
❸ My friend is Laura.
❹ Laura is thirsty, so she needs a drink.
❺ I want an apple.
❻ Apples are sweet.
❼ Laura wants a coffee.
❽ Coffee is delicious.

5. Reading Comprehension Questions (answers)

1. Is José sleepy?
   No, él / José tiene hambre. (No, he / José is hungry.)
2. What does Laura need?
   Ella / Laura necesita una bebida. (She / Laura needs a drink.)
3. What does José need?
   Él / José necesita comida. (He needs food.)
4. Is Laura hungry?
   No, ella / Laura tiene sed. / No, tiene sed. (No, she / Laura is thirsty.)
5. What does Laura want?
   Ella / Laura quiere un café. (She / Laura wants a coffee.)
6. What does José want?
   Él / José quiere una manzana. (He / José wants an apple.)

6. Spanish Translation (answers)

1. A: Do you have homework?
   B: Yes, I have homework.
   A: Is your homework difficult.
   B. No, my homework is easy. And you? Do you have homework?
   A: No, I don't.

2. A: ¿Usted necesita algo?
   B: Sí, yo necesito una bebida.
   A: ¿Usted quiere café?
   B. No, yo no bebo café. Yo quiero un jugo.

7. English Translation (answers)

1. Querer (to want)	
yo	quiero
tú	quieres
él / ella / usted	quiere
nosotros	queremos
ustedes	quieren
ellos / ellas	quieren

2. Necesitar (to need)	
yo	necesito
tú	necesitas
él / ella / usted	necesita
nosotros	necesitamos
ustedes	necesitan
ellos / ellas	necesitan

3. Tener (to have)	
yo	tengo
tú	tienes
él / ella / usted	tiene
nosotros	tenemos
ustedes	tienen
ellos / ellas	tienen

Vocabulary Builder 7:
Group L

Group L More places

el edificio	building
el mercado	market
la farmacia	drugstore
el cine	movie theather
el cajero automático	ATM
el centro comercial	mall
el supermercado	supermarket
el estacionamiento	parking lot
el banco	bank
la plaza	plaza

This is often shortened to ***cajero***.

15 PAGES	12 USAGE SECTIONS	23 NEW WORDS

13 Lesson 13: Locations, de, and Estar

From the teacher...

In this lesson we introduce the other "to be" verb ***estar***. It's used differently from ***ser***. For natural sounding Spanish, it's important to eventually learn when to use one over the other. Also, this lesson is huge and it might take a bit of time to fully understand it entirely.

13 New Words *Palabras Nuevas*

Nouns etc.

¿dónde?	where?	**la tarea**	homework
afuera	out; outside	**el hombre**	man
la cama	bed	**la mujer**	woman
entre	between	**arriba**	above; upstairs
izquierda	left	**derecha**	right
abajo, debajo	below; under	**adentro**	inside

Adjectives

azúl	blue	**rosa**	pink
triste	sad	**feliz**	happy
amable	kind	**pequeño**	small
mediano	medium	**chico**	small

Prepositions

de	of	**a**	to, (as in "to the right")

Verbs

estar	to be (is, am, are)

chico

mediano

grande

extra grande

13 Culture Clip *Clip Cultural*

● 13-1. Spanish Cities in the USA

A large part of the USA used to be part of Mexico, and many areas are named in Spanish. For example, areas with ***san*** in their name mean "saint" something. For example, ***San Francisco*** and ***San Diego***. Two of the most famous cities with fully Spanish names are ***Los Angeles***, which means "the angels", and ***Las Vegas***, which means "the meadows."

13 New Expressions *Expresiones Nuevas*

Don't worry about the grammar here. Just learn the phrases for communication.

1. **Yo no sé. / No sé.** **I don't know.**
   When you don't know the answer to something, this is the standard way to say so.

2. **Bueno.** **Okay.**
   Bueno means "good" but it's also just a way to acknowledge what someone has said. We will learn more about ***bueno*** in the next lesson.

13 Word Usage *Uso de Palabras*

W-1	entonces	so; therefore

We learned ***entonces*** as "well; well then." It can also mean "so; therefore" to show the result of the previous statement.

EXAMPLE SENTENCES

1. Yo soy estudiante, entonces yo estudio todos los días.
   I'm a student, so I study every day.
2. Yo soy australiano, entonces yo hablo inglés.
   I'm Australian, so I speak English.
3. Yo tengo novia, entonces no tengo dinero.
   I have a girlfriend, so I don't have money.

13 Verb Usage *Uso de Verbos*

13-2. The other "to be" verb *estar*

Before we learn the second "to be" verb, let's review ***ser***, our first "to be" verb.

EXAMPLE SENTENCES (SER)

1. Yo soy mexicano. — I am Mexican.
2. Tú eres mi amiga. — You are my friend.
3. Él es abogado. — He is a lawyer.
4. Nosotros somos hermanos. — We are brothers.
5. ¿Ustedes son hermanas? — Are you guys sisters?

Spanish has an additional "to be" verb, ***estar***. Let's look at the conjugations of both verbs.

Ser y Estar (to be)			
pronoun	ser	estar	English
yo	soy	***estoy***	I am~
tú	eres	***estás***	You are~
él / ella / usted	es	***está***	he/she/you are~
nosotros / nosotras	somos	***estamos***	we are~
ustedes / ellos / ellas	son	***están***	you guys / they are~

Ser is generally used for things that don't change. For example, nationality, gender, occupation, relationships, color of objects, etc. are considered permanent.

EXAMPLE SENTENCES (SER)

1. Yo soy estadounidense. — I am American. (nationality)
2. Yo soy estudiante. — I am a student. (occupation)
3. Ellas son mis hermanas. — They are my sisters. (relationship)
4. Mi auto es azúl. — My car is blue. (color)

Estar is for states that can change such as location, feelings, temperature, health, etc.

EXAMPLE SENTENCES (ESTAR)

1. Yo estoy en México. — I'm in Mexico. (location)
2. ¿Tú estás feliz? — Are you happy? (feelings)
3. Mi comida está fría. — My food is cold. (temperature)
4. Mis piernas están débiles. — My legs are weak. (health)

For locations, even those that seem permanent, ***estar*** is always used.

EXAMPLE SENTENCES

1. Mi casa está en México.	My house is in Mexico.
2. Mis hermanos están en sus casas.	My brothers are in their houses.
3. Nosotros estamos en el parque ahora.	We are in the park now.
4. ¿Tu escuela está en la ciudad?	Is your school in the city?
5. ¿Tú estás en la ciudad?	Are you in the city?

In sentence 4 we are asking about ***escuela*** (school) so we use ***está***, but in sentence 5 we are asking about ***tú*** (you) so we use ***estás***.

13-3. To *Ser* or not to *Estar*

Here's a mental hint to remind you of when to use ***estar***. "States" are places, like the "state" of California, and emotions can also be a mental "state". In both cases, whether talking about locations such as a "state" or which mental "state" you are in, you use ***estar***.

location "states"

Yo **estoy** en (location)

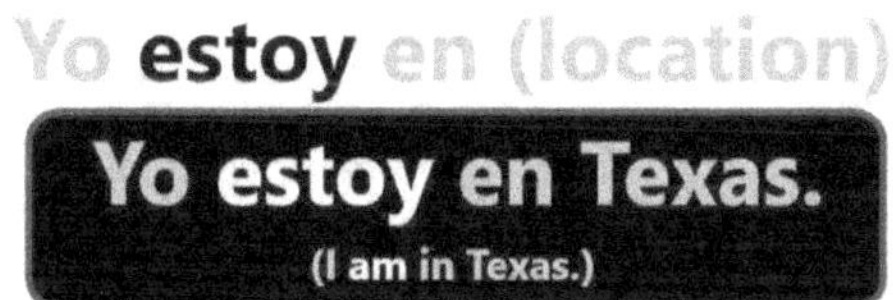

emotion "states"

Yo **estoy** (emotion)

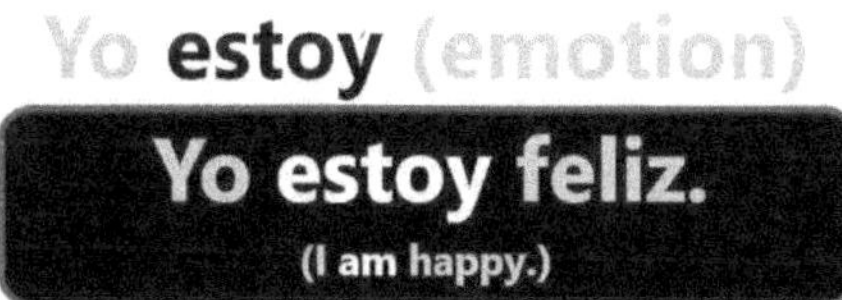

 *Más Detalles* **More Details** 

Life state VS current state

Ser and ***estar*** are used differently depending on what you want to say. For example, in the case of happiness, ***ser*** is for life happiness, and ***estar*** is for momentary happiness.

EXAMPLE SENTENCES

1. Yo soy feliz.	I'm happy. (overall in my life)
2. Yo estoy feliz.	I'm happy. (because of a recent event)

13 Grammar and Usage *Gramática y Uso*

● 13-4. Spanish "the" is sometimes different

Spanish and English use "a" (a dog, etc.) in the same way. However, "the" has some differences. To understand the logic, read the text conversations in order 1-6.

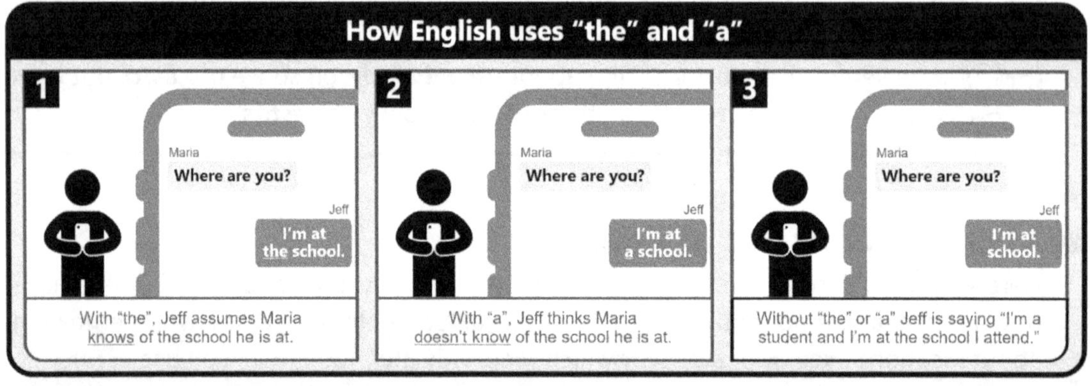

To show the impact of "the," say the following out loud without "the." Weird right?

I'm at ~~the~~ store.	I'm at ~~the~~ park.	I'm at ~~the~~ bank.
I'm at ~~the~~ festival.	I'm at ~~the~~ party.	I'm at ~~the~~ hospital.

Now consider how "the" changes the meaning. Say these with and without "the".

I'm in (the) church.	I'm at (the) work.	I'm in (the) jail.
I'm in (the) bed.	I'm in (the) college.	I'm in (the) space.

As you can see, in English "the" has impact. For example, "I'm in college" means "I'm a college student" whereas "I'm in the college" only refers to your location and not your status as a student. Spanish always has ***el / la*** (the) with no other implications.

In these next examples, remember that even if English doesn't have "the," Spanish does.

EXAMPLE SENTENCES

1. Mi amigo está en la cárcel. — My friend is in (the) jail.
   This can mean the friend is a prisoner in jail, or he is just visiting.

2. Yo estoy en la cama ahora. — I'm in (the) bed now.
   This can mean the person is in bed, or in a specific bed both people know.

3. ¿Tú estás en el trabajo? — Are you at (the) work?
   This can just mean, "are you working?" or "Are you at the job site we both know?"

4. Mis padres están en la iglesia. — My parents are in (the) church.
   This means the parents are attending church or are at a specific church.

13-5. More on possession - *de*

We previously learned ***mi*** (my~), ***tu*** (your~) and ***su*** (his / her / their). We can also make possession with ***de***. In some cases, ***de*** translates to "of" and in others as **'s** (apostrophe s).

EXAMPLES

1. los perros **de** María	María**'s** dogs / the dogs **of** María
2. la casa **de** mi amigo	my friend**'s** house / the house **of** my friend
3. el amigo **de** tu hermana	your sister**'s** friend / the friend **of** your sister
4. las hermanas **de** mi madre	my mother**'s** sisters / the sisters **of** my mother

Now we can use the ***de*** (possession) in sentences. Notice that we don't use "of" in the following examples since **'s** (apostrophe s) is more natural in English.

EXAMPLE SENTENCES

1. El auto **de** mi mamá es un Toyota.	My mom**'s** car is a Toyota.
2. El padre **de** la niña es fuerte.	The girl**'s** father is strong.
3. Los zapatos **de** Ema están en tu auto.	Ema**'s** shoes are in your car.
4. La novia **de** mi hermano es mexicana.	My brother**'s** girlfriend is Mexican.
5. La tarea **de** mis hijos es difícil.	My children**'s** homework is difficult.

NOTE: The apostrophe s way of making possession does NOT exist in Spanish.

13-6. Shortening of *de el~*

When ***de*** is followed immediately with ***el***, both are combined into ***del***.

EXAMPLES (DE + EL = DEL)

1. el auto **del** maestro — the teacher**'s** car
2. las mascotas **del** niño — the boy**'s** pets
3. las mascotas **de la** niña — the girl**'s** pets

de la doesn't shorten to ***dela***.

EXAMPLE SENTENCES

1. El helado **del** niño es rosa. — The boy**'s** ice cream is pink.
2. La casa **del** doctor es grande. — The doctor**'s** house is big.
3. La camisa **del** hombre es azul. — The man**'s** shirt is blue.

13-7. An unneccessary "the"?

Students often forget the need for ***el*** or ***la*** when using ***de***. This is because often ***de*** is translated to **'s** (apostrophe s). It leads to what looks like an unneccessary ***el*** or ***la*** (the) in the sentence. Consider the following English-Spanish breakdown.

Let's start with this sentence:
My friend's house is big.

Since ***de*** can be translated as **'s**, you might translate the sentence to:
Casa de mi amigo es grande. (incorrect)

However, this is incorrect. And instead must say:
La casa de mi amigo es grande. (correct)

You'll notice ***la*** was added. If we directly translate this to English, it becomes:
My friend's the house is big.

Of course that doesn't work in English, but makes sense when you consider ***de*** as "of":
The house of my friend is big.

13-8. Another way to say his~ and her~

We know ***su*** can mean, "his~", "her~", or "their~" but as to which meaning it is, can be unclear. To be more specific, we can use ***de él*** (his~, ~of his) and ***de ella*** (her~, ~of her).

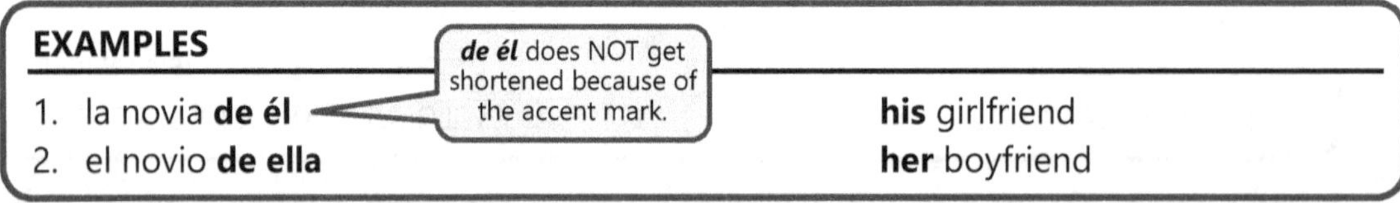

EXAMPLE SENTENCES

1. El helado **de ella** es rosa.	**Her** ice cream is pink.
2. La casa **de él** es grande.	**His** house is big.
3. La camisa **de usted** es azul.	**Your** shirt is blue.
4. El cuarto **de ellos** es grande. (all male or mixed)	**Their** room is big.
5. El cuarto **de ellas** es grande. (only females)	**Their** room is big.
6. El cuarto **de ustedes** es grande.	**You guys'** room is big.

de usted can also be used instead of ***su***.

 *Más Detalles* More Details 

Translating *de* to "of"

As stated before, it's often easier to think of ***de*** as "of" since sentence order then perfectly matches Spanish.

1. El auto **de** George es un Toyota.	The car **of** George is a Toyota.
2. El padre **de** Carla es fuerte.	The father **of** Carla is strong.

The problem is this often makes unnatural English, so we instead use apostrophe "s".

3. El auto **de** Jorge es un Toyota.	Jorge**'s** car is a Toyota.
4. El padre **de** Carla es fuerte.	Carla**'s** father is strong.

13-9. Locations

We can use ***de*** (of) to say where something is. But first we need to know some location words. Location words are considered adverbs, so they don't have gender or plurals.

arriba
above; on top; up

debajo, abajo
below; under; down

adentro
inside; in

EXAMPLES

1. **arriba** del escritorio	**on top of** the desk
2. **debajo** del escritorio	**under** the desk
3. **adentro** del escritorio	**inside** the desk

Remember, locations use ***estar***.

EXAMPLE SENTENCES

1. El gato está **arriba** del escritorio.
   The cat is **on top** of the desk.

2. El ratón está **debajo** del escritorio.
   The mouse is **under** the desk.

3. El pingüino está **adentro** del escritorio.
   The penguin is **inside** the desk.

Now that we know the pattern, let's look at more variety.

4. Nosotros estamos **arriba** de la montaña.	We are **on top** of the mountain.
5. Mi padre está **arriba** de la casa.	My father is **on top** of the house.
6. Tus calcetas están **debajo** de mi camisa.	Your socks are **under** my shirt.
7. El niño y la niña están **abajo** del escritorio.	The boy and girl are **under** the desk.
8. Tú comida está **adentro** del refrigerador.	Your food is **in** the fridge.
9. Yo estoy **adentro** de la iglesia.	I'm **inside** the church.

 *Más Detalles* More Details 

Debajo vs Abajo

Debajo and ***abajo*** both mean "below" or "under". However, ***abajo*** is more commonly used just to express "direction" as in "go down". Despite these distinctions, Spanish speakers will use either without concern of their differences.

Arriba for "upstairs"

It's common to use arriba to just mean "upstairs". For example, ***Mi cuarto está arriba.*** My room is upstairs.

● 13-10. More locations

Here are three more location words.

la izquierda
left

entre
between

la derecha
right

Since ***izquierda*** (left) and ***derecha*** (right) are nouns we must use their gender companion words. And when using *left* and *right*, we must also use ***a*** (to).

EXAMPLES

1. **a la izquierda** del escritorio	**to the left** of the desk
2. **a la derecha** del escritorio	**to the right** of the desk

EXAMPLE SENTENCES

1. El león está **a la izquierda** del escritorio.
   The lion is **to the left of** the desk.
2. El canguro está **a la derecha** del escritorio.
   The kangaroo **is to the right** of the desk.

Entre (between) is a bit special. It doesn't require ***de*** (of). Also, if something is between two of the same things, there are a few ways the sentence can be made.

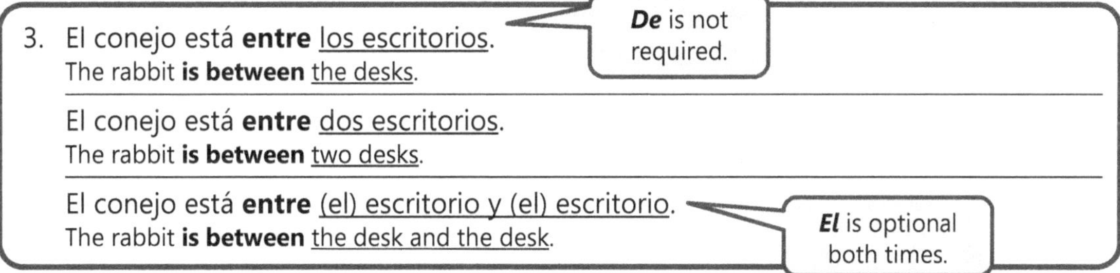

3. El conejo está **entre** los escritorios.
   The rabbit **is between** the desks.

   De is not required.

   El conejo está **entre** dos escritorios.
   The rabbit **is between** two desks.

   El conejo está **entre** (el) escritorio y (el) escritorio.
   The rabbit **is between** the desk and the desk.

   El is optional both times.

Now that we hopefully understand how to make these sentences, let's look at more. Cover the Spanish, look at just the English, and see if you can make the Spanish sentences.

EXAMPLE SENTENCES

1. My school is to the right of my house.
   Mi escuela está a la derecha de mi casa.
2. I have a light to the left of my bed.
   Yo tengo una luz a la izquierda de mi cama.
3. My cats are under the table.
   Mis gatos están debajo de la mesa.
4. My dad is between my uncle and my aunt.
   Mi papá está entre mi tío y mi tía.
5. The bathroom is between the kitchen and the living room.
   El baño está entre la cocina y la sala.
6. The store is to the right of the bank.
   La tienda está a la derecha del banco.

13-11. The question word "where" - *dónde*

Dónde (where) is used just like in English, to ask *where* something is. Since "where" is a *location*, we almost always use ***estar***.

EXAMPLE Q&A

1. **¿Dónde estás tú?** — **Where are you?**
   - Yo estoy en mi casa. — I'm in my house.
   - Yo estoy en la escuela. — I'm at (the) school.

En can be "in" "on" and "at".

La isn't optional.

2. **¿Dónde está tu casa?** — **Where is your house?**
   - Mi casa está en España. — My house is in Spain.
   - Yo vivo en México. — I live in Mexico.
   - Mi casa está en Estados Unidos. — My house is in the United States.

3. **¿Dónde está el baño?** — **Where is the bathroom?**
   - El baño está afuera. — The bathroom it's outside.
   - El baño está adentro del restaurante. — The bathroom is inside the restaurant.

4. **¿Dónde está tu novia?** — **Where is your girlfriend?**
   - Ella está en la librería. — She is in the bookshop.
   - Ella está en su auto. — She is in her car.
   - Ella está en el centro comercial. — She's at the shopping mall.

5. **¿Dónde están tus hijos?** — **Where are your children?**
   - Ellos están en la escuela. — They're at school.
   - Ellos están debajo de sus camas. — They're under their beds.
   - Yo no tengo hijos. — I don't have children.

Más Detalles More Details 

El Baño

When at someone's house you can ask:

¿Dónde está el baño?	Where's the bathroom?

However, in public places, since there are ***baños de hombres*** (men's room) y ***baños de mujeres*** (women's room) people usually ask in plural:

¿Dónde están los baños?	Where are the restrooms?

13-12. Using *dónde* in questions with verbs

We learned how question words change sentence order with ***qué*** (what). Since ***dónde*** (where) is also a question word, it changes sentence order as well.

EXAMPLE SENTENCES

1. ¿Dónde comes tú? (Literally: Where eat you?)
   Where do you eat?

2. ¿Dónde vive ella? (Literally: Where live she?)
   Where does she live?

3. ¿Dónde escribes tú la novela? (Literally: Where write you the novel?)
   Where do you write the novel?

4. ¿Dónde cocina tu mamá todos los días? (Literally: Where cook your mom...)
   Where does your mom cook every day?

Remember, without a question word like ***dónde***, the order switches to match English.

5. ¿Tu mamá cocina todos los días? (Literally: Your mom cooks every day?)
   Does your mom cook every day?

13 Practice and Review *Práctica y Repaso*

1. Question and Answer (Spanish → English)

Each question has multiple answers. Cover up the right side and try to translate.

1. ¿Dónde estás tú ahora?	**Where are you now?**
Ahora yo estoy en la estación.	Now I am at the station.
Yo estoy en el parque ahora.	I am at the park now.
Yo estoy en la librería.	I am in the bookstore.
2. ¿Dónde está el baño?	**Where is the bathroom?**
El baño está a la derecha.	The bathroom is to the right.
Nosotros no tenemos baño.	We don't have a bathroom.
El baño está afuera.	The bathroom is outside.
No sé.	I don't know.
3. ¿La tarea de tu hijo es fácil?	**Is your son's homework easy?**
Sí, la tarea es fácil.	Yes, the homework is easy.
No, la tarea de mi hijo es difícil.	No, my son's homework is easy.
Mi hijo no tiene tarea.	My son doesn't have homework.

4. **¿Tus padres son amables?** — **Are your parents kind?**
   - Mi papá es amable, pero mi mamá no es. — My dad is kind, but my mom isn't.
   - Sí, ellos son amables. — Yes they are kind.
   - Mi mamá es amable. Yo no tengo papá. — My mother is kind. I don't have a dad.

5. **¿Usted está en <u>su</u> casa?** — **Are you in your house?**

   Remember ***su*** is used with ***usted*** for "your".

   - Sí, yo estoy en mi casa. — Yes, I'm in my house.
   - No, yo estoy en mi auto. — No, I'm in my car.
   - No, yo estoy en un restaurante. — No, I'm at a restaurant.

6. **¿Dónde están tus maestros?** — **Where are your teachers?**
   - Ellos están en la librería. — They are in the bookstore.
   - Ellos están en la escuela. — They are at the school.
   - Uno está en el baño, una está afuera. — One's in the bathroom, one's outside.

2. Question and answer (English → Spanish)

Each question has multiple answers. Cover up the right side and try to translate.

1. **Are you guys (in) downtown?** — **¿Ustedes están en el centro?**
   - No, we are at school. — No, nosotros estámos en la escuela.
   - No, we are at our house. — No, nosotros estámos en nuestra casa.
   - Yes, we are downtown. — Sí, nosotros estámos en el centro.

2. **Is Sofia's car pink?** — **¿El auto de Sofía es rosa?**
   - No, Sofía's car is not pink. — No, el auto de Sofía no es rosa.
   - No, Sofía's car is blue. — No, el auto de Sofía es azul.
   - Yes, Sofía's car is pink. — Sí, el carro de Sofía es rosa.

3. **Where does your brother live?** — **¿Dónde vive tu hermano?**
   - My brother lives in England. — Mi hermano vive en Inglaterra.
   - My brother is in Korea. — Mi hermano está en Corea.
   - He lives in France. — Él vive en Francia.

4. **Where are my shoes?** — **¿Dónde están mis zapatos?**
   - Your shoes are in your room. — Tus zapatos están en tu cuarto.
   - Your shoes are in the kitchen — Tus zapatos están en la cocina.
   - Your shoes are in the living room. — Tus zapatos están en la sala.

5. **Is she your girlfriend's friend?** — **¿Ella es amiga de tu novia?**
   - Yes, she is my girlfriend's friend. — Sí, ella es la amiga de mi novia.
   - No, she's my girlfriend. — No, ella es mi novia.
   - No, she's my girlfriend's mom. — No, ella es la mamá de mi novia.

6. **Where is your house?** — **¿Dónde está tu casa?**
   - My house is in Mexico. — Mi casa está en México.
   - My house is to the right of the drugstore. — Mi casa está a la derecha de la farmacia.
   - It's to the left of the station. — Está a la izquierda de la estación.

3. Spanish to English Conversation

Try translating the entire conversation before looking at the translation.

1. Conversation between people who met online.

¿Dónde vives tú?	Where do you live?
Yo vivo en estados unidos ahora.	I live in the United States now.
¿Tú tienes mascotas?	Do you have pets?
Sí, yo tengo dos gatos.	Yes, I have two cats.

2. Conversation between a man in a car and another looking for his driver.

¿Tú nombre es Jorge?	Is your name Jorge?
No disculpa, yo no soy Jorge.	No sorry, I'm not Jorge.
Entonces, ¿cuál es tu nombre?	Well then, what's your name?
Yo soy Carlos.	I'm Carlos.

3. Conversation between friends at a party.

Hola. ¿Dónde está tu novia?	Hello. Where's your girlfriend?
Ella está en su casa.	She's at her house.
¿Y tu hermano?	And your brother?
Él está en el baño ahora.	He's in the bathroom now.

4. Conversation between a male customer who had too many lemonades.

Disculpe ¿dónde están los baños?	Excuse me, where are the restrooms?
El baño de mujeres está a la derecha.	The women's restroom is to the right.
¡¿Y el baño de hombres?!	And the men's restroom?!
Está arriba.	The men's restroom is upstairs.

4. English to Spanish conversation

Try translating the entire conversation before looking at the translation.

1. Conversation between a couple in a shopping mall.

Are you hungry?	¿Tú tienes hambre?
Yes, I'm hungry, and I'm thirsty.	Sí, yo tengo hambre, y yo tengo sed.
Do we have food in our house?	¿Nosotros tenemos comida en nuestra casa?
Yes, we have meat and vegetables.	Sí, nosotros tenemos carne y verduras.

2. Conversation between players meeting at a chess tournament finals.

Hi, how old are you?	Hola, ¿cuántos años tienes?
I'm twenty-one years old. And you?	Yo tengo vientiún años. ¿Y tú?
I'm seven years old.	Yo tengo siete años.
You're seven?!?!?!	¿¡¿¡¿Tú tienes siete?!?!?

3. Conversation between an angry friend who is owed money.

Do you have money?	¿Tú tienes dinero?
I don't have, but Carlos does.	Yo no tengo, pero Carlos tiene.
Well then, where is Carlos now?	Entonces, ¿dónde está Carlos ahora?
He and my brother are in the car.	Él y mi hermano están en el auto.

4. Conversation between a local and a clueless tourist.

Excuse me, where is the bank?	Disculpe, ¿dónde está el banco?
The bank is to the right of the the supermarket.	El banco está a la derecha del supermercado.
Thanks, and where is the ATM?	Gracias, ¿y dónde está el cajero automático?
The ATM is inside the bank...	El cajero está adentro del banco...

5. Conversation between a person walking down the street and a lost driver.

Where's the parking lot?	¿Dónde está el estacionamiento?
The parking lot is to the right of the mall.	El estacionamiento está a la derecha del centro comercial.
Well, then where is the mall?	Entonces, ¿dónde está el centro comercial?
It's on the left of the parking lot.	Está a la izquierda del estacionamiento.

13 Workbook 13: Lesson Activities

13 Vocabulary Drills *Ejercicios de Vocabulario*

1. Writing and Vocabulary

Write the Spanish for each of the pictures. Make sure to add accent marks when needed.

homework, woman, bank, pharmacy, below, left, right, up, bed, man

1.__________ 2.__________ 3.__________ 4.__________ 5.__________

Pharmacy

6.__________ 7.__________ 8.__________ 9.__________ 10.__________

2. Gender Matching

Write the following words and circle the gender companion word for each one.

parque, librería, centro, iglesia, parada, estación, cuarto, sala, restaurante, jardín

1) el / la ____________________
(park)

2) el / la ____________________
(station)

3) el / la ____________________
(downtown)

4) el / la ____________________
(church)

5) el / la ____________________ (livingroom)

6) el / la ____________________ (bookstore)

7) el / la ____________________ (room)

8) el / la ____________________ (stop [bus, etc.])

9) el / la ____________________ (garden)

10) el / la ____________________ (restaurant)

13 Usage Activities *Actividades de Uso*

● 3. Reading Comprehension

Translate the following on a separate piece of paper or type in an electronic device.

Las mascotas de Dora

Dora obviously loves animals. She has airtags on each of her animals so she always knows exactly where they are.

❶ Mi nombre es Dora. Yo soy doctora de animales.

❷ Yo no tengo amigos, entonces, yo tengo seis mascotas.

❸ Mis mascotas son un perro, un gato, una gata, un conejo, un hámster y una jirafa.

❹ Mis gatos están en el comedor ahora.

❺ Mi gata está arriba de la mesa y mi gato está abajo de la mesa.

❻ Mi hámster está en mi cuarto, abajo de mi cama.

❼ Mi jirafa y mi conejo están afuera.

❽ Mi jirafa está en mi jardín, a la derecha del árbol grande.

❾ Y mi conejo está a la izquierda del árbol.

❿ Mi perro está adentro de su casa de perro.

4. Reading Comprehension Questions

Answer the following questions about the reading comprehension in Spanish.

1. ¿Dónde está el gato de Dora?

____

2. ¿Dónde está el hámster de Dora?

____

3. ¿Dora tiene siete mascotas?

____

4. ¿La jirafa de Dora está a la derecha del árbol?

____

5. ¿Dónde está la gata de Dora?

____

6. ¿Dónde está el conejo?

____

7. ¿Dora es abogada?

____

8. ¿Dónde está el perro de Dora?

____

9. ¿Dora tiene dos gatas?

____

10. ¿El perro de Dora tiene hambre?

____

5. Spanish translation

Translate the following conversations into English.

1.
A: ¿Dónde estás tú ahora? B: Yo estoy en el centro. A: ¿En el supermercado? B: No, en la librería.
A:
B:
A:
B:

6. Spanish translation 2

Translate the following conversations into Spanish.

1.
A: ¿¡Nuestra maestra de inglés es tu mamá!? B: No, la maestra de inglés es mí tía. A: ¿Cuántos años tiene tu tía? B: Mi tía tiene 31 años.
A:
B:
A:
B:

7. English Translation

Translate the following conversations into Spanish.

1.
A: ¿Tú tienes un auto? B: Sí, tengo un auto. Mi auto es azul. A: ¿En dónde está tu auto ahora? B: Mi auto está en el estacionamiento de la casa de mi amigo.
A:
B:
A:
B:

8. *Ser* and *Estar* practice

Write the proper verb in each sentence.

1. El gato __________ en la habitación.
   The cat is in the room.

2. Yo __________ mexicano.
   I am Mexican.

3. Tú __________ en Chile.
   You are in Chile.

4. Carlos __________ abogado.
   Carlos is a lawyer.

5. Tú perro __________ triste.
   Your dog is sad.

6. Mis gatos __________ en mi cuarto.
   My cats are in my room.

7. Todos los autos de mi papá__________ Toyota.
   All of my dad's cars are Toyota.

9. Verb conjugation drills

Fill in the blanks with the proper verb conjugations.

1. Estar (to be)	
Pronouns	**Present Tense**
yo	
tú	estás
él / ella / usted	
nosotros	
ustedes	
ellos / ellas	

2. Ser (to be)	
Pronouns	**Present Tense**
yo	
tú	
él / ella / usted	
nosotros	somos
ustedes	
ellos / ellas	

3. Tener (to have)	
Pronouns	**Present Tense**
yo	
tú	
él / ella / usted	
nosotros	
ustedes	tienen
ellos / ellas	

13 Answer Key *Clave de Respuestas*

1. Writing and vocabulary (answers)

1. cama
bed

2. izquierda
left

3. hombre
man

4. tarea
homework / chores

5. derecha
right

6. arriba
up / above

7. farmacia
pharmacy

8. debajo
down / below

9. banco
bank

10. mujer
woman

2. Gender Matching (answers)

1) el parque
2) la estación
3) el centro
4) la iglesia
5) la sala
6) la librería
7) el cuarto
8) la parada
9) el jardín
10) el restaurante

3. Reading Comprehension Translation

❶ My name is Dora. I am an animal doctor.
❷ I don't have friends so, I have six pets.
❸ My pets are a dog, a cat, a (female) cat, a rabbit, a hamster, and a giraffe.
❹ My cats are in the dining room now.
❺ My (female) cat is on the table and my (male) cat is under the table.
❻ My hamster is in my room, under my bed.
❼ My giraffe and my rabbit are outside.
❽ My giraffe is in the garden, to the right of the tree.
❾ And my rabbit is to the left of the tree.
❿ My dog is inside his dog house.

4. Reading Comprehension Questions (sample answers)

1. Where is Dora's cat? — El gato de Dora está abajo de la mesa.
2. Where is Dora's hamster? — El hámster de Dora está en su cuarto, abajo de su cama.
3. Does Dora have seven pets? — No, Dora tiene seis mascotas.
4. Is Dora's giraffe to the right of the tree? — No, la jirafa de Dora está a la izquierda del árbol.

5. Where is Dora's (female) cat? La gata de Dora está arriba de la mesa.
6. Where is the rabbit? El conejo está en el jardín a la izquierda del árbol.
7. Is Dora a lawyer? No, Dora es doctora de animales.
8. Where is Dora's dog? El perro de Dora está adentro de su casa de perro.
9. Does Dora's have two female cats? No, Dora tiene un gato y una gata.
10. Is Dora's dog hungry? No sé. (We can't know the answer)

5. Spanish Translation (answers)

1. A: Where are you now?
   B: I'm at the city center.
   A: In the supermarket?
   B: No, in the bookstore.

6. Spanish translation 2 (answers)

1. A: Is our English teacher your mom!?
   B: No, the English teacher is my aunt.
   A: How old is your aunt?
   B: She's 31 years old.

7. English Translation (answers)

1. A: Do you have a car?
   B: Yes, I have a car. My car is blue.
   A: Where is your car now?
   B: My car is in the parking lot at my friend's house.

8. Ser and Estar practice (answers)

1. El gato <u>está</u> en la habitación.
2. Yo <u>soy</u> mexicano.
3. Tú <u>estás</u> en Chile.
4. Carlos <u>es</u> abogado.
5. Tú perro <u>está</u> triste.
6. Mis gatos <u>están</u> en mi cuarto.
7. Todos los autos de mi papá <u>son</u> Toyota.

9. Verb conjugation drills (answers)

1. estar (to be)	
yo	estoy
tú	estás
él / ella / usted	está
nosotros	estamos
ustedes	están
ellos / ellas	están

2. ser (to be)	
yo	soy
tú	eres
él / ella / usted	es
nosotros	somos
ustedes	son
ellos / ellas	son

3. tener (to have)	
yo	tengo
tú	tienes
él / ella / usted	tiene
nosotros	tenemos
ustedes	tienen
ellos / ellas	tienen

Vocabulary Builder 8:

Groups M and N

Group M Similar words to English

There are a ton of Spanish words that are the same as English but with Spanish pronunciation.

el color	color	**el chocolate**	chocolate
la pasta	pasta	**el horror**	horror
el pepperoni	pepperoni	**el drama**	drama
el animal	animal	**el hotel**	hotel
la cafetería	cafeteria	**el internet**	internet

Group N Colors

rojo	red	**blanco**	white
verde	green	**negro**	black
amarillo	yellow	**café**	brown
naranja	orange		

animal

pepperoni

hotel

16 PAGES	10 USAGE SECTIONS	26 NEW WORDS

14 Lesson 14: More about adjectives

14 New Words *Palabras Nuevas*

Nouns etc.

muy	very~; too~	**la fresa**	strawberry
la computadora	computer	**la naranja**	orange (the fruit)
el celular	smart phone	**el teléfono**	telephone
la película	movie	**la noche**	night
aquí	here	**allí**	over there
ahí	there		

Adjectives

bueno	good	**malo**	bad
caliente	hot; warm	**frío**	cold
bonito	beautiful	**feo**	ugly
caro	expensive	**barato**	cheap; inexpensive
alto	tall	**bajo**	short
delicioso	delicious	**tonto**	dumb
genial	cool; nice	**popular**	popular

Verb

trabajar	to work

14 Culture Clip *Clip Cultural*

● 14-1. Coffee grains?

In one of the vocab builders we learned "bean" is ***frijol***. The plural of ***frijol*** is ***frijoles***. We also learned ***café*** is coffee. But interestingly in Spanish "coffee beans" are called ***granos de café*** (coffee grains) and not ***frijoles de café*** (coffee beans).

14 Word Usage *Uso de Palabras*

14-2. Gender for adjectives

Until now, all the adjectives we've learned were gender neutral, meaning we didn't have to consider gender when using them. In this lesson we introduce adjectives with gender.

NEUTRAL ADJECTIVES

Neutral adjectives end in any letter other than ***-o***. They never change gender.

genial	cool; nice
excelente	excellent
fácil	easy

interesante	interesting
popular	popular
difícil	difficult; hard

GENDER-BASED ADJECTIVES

When adjectives are introduced in this book, if they can change gender, they are always introduced first in their masculine form, which ends in ***o***. With mixed gender groups, then masculine is used for the group.

bonito / bonita	beautiful
caro / cara	expensive
alto / alta	tall

feo / fea	ugly
barato / barata	inexpensive; cheap
bajo / baja	short; low

Let's look at some sentences using adjectives that change based on the object gender.

EXAMPLE SENTENCES (NEUTRAL ADJECTIVES)

1. Mi padre es alto. — My father is tall.
2. La tarea de mi hija es simple. — My daughter's homework is simple.
3. La película es interesante. — The movie is interesting.
4. Mi hijo es popular en la escuela. — My son is popular in school.
5. Tu auto es genial. — Your car is cool.

EXAMPLE SENTENCES (O-ADJECTIVES)

6. Tu novia es bonita. — Your girlfriend is beautiful.
7. Tu auto es bonito. — Your car is beautiful.
8. ¿Tu hermano es bajo? — Is your brother short?
9. Mi hermano es alto. — My brother is tall.
10. Mi hermana es baja. — My sister is short.
11. Su mascota es fea. — His/her/their/ your (polite) pet is ugly.

W-1 **caliente** **hot; warm**

We learned ***el calor*** as a noun meaning "heat; hotness". ***Caliente*** is the adjective for "hot" and is a neutral adjective only having to match the plurality of the noun.

EXAMPLE SENTENCES

Estar is used because temperature can change.

1. Mi sopa está caliente. — My soup is hot.
2. Mi té está caliente. — My tea is hot.
3. La nariz de mi gato está caliente. — My cat's nose is warm.
4. Mis pies están calientes. — My feet are hot.
5. Tus manos están calientes. — Your hands are warm.

Congratulations if you remembered ***pies*** meant "feet".

Remember, if you want to say "I'm hot" you have to say "I have heat".

6. Yo tengo calor. — I'm hot.

Más Detalles More Details

How to handle "hot" and "warm"

Caliente can mean both *hot* and *warm*. It's up to you how you translate it. However, there are ways to make ***caliente*** mean "hot" instead of "warm". If you want to say your soup is *very hot* we can add ***muy*** (very) in front. This makes ***caliente*** mean "hot".

1. Mi sopa está muy caliente. — My soup is very hot.

There is also an unofficial way to say "warm" with a modification of ***caliente*** to ***calientito***, which always means just "warm". However, the ***calientito*** must match the gender of the noun.

2. Mi sopa está calientita. — My soup is warm.
3. Mi café está calientito. — My coffee is warm.

W-2

el celular | smartphone; cell phone; phone

Mobile phones are called ***celular*** and similar to English, you can also just say ***teléfono***.

EXAMPLE Q&A

1. ¿Tú tienes un celular?	**Do you have a cell phone?**
Sí, yo tengo un iPhone.	Yes, I have an iPhone.
Sí, yo tengo dos.	Yes, I have two.
No, mis padres no tienen dinero.	No, my parents don't have money.

W-3

frío | cold

We learned ***el frío*** as a noun meaning "coldness". ***Frío*** is also an adjective meaning "cold". ***Frío*** must match its gender and plurality to the noun.

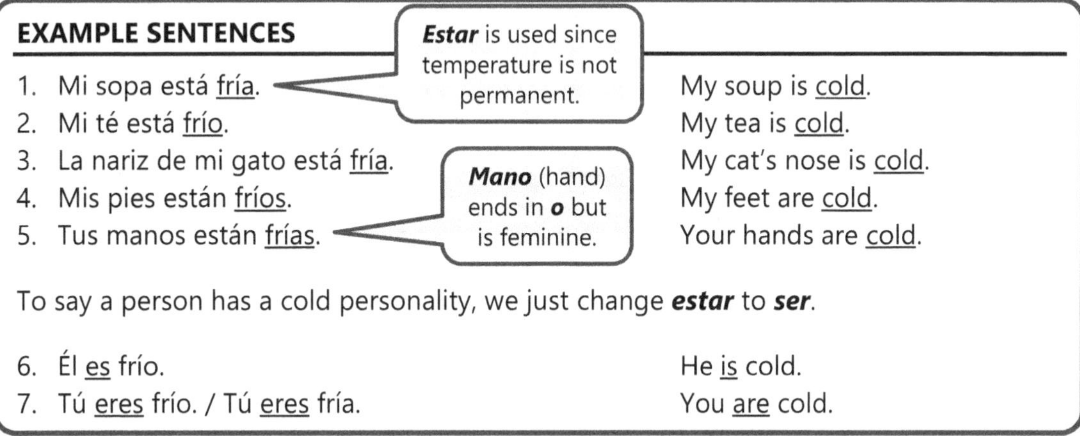

EXAMPLE SENTENCES

1. Mi sopa está fría.	My soup is cold.
2. Mi té está frío.	My tea is cold.
3. La nariz de mi gato está fría.	My cat's nose is cold.
4. Mis pies están fríos.	My feet are cold.
5. Tus manos están frías.	Your hands are cold.

To say a person has a cold personality, we just change ***estar*** to ***ser***.

6. Él es frío.	He is cold.
7. Tú eres frío. / Tú eres fría.	You are cold.

W-4

brown | café

We already learned ***café*** as "coffee", but it also means "brown" in Spanish.

EXAMPLE SENTENCES (NEUTRAL ADJECTIVES)

1. Mi chaqueta es café.	My jacket is brown.
2. Mis zapatos son cafés.	My shoes are brown.
3. Tu café es café.	Your coffee is brown.

In sentence 2 we use the plural ***cafés*** (brown) to match the plural noun. Sometimes native Spanish speakers incorrectly say the plural as ~~***cafeses***~~.

W-5	
aquí	**here**
ahí	**there**
allí	**over there**

For the most part these words work exactly like you would expect them to. Just remember that ***aqui*** is pronounced *ah-kee* , ***ahí*** is pronounced *ah-ee,* and ***allí*** is pronounced *ah-yee.*

EXAMPLE SENTENCES

1. Yo como aquí todos los días con mi amigo.
   I eat here every day with my friend.
2. Nosotros comemos ahí mañana.
   We're going to eat there tomorrow.
3. Mi casa está allí.
   My house is over there.

14 Verb Usage *Uso de Verbos*

V-1 **trabajar**	**to work**	**regular**
Yo **trabajo**.	I **work**.	
Tú **trabajas**.	You **work**.	
Él / Ella / Usted **trabaja**.	He / She / You (polite) **work(s)**.	
Nosotros **trabajamos**.	We **work**.	
Ustedes **trabajan**.	You guys **work**.	

EXAMPLE SENTENCES

1. Yo trabajo todos los días.	I work every day.
2. Ellas trabajan en la biblioteca.	They work in the library.
3. Mi papá trabaja en mi escuela.	My dad works in my school.
4. Nosotros trabajamos aquí.	We work here.
5. ¿Dónde trabajas tú?	Where do you work?

14 Grammar and Usage *Gramática y Uso*

14-3. How Spanish adjectives work

In English we say "hot soup" or "kind person" with the first word as the *descriptive word* BEFORE the item. In most cases, Spanish puts the descriptive word AFTER the item.

hot **soup**
sopa caliente

kind **person**
persona amable

EXAMPLES

Notice how the adjective matches noun gender.

1. un auto rojo	a red car
2. una chaqueta roja	a red jacket

EXAMPLE SENTENCES

1. Yo quiero una novia amable.	I want a kind girlfriend.
2. ¿Tú quieres sopa caliente?	Do you want hot soup?
3. Mi hermano es una persona interesante.	My brother is an interesting person.
4. ¿Ustedes tienen café negro?	Do you (guys) have black coffee?
5. Carla es una mujer muy alta.	Carla is a very tall woman.

14-4. Using nouns as adjectives

In English, *cheese* and *pizza* are both nouns. But when *cheese* is in front of *pizza*, it becomes an adjective, making the pizza a "cheese one". In Spanish, when a noun is used as an adjective in this way, you must add ***de*** in front of it. So, "cheese" as in "cheese-flavored" is ***de queso***. Also, instead of being in front, it must be AFTER the item it's modifying.

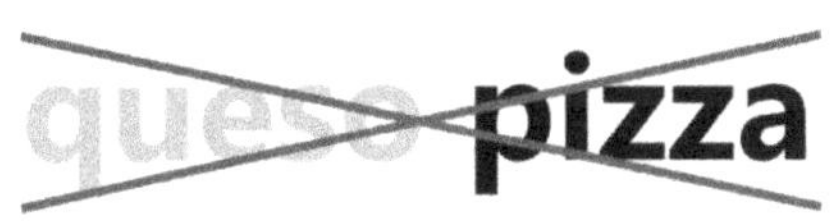

pizza de queso

EXAMPLES

Spanish	Natural English	Literal English
jugo de naranja	orange juice	juice of orange
ropa de niño	boy clothes	clothes of boy
sopa de verduras	vegetable soup	soup of vegetable
libro de español	Spanish book	book of Spanish
película de horror	horror movie	movie of horror

Let's look at a few more examples where the noun is changed into an adjective using ***de***.

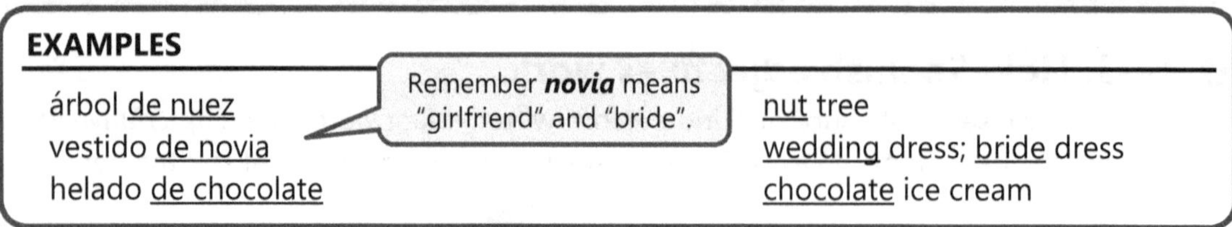

EXAMPLES

árbol de nuez	nut tree
vestido de novia	wedding dress; bride dress
helado de chocolate	chocolate ice cream

Remember ***novia*** means "girlfriend" and "bride".

Ok! Enough practice! Let's put these into sentences using verbs we already know.

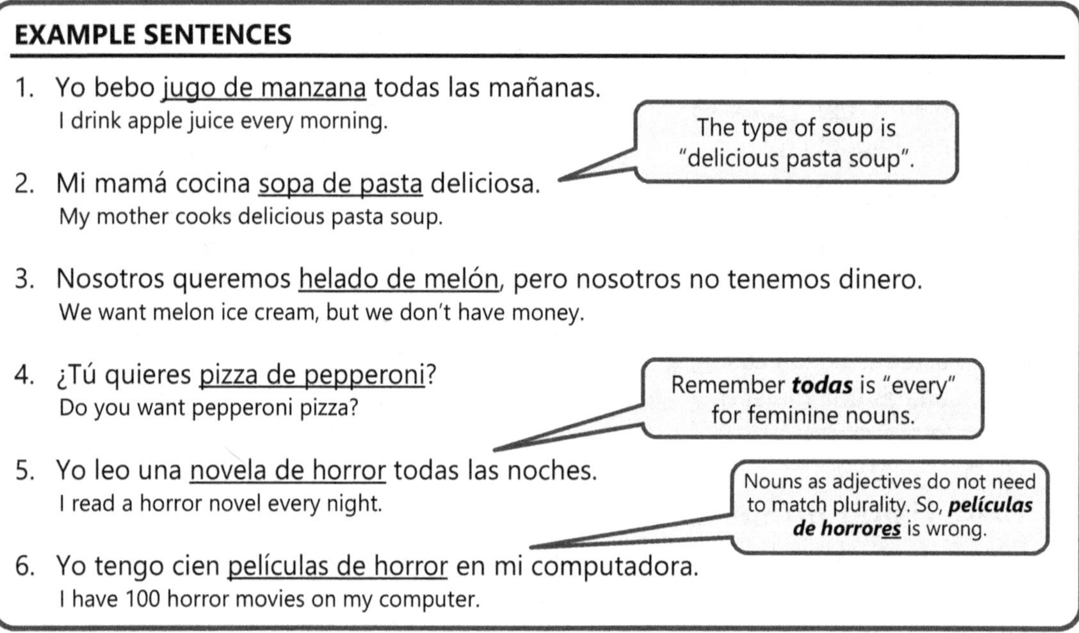

EXAMPLE SENTENCES

1. Yo bebo jugo de manzana todas las mañanas.
   I drink apple juice every morning.
2. Mi mamá cocina sopa de pasta deliciosa.
   My mother cooks delicious pasta soup.
3. Nosotros queremos helado de melón, pero nosotros no tenemos dinero.
   We want melon ice cream, but we don't have money.
4. ¿Tú quieres pizza de pepperoni?
   Do you want pepperoni pizza?
5. Yo leo una novela de horror todas las noches.
   I read a horror novel every night.
6. Yo tengo cien películas de horror en mi computadora.
   I have 100 horror movies on my computer.

The type of soup is "delicious pasta soup".

Remember ***todas*** is "every" for feminine nouns.

Nouns as adjectives do not need to match plurality. So, ***películas de horrores*** is wrong.

 *Más Detalles* **More Details** 

What is pasta soup?

In Mexico, *pasta soup* is any soup that has "noodles" in it that are typically used in pasta such as macaroni, penne, spaghetti, etc. The soup is a chicken broth with tomato and spices. It usually doesn't have any other ingredients beyond the broth and noodles.

14-5. Noun adjectives used alone

If you ask, "What kind of pizza do you want?" in English we can say, "I want cheese", but in Spanish, cheese must be in its adjective form ***de queso***, or else the meaning changes.

Any time a noun is used as an adjective, it must keep the ***de*** before it.

EXAMPLE Q&A

1.	**¿Tú quieres pizza de pepperoni?**	**Do you want pepperoni pizza?**
	No, yo quiero de queso.	No, I want cheese.
	Sí, de pepperoni, por favor.	Yes, pepperoni, please.
2.	**¿Quieres helado de chocolate?**	**Do you want chocolate ice cream?**
	No, yo quiero de fresa.	No, I want strawberry.
	Sí, de chocolate.	Yes, chocolate.
3.	**¿Tú lees novelas de horror?**	**Do you read horror novels?**
	Sí, yo leo de horror y de drama	Yes, I read horror and drama.
	No, de drama.	No, drama.

14-6. Using multiple nouns in a row as adjectives

We already learned that *possession* is ***~de (name).***

EXAMPLES

auto de María	Maria's car
amigo de Jorge	Jorge's friend
libros de Juan	Juan's books

We can "stack" possession (George's mother's car) like English, except the order is reversed.

EXAMPLES (STACKED POSSESSION)

auto ① de la hermana ② de María	② María's ① sister's car
amigo ① del tío ② de George	② George's ① uncle's friend
libros ① de los hijos ② de Juan	② Juan's ① children's books

Remember ***de*** + ***el*** becomes ***del***.

We can also "stack" noun adjectives similar to how we did with possession.

EXAMPLE SENTENCES

1. El vestido de novia de Sofía es muy bonito.
   Sofía's wedding dress is very beautiful.
2. El libro de francés de Carlos es difícil.
   Carlos's French book is difficult.
3. La computadora de escritorio de mi papá es muy cara.
   My father's desktop computer is very expensive.

"Desktop computer" in Spanish is literally "Desk computer".

14-7. Putting the adjective first

Adjectives normally come after the noun, but there are three adjectives that commonly go in front. They must also change form when used as singular masculine.

gender	most common	okay to say	English	Note
F	mala amiga	amiga mala	bad friend	***malo*** must be ***mal*** for singular masculine
M	mal amigo	amigo malo	bad friend	
F	buena amiga	amiga buena	good friend	***bueno*** must be ***buen*** for singular masculine
M	buen amigo	amigo bueno	good friend	
F	gran amiga	amiga grande	great friend	***grande*** changes to ***gran*** for both genders
M	gran amigo	amigo grande	great friend	

EXAMPLES

1. mal maestro	bad teacher (male)
mala maestra	bad teacher (female)
malos maestros	bad teachers (male or mixed)
2. buen doctor	good doctor (male)
buena doctora	good doctor (female)
buenos doctores	good doctors (male or mixed)
3. gran amigo	great friend (male)
gran amiga	great friend (female)
grandes amigos	great friends (male or mixed)

Plural doesn't drop the "o" in ***malos***.

14-8. How to say "or" in Spanish

Spanish has two ways to say "or". The first is ***o***.

EXAMPLES

1. gatos o perros	cats or dogs
2. tú, yo o ella	you, I, or she
3. manzanas o naranjas	apples or oranges

EXAMPLE SENTENCES

1. ¿Tú quieres carne o verduras?
   Do you want meat or vegetables?
2. ¿Tu gato es blanco o negro?
   Is your cat white or black?

The second "or" is ***u***, only used when the next word starts with ***o*** or ***ho***.

EXAMPLE SENTENCES

1. ¿Tú quieres un conejo u oso?
   Do you want a rabbit or bear?
2. ¿Él trabaja en Miami u Orlando?
   Does he work in Miami or Orlando?

Having ***un*** or ***en*** can cancel the need for ***u*** since the sound is different.

3. ¿Tú quieres un conejo o un oso?
   Do you want a rabbit or a bear?
4. ¿Él trabaja en Miami o en Orlando?
   Does he work in Miami or in Orlando?

14-9. Removing pronouns in Spanish

Pronouns are often dropped in Spanish because the verb ending alone indicates which pronoun is being used.

None of these Spanish sentences need pronouns because the verb ending handles it.

EXAMPLE SENTENCES

1. ¿Dónde trabajas?	Where do (you) work?
2. Trabajo en una escuela.	(I) work at a school.
3. Trabajamos en la librería.	(We) work at the bookstore.

If there might be confusion as to "who" is doing the action, then the pronoun should be included. For example, a pronoun is helpful for third person verb conjugations that have multiple possible pronouns such as "***trabaja***" which can use "he", "she", or polite "you".

¿Él / ella / usted trabaja?
(optional but sometimes neccessary) ¿trabaja?
} **He / she / you** work?

If a mother was talking about her son, and you asked ***¿Trabaja?*** it's easy to know it means "Does he work?" because of the conversation's context, so no pronoun is needed.

Talking ONLY about son. **Pronoun not needed.**

HOWEVER, when talking about a person's son AND daughter, we would need to specify ***él*** or ***ella*** to avoid confusion. Also, since ***usted*** (polite "you") also uses ***trabaja*** conjugation, the person might think you're asking "Do you work?" instead of "Does he work?"

Talking about son and daughter.

Pronoun needed for clarity.

OR

Trabajan **is only used with "they" so no pronoun needed.**

 *Más Detalles* More Details 

English-style Spanish

Overusing pronouns makes Spanish sound "funny" from a native's perspective. But you should be aware that some Spanish speakers, when having lived in an English-speaking country for a long time, might *Englishify* their Spanish by using pronouns in every sentence similarly to English, while most natives would not.

ENGLISH-STYLE SPANISH	NATIVE SPEAKER
1. ¿Tú tienes frío? Are you cold?	¿Tienes frío? Are you cold?
2. Yo estoy en mi casa. I'm at my house.	Estoy en mi casa. I'm at my house.
3. Yo tengo hambre y yo quiero una pizza. I'm hungry and I want a pizza.	Yo tengo hambre y quiero una pizza. I'm hungry and I want a pizza.

The second ***yo*** is excessive.

14-10. Question order in Spanish

Remember that with question words like ***dónde*** (where), the sentence order changes. The subject ALWAYS comes after the verb in these cases.

EXAMPLE SENTENCES	
1. ¿Dónde trabajas tú?	Where do you work?
2. ¿Dónde vive tu hermano?	Where does your brother live?
3. ¿Dónde estudian ustedes?	Where do you guys study?
4. ¿Dónde estás?	Where are (you)?

Pronoun ***tú*** can be dropped.

14 Practice and Review *Práctica y Repaso*

● 1. Question and Answer (Spanish → English)

Each question has multiple answers. Cover up the right side and try to translate.

1. **¿Dónde trabaja tu hermana?** — **Where does your sister work?**
   - Ella trabaja en un restaurante. — She works at a restaurant.
   - Trabaja en una librería muy grande. — She works at a very big bookshop.
   - Trabaja en un edificio muy alto. — She works in a very tall building.

2. **¿Hablas español?** — **Do you speak Spanish?**
   - Sí, el español es muy fácil. — Yes, Spanish is very easy.
   - No, pero hablo francés. — No, but I speak French.
   - Sí, hablo español e inglés. — Yes, I speak Spanish and English.

3. **¿Quieres un burrito delicioso?** — **Do you want a delicious burrito?**
   - Sí, pero no tengo hambre ahora. — Yes, but I'm not hungry now.
   - No, no tengo hambre. — No, I'm not hungry.
   - Sí, tengo hambre. Dos por favor. — Yes, I'm hungry. Two please.

4. **¿Dónde está tu madre?** — **Where is your mother?**
   - Ella está en el trabajo. — She's at work.
   - Está en casa. — She's at home.
   - Está en la casa de mi hermana. — She's at my sister's house.

5. **¿La película es interesante?** — **Is the movie interesting?**
   - No, es una mala película. — No, it's a bad movie.
   - Sí, es una muy buena película. — Yes, it's a very good movie.
   - Sí, es interesante. — Yes, it's interesting.

● 2. Question and answer (English → Spanish)

Each question has multiple answers. Cover up the right side and try to translate.

1. **Where does your friend work?** — **¿Dónde trabaja tu amigo?**
   - My friend works at a restaurant. — Mi amigo trabaja en un restaurante.
   - My friend works at the station. — Mi amigo trabaja en la estación.
   - He works at the station. — Él trabaja en la estación.

2. **Do you want pizza?** — **¿Quieres pizza?**
   - No, I want vegetables. — No, quiero verduras.
   - No, I'm not hungry now. — No, no tengo hambre ahora.
   - Yes, I want cheese. — Sí, quiero de queso.

3. **Where is your dog?** — **¿Dónde está tu perro?**
   - My dog is at my house. — Mi perro está en mi casa.
   - At my house. — En mi casa.
   - My dog is under the table. — Mi perro está debajo de la mesa.
   - He's to the right of the white car. — Él está a la derecha del auto blanco.

4. **Do you want soup?** — **¿Quieres sopa?**
   - Yes, I want pasta (soup). — Sí, quiero de pasta. (They want pasta style soup.)
   - No, I want pasta. — No, quiero pasta. (They want pasta, NOT soup.)
   - Yes, I want vegetable (soup). — Sí, quiero de verduras.
   - No, I want bean soup. — No, quiero sopa de frijoles.

5. **Is your phone good?** — **¿Tu celular es bueno?**
   - Yes, it's cheap and good. (iPhone? 😉) — Sí, es barato y bueno.
   - No, my phone is expensive and bad. — No, mi celular es caro y malo.
   - Yes, I have an excellent phone. — Sí, tengo un celular excelente.

● 3. English to Spanish conversation

Try translating the entire conversation before looking at the translation below.

1. Conversation between friends at a high school reunion.

¿Dónde trabajas?
En una escuela.
¿Eres maestra?
No, no soy. Soy chofer de autobús.

Where do you work?
At a school.
Are you a teacher?
No, I'm not. I'm a bus driver.

2. Conversation between friends at school.

¿Tu papá es alto o bajo?
Es muy alto.
¿Él es popular en su trabajo?
¡No, no es popular!

Is your dad tall or short?
He's very tall.
Is he popular at his job?
No, he's not popular!

3. Conversation between coworkers at a company

¿Tú tienes una computadora?
Sí, es muy cara, pero no buena.
Mi computadora es muy buena. Pero no es cara.
Quiero tu computadora.

Do you have a computer?
Yes, it's very expensive, but it's not good.
My computer is good. But it's not expensive.
I want your computer.

4. Conversation between new friends in a cafe.

¿Tú lees novelas de horror?
No, pero leo novelas de drama.
¿Las novelas de drama son interesantes?
¡Sí, son muy buenas!

Do you read horror novels?
No, but I read drama novels.
Are drama novels interesting?
Yes, they are very good!

4. Spanish to English Conversation

Try translating the entire conversation before looking at the translation below.

1. Conversation at a restaurant.

¿Tu sopa está fría?
No, mi sopa está caliente y deliciosa.
Mi sopa no está caliente. Está muy fría.
¡Mesero!
Sí, señor.
La sopa de ella está fría. / Su sopa está fría.

Is your soup cold?
No, my soup is hot and delicious.
My soup isn't hot. It's very cold.
¡Waiter!
Yes, sir.
Her soup is cold.

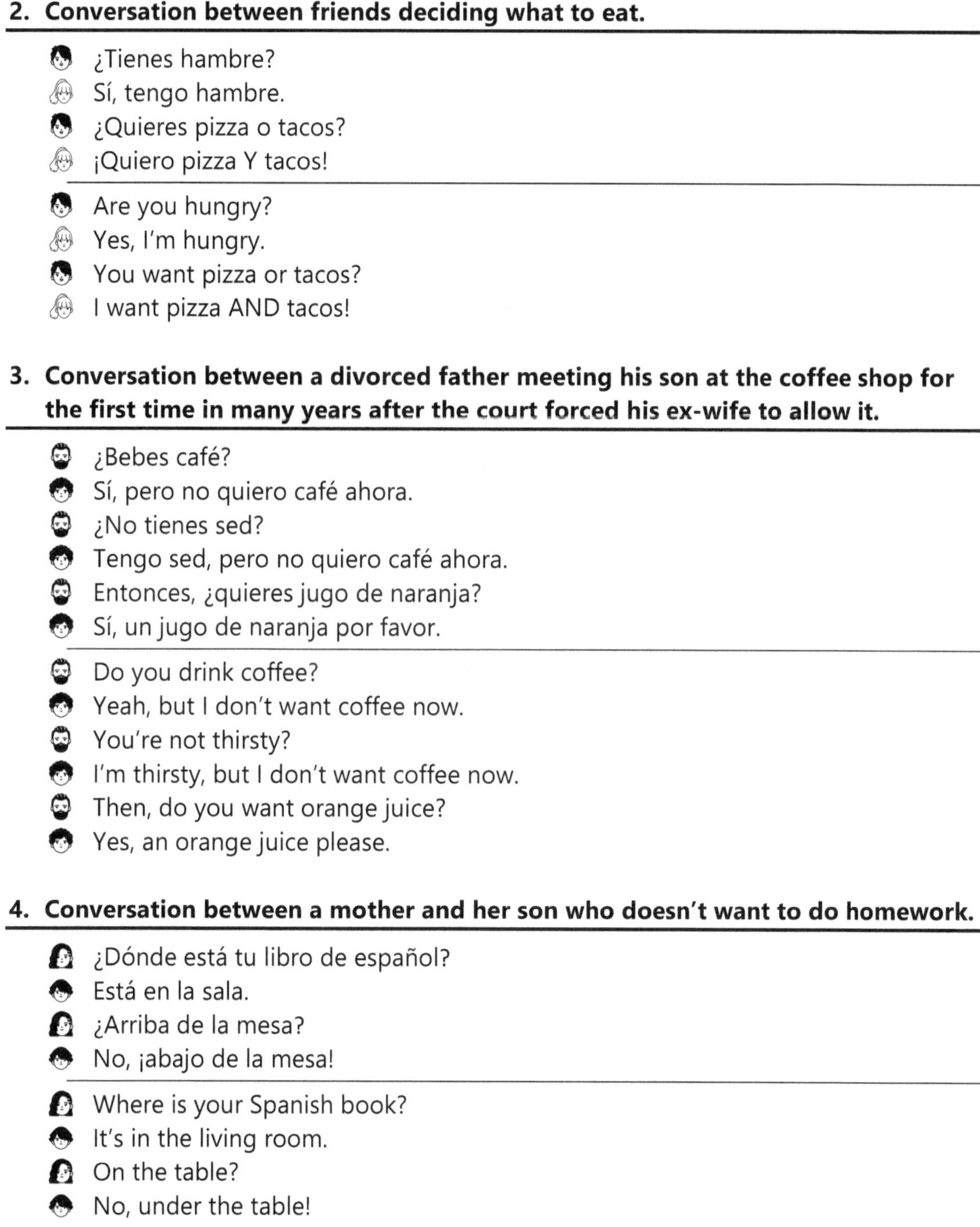

2. Conversation between friends deciding what to eat.

¿Tienes hambre?
Sí, tengo hambre.
¿Quieres pizza o tacos?
¡Quiero pizza Y tacos!

Are you hungry?
Yes, I'm hungry.
You want pizza or tacos?
I want pizza AND tacos!

3. Conversation between a divorced father meeting his son at the coffee shop for the first time in many years after the court forced his ex-wife to allow it.

¿Bebes café?
Sí, pero no quiero café ahora.
¿No tienes sed?
Tengo sed, pero no quiero café ahora.
Entonces, ¿quieres jugo de naranja?
Sí, un jugo de naranja por favor.

Do you drink coffee?
Yeah, but I don't want coffee now.
You're not thirsty?
I'm thirsty, but I don't want coffee now.
Then, do you want orange juice?
Yes, an orange juice please.

4. Conversation between a mother and her son who doesn't want to do homework.

¿Dónde está tu libro de español?
Está en la sala.
¿Arriba de la mesa?
No, ¡abajo de la mesa!

Where is your Spanish book?
It's in the living room.
On the table?
No, under the table!

Workbook 14: Lesson Activities

14 Vocabulary Drills *Ejercicios de Vocabulario*

1. Writing and Vocabulary

Write the Spanish for each of the pictures. Make sure to add accent marks when needed.

computer, movie, cell phone, night, strawberry, phone, orange, parking lot, building, ATM

1.__________ 2.__________ 3.__________ 4.__________ 5.__________

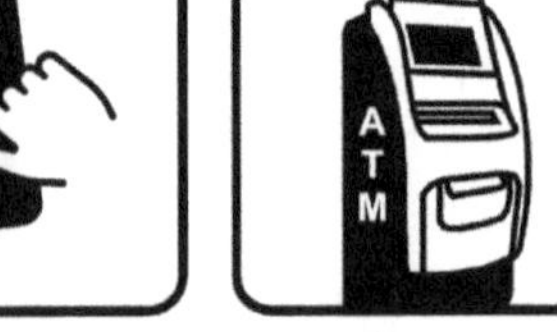

6.__________ 7.__________ 8.__________ 9.__________ 10.__________

2. Gender Matching

Write the following words and circle the gender companion word for each one.

banco, farmacia, plaza, mercado, cajero, noche, día, sopa, dulce, idioma

1) el / la ____________________
(bank)

2) el / la ____________________
(plaza)

3) el / la ____________________
(night)

4) el / la ____________________
(day)

5) el / la ____________________
(ATM)

6) el / la ____________________
(pharmacy)

7) el / la ____________________
(language)

8) el / la ____________________
(candy)

9) el / la ____________________
(market)

10) el / la ____________________
(soup)

14 Usage Activities *Actividades de Uso*

3. Reading Comprehension

Translate the following on a separate piece of paper or type in an electronic device.

My School

Laura attends a private school. She wants to tell you all about it.

❶ Mi escuela está en la ciudad y es muy buena.

❷ Todas mis clases son interesantes y todas las computadoras son muy veloces.

❸ Todos los maestros hablan español e inglés.

❹ Todos los estudiantes son amables.

❺ También, la escuela tiene un jardín muy grande. Es muy bonito.

❻ Yo como en la cafetería todos los días. La comida es deliciosa.

❼ Mi escuela no es barata, pero es una escuela excelente.

4. Reading Comprehension Questions

Answer the following questions in Spanish about the reading comprehension.

1. ¿La escuela de Laura tiene algo bonito?

____

2. ¿Los estudiantes en la escuela de Laura son interesantes?

3. ¿Los maestros de la escuela de Laura hablan francés?

4. ¿Dónde está la escuela de Laura?

5. ¿En dónde come Laura todos los días?

6. ¿La comida de la escuela de Laura es cara?

7. ¿La escuela de Laura es fácil?

5. Spanish translation

Translate the following conversations into Spanish.

1.
A: ¿Dónde trabaja tu amigo? B: Mi amigo trabaja en el edificio a la izquierda del centro comercial. A: ¿El edificio rojo? B: No, el edificio alto y blanco.
A:
B:
A:
B:

6. English Translation

Translate the following conversations into Spanish.

1.
A: ¿Quieres sopa de tomate? B: No, no tengo hambre, gracias. A: Bueno, y ¿quieres una bebida? B: Sí, un café frío, por favor.
A:
B:
A:
B:

7. Spanish translation 2

Translate the following conversations into English.

1.
A: ¿Tienes un celular? B: Sí, tengo un celular muy bueno. A: ¿Tu celular es caro? B: No, es barato y excelente.
A:
B:
A:
B:

8. Adjective Practice

Write each adjective in the form that matches each noun correctly.

1) la sopa __________________
(hot)

2) el edificio __________________
(tall)

3) el repartidor __________________
(nice; kind)

4) la repartidora __________________
(nice; kind)

5) la manzana ______________ (sweet)

6) el café ______________ (strong)

7) el examen ______________ (hard)

8) el hombre ______________ (big)

9) la gata ______________ (smart)

10) el restaurante______________ (delicious)

9. Verb conjugation drills

Fill in the blanks with the proper verb conjugations.

1. Necesitar (to need)	
Pronouns	**Present Tense**
Yo	
Tú	
Él / ella / usted	
nosotros	
ustedes	
ellos / ellas	

2. Trabajar (to work)	
Pronouns	**Present Tense**
Yo	
Tú	
Él / ella / usted	
nosotros	
ustedes	
ellos / ellas	

14 Answer Key *Clave de Respuestas*

1. Writing and Vocabulary (answers)

1. edificio
building

2. estacionamiento
parking lot

3. computadora
computer

4. noche
night

5. fresa
strawberry

6. naranja
orange

7. celular
cell phone

8. cajero
ATM / cash machine

9. teléfono
phone / telephone

10. película
movie

2. Gender Matching (answers)

1) el banco
2) la plaza
3) la noche
4) el día
5) el cajero
6) la farmacia
7) el idioma
8) el dulce
9) el mercado
10) la sopa

3. Reading Comprehension (answers)

❶ My school is in the city and it is very good.
❷ All my classes are interesting and all the computers are very fast.
❸ All the teachers speak Spanish and English.
❹ All the students are kind.
❺ Also, the school has a very big garden. It's very beautiful.
❻ I eat at the cafeteria every day. The food is delicious.
❼ My school is not cheap, but it's an excellent school.

4. Reading Comprehension Questions (sample answers)

1. Does Laura's school has something beautiful?	Sí, el jardín de la escuela es bonito.
2. Are the students at Laura's school interesting?	No, los estudiantes son amables.
3. Do the teachers at Laura's school speak French?	No, los maestros hablan español e inglés.
4. Where is Laura's school?	La escuela está en la ciudad.
5. Where does Laura eat everyday?	Laura come en la cafetería todos los días.
6. Is the food of Laura's school's expensive?	No sé. / No sé, pero es deliciosa.
7. Is Laura's school easy?	No sé.

5. Spanish translation (answers)

1. A: Where does your friend work?
   B: My friend works in the building to the left of the shopping mall.
   A: The red building?
   B: No, the tall white building.

6. English Translation (answers)

1. A: Do you want tomato soup?
   B: No, I'm not hungry, thank you.
   A: Okay, and do you want a drink?
   B: Yes, a cold coffee please.

7. Spanish translation 2 (answers)

1. A: Do you have a phone?
   B: Yes, I have a very good phone.
   A: Is your cellphone expensive?
   B: No, it is cheap and excellent.

8. Adjective Practice (answers)

1) la sopa caliente
2) el edificio alto
3) el repartidor amable
4) la repartidora amable
5) la manzana dulce
6) el café fuerte
7) el examen difícil
8) el hombre grande
9) la gata inteligente
10) el restaurante delicioso

9. Verb conjugation drills (answers)

1. necesitar (to need)	
yo	necesito
tú	necesitas
él / ella / usted	necesita
nosotros	necesitamos
ustedes	necesitan
ellos / ellas	necesitan

2. trabajar (to work)	
yo	trabajo
tú	trabajas
él / ella / usted	trabaja
nosotros	trabajamos
ustedes	trabajan
ellos / ellas	trabajan

15

14 PAGES	10 USAGE SECTIONS	29 NEW WORDS

Lesson 15: This and That

15 New Words *Palabras Nuevas*

Nouns etc.

¿quién?	who?	**la semana**	the week
esto	this (one)	**el fin**	the end
eso	that (one)	**la clase**	class
aquello	that (one) over there	**tuyo**	yours
mío	mine	**suyo**	his; hers; theirs
solo	only; just	**hoy**	today

Days of the Week

el lunes	Monday	**el viernes**	Friday
el martes	Tuesday	**el sábado**	Saturday
el miércoles	Wednesday	**el domingo**	Sunday
el jueves	Thursday		

Adjectives

favorito	favorite	**mexicano**	Mexican
picante	spicy; hot	**fresco**	fresh
nuevo	new	**viejo**	old

Verbs

ir	to go

Prepositions

con	with	**a**	to
de	from		

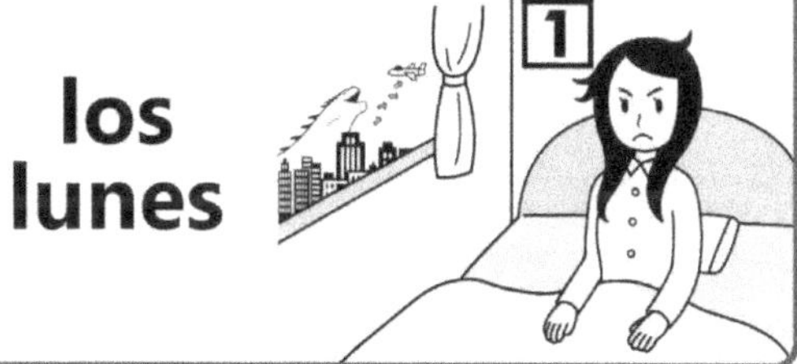

15 Word Usage *Uso de Palabras*

15-1. Days of the week

In Spanish, days of the week have different rules from English.

RULE 1 The days aren't capitalized (unless at the beginning of a sentence).

EXAMPLE SENTENCE

1. Hoy es lunes. Y mañana es martes.
   Today is Monday. And tomorrow is Tuesday.

RULE 2 When saying "on (day)" use ***el / los*** (day) not ~~***en*** (day)~~.

EXAMPLE SENTENCE

2. Trabajo el miércoles. Pero, no trabajo el jueves.
   I work on Wednesday. But I don't work on Thursday.

Here ***el*** means "on" and takes the place of ***en***. ***En*** is never needed.

RULE 3 The *weekdays* all end in "s", and are both singular and plural without adding "es".

EXAMPLE SENTENCE

3. Trabajo los miércoles. Pero, no trabajo el jueves.
   I work on Wednesdays. But I don't work on Thursday.

Use ***los*** for plural form. For only one day, use ***el*** (***los*** and ***el*** mean "on" for days of the week.

RULE 4 ***Sábado*** *(Saturday)* and ***domingo*** *(Sunday)* need an "s" to make plural versions.

EXAMPLE SENTENCE

4. Trabajo los sábados y mi novia trabaja los domingos.
   I work on Saturdays and my girlfriend works on Sundays.

Now let's look at some more sentences using days of the week in a variety of ways.

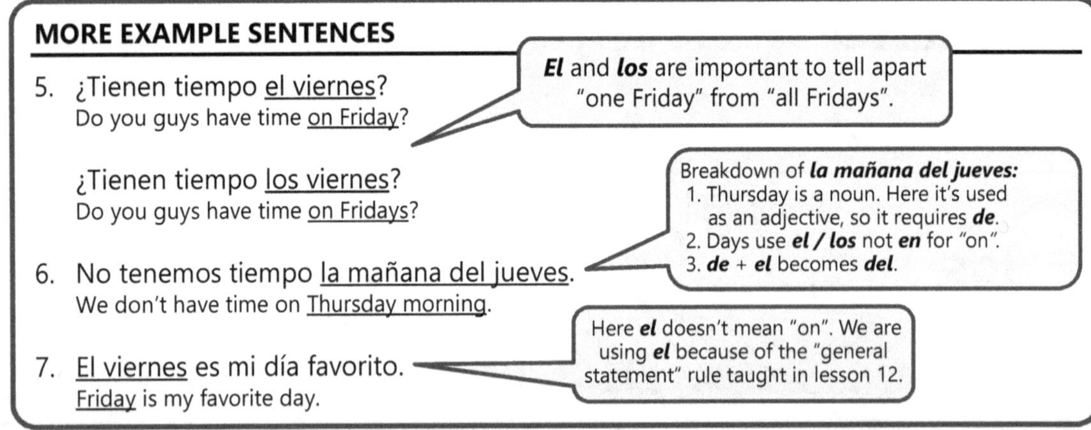

MORE EXAMPLE SENTENCES

5. ¿Tienen tiempo el viernes?
   Do you guys have time on Friday?

   ¿Tienen tiempo los viernes?
   Do you guys have time on Fridays?

El and ***los*** are important to tell apart "one Friday" from "all Fridays".

6. No tenemos tiempo la mañana del jueves.
   We don't have time on Thursday morning.

Breakdown of ***la mañana del jueves:***
1. Thursday is a noun. Here it's used as an adjective, so it requires ***de***.
2. Days use ***el / los*** not ***en*** for "on".
3. ***de*** + ***el*** becomes ***del***.

7. El viernes es mi día favorito.
   Friday is my favorite day.

Here ***el*** doesn't mean "on". We are using ***el*** because of the "general statement" rule taught in lesson 12.

15-2. New ways to use *de*

Let's review what ***de*** can do, from showing possession to making nouns into adjectives.

1. Possession

auto de mamá	Mom's car
amigo de Carlos	Carlos's friend
novia de mi amigo	my friend's girlfriend

2. Turning nouns into adjectives

helado de chocolate	chocolate ice cream
árbol de manzana	apple tree
libro de español	Spanish book

De can also translate to "of." Of course you already know this, but let's review!

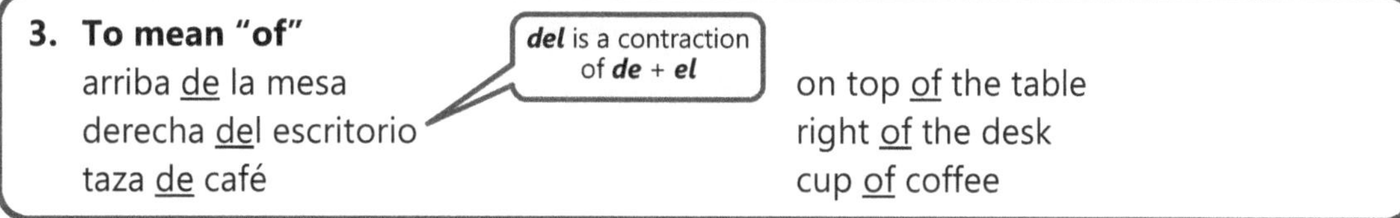

3. To mean "of"

arriba de la mesa	on top of the table
derecha del escritorio	right of the desk
taza de café	cup of coffee

del is a contraction of ***de*** + ***el***

And now for a new usage of ***de. De*** can also translate to "from."

4. To mean "from"

comida de México	food from Mexico
una persona de mi escuela	a person from my school

Más Detalles More Details

What is really happening with *de*?

We've learned that Spanish ***de*** in English can be "of", "from", or "~'s". So, how do you know *which version* it is in English for something like ***comida de México***? Is it, "food from Mexico" or "Mexican food" or another. The answer is always "context".

comida de México	
Context	Translation
(as an adjective)	Mexican food
(as possession)	Mexico's food
(as a characteristic)	food of Mexico
(as an origin)	food from Mexico

In a textbook, knowing how to translate ***comida de México*** might be a challenge as context is often missing.

However, in an actual conversation, there are context clues such as smell, location, food on the table, time of day etc.

Such context makes it easy to know what English is best for ***de***. (of / from / 's)

W-1

solo — only; just

Solo can be used in the exact spot you would use "only" or "just" in English.

EXAMPLE SENTENCE

1. Él solo habla inglés.	He only speaks English.
2. Mi novia solo come verduras.	My girlfriend only eats vegetables.
3. Ella solo tiene cinco minutos.	She only has five minutes.
4. Trabajo solo los lunes y los jueves.	I work only Mondays and Thursdays.
5. Mi mamá solo cocina el fin de semana.	My mom only cooks on the weekend.
6. Yo solo quiero comida.	I just want food.
7. Nosotros solo necesitamos dinero.	We just need money.
8. Solo bebo agua.	I only drink water.

W-2

fin — the end

We can use ***fin*** to say something is at its end.

EXAMPLES

1. el fin de la película	the end of the movie
2. el fin de mi clase	the end of my class
3. el fin del día	the end of the day

Final can also be used to say "end".

EXAMPLES

4. el final de la película	the end of the movie
5. el final de mi clase	the end of my class
6. el final del día	the end of the day

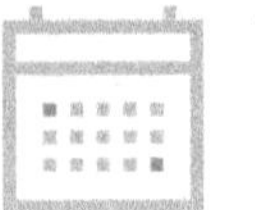

You had to learn ***fin*** to know how to say "the weekend" which is ***fin de semana***. But since ***fin*** and ***final*** both mean "end", you might think ***final de semana*** also means "the weekend"; however ***final de semana*** means "the end of the week".

15 Verb Usage *Uso de Verbos*

15-3. Shortcut to other verb tenses

DON'T SKIP THIS: For each sentence, either say the English out loud or write it on the right.

1. Mi mamá *cocina* todos los días.
2. Mi mamá *cocina* ahora.
3. Mi mamá *cocina* mañana.

If you didn't skip, you probably changed the English verb in each sentence as below.

1. My mom *cooks* every day. ➡ *cooks* for "habitual" action.
2. My mom *is cooking* now. ➡ *cooking* for "on-going" action.
3. My mom *will cook* tomorrow. ➡ *will cook* for "future" action.

So *cocina* can mean, "cooks", "cooking" and "will cook" depending on the *time word*. This shortcut allows you to say more in Spanish without learning new verb conjugations.

NOTE: There are other *on going tense* and *future tense* patterns (taught in book 2), but these shortcut versions are commonly used and work with all verbs.

V-1

ir	to go	irregular
Yo	***voy*** a (place).	I **go** to (place).
Tú	***vas*** a (place).	You **go** to (place).
Él / Ella / Usted	***va*** a (place).	He / She / You (polite) **go(es)** to (place).
Nosotros	***vamos*** a (place).	We **go** to (place).
Ustedes	***van*** a (place).	You guys **go** to (place).

Ir (to go) is irregular, so you'll have to spend a bit of time memorizing its conjugations. The Spanish word "to" is ***a*** and is used when going "to" a place.

EXAMPLE SENTENCES

1. Yo voy a México el viernes.
   I'll go to Mexico on Friday.
2. ¿Tú vas a la escuela el miércoles?
   Will you go to school on Wednesday?
3. Mi amigo va a las montañas todos los sábados.
   My friend goes to the mountains every Saturday.
4. Yo voy a la casa de mi novia ahora.
   I'm going to my girlfriend's house now.
5. Mis padres van a Madrid el domingo.
   My parents are going to Madrid on Sunday.

15 Grammar and Usage *Gramática y Uso*

15-4. This, that, and that over there

In Spanish, "this", "that", and "that over there" change based on gender and plurality.

	THIS (singular / plural)		THAT (singular / plural)		THAT OVER THERE (singular / plural)	
Masculine	**este**	est<u>os</u>	**ese**	es<u>os</u>	**aquel**	aquel<u>los</u>
Feminine	esta	est<u>as</u>	esa	es<u>as</u>	aquella	aquel<u>las</u>
? Unknown	esto	esto<u>s</u>	eso	eso<u>s</u>	aquello	aquel<u>los</u>

All versions of "This" and "That" are the same, except for a "T". This phrase can help!

"THIS" has a T, the others don't

Beware! (a personal note)

Masculine normally ends in ***o***, so instead of ***este*** (this) and ***ese*** (that) I would always mistakenly say, ***esto*** and ***eso***. But those are for objects of *unknown gender*. UGGH! Luckily, for me (and you), the plural versions end in ***os***. So, at least they feel masculine!

Anyways... as with most things, for *this* and *that* we must match gender and plurality.

EXAMPLE SENTENCES

1. <u>Este</u> es mi gato. — <u>This</u> is my cat. (male)
2. <u>Esta</u> es mi gata. — <u>This</u> is my cat. (female)
3. <u>Esos</u> son mis gatos. — <u>Those</u> are my cats. (male / mixed)
4. <u>Esas</u> son mis gatas. — <u>Those</u> are my cats. (female)
5. <u>Aquel</u> es mi gato. — <u>That's</u> my cat <u>over there</u>. (male)
6. <u>Aquella</u> es mi gata. — <u>That's</u> my cat <u>over there</u>. (female)

When the gender of the object is unknown, we don't use the gendered versions but instead use the "unknown" versions ***esto*** (this), ***eso*** (that), and ***aquello*** (that over there).

EXAMPLE Q&A - A FRIEND HANDS YOU A PACKAGE WITH NO MARKINGS ON IT.

1. **¿Qué es esto?** — **What is this?**
   A) <u>Esa</u> es mi comida favorita. — <u>That's</u> my favorite food.
   <u>Ese</u> es mi dulce favorito. — <u>That's</u> my favorite candy.
   B) <u>Eso</u> es mi comida favorita. — <u>That's</u> my favorite food.
   C) <u>Es</u> mi comida favorita. — <u>It's</u> my favorite food.

Comida (food) is feminine.

Dulce (candy) is masculine.

Let's analyze this Q&A to make sure we understand what's happening.
In the question, the person doesn't know what the object is. As a result, the gender is unknown, so ***esto*** (neutral for "this") is used. Let's break down the possible answers.

> For A) ***ese*** or ***esa*** is used depending on the object's gender.
> For B) ***eso*** is used to match the style of the question. This is very common even if the person being asked knows the gender.
> For C) ***eso***, ***esa***, ***ese*** are skipped by just saying ***es*** (It's a...). This is the easy way!

● 15-5. Specifying certain objects with *this~* and *that~*

Just like English, we can also use *this* and *that* to specify certain items. The gender of the word used for *this* and *that* is based on the noun its used with.

use *feminine* *this / that* to match *feminine* objects	***esta* persona** *this* person	***esa* mujer** that woman	***aquella* gata** *that* cat *over there*
use *masculine* *this / that* to match *masculine* objects	***este* hombre** *this* man	***ese* libro** *that* book	***aquel* gato** *that* cat *over there*

EXAMPLE SENTENCES

1. Esta pizza es muy deliciosa.	This pizza is very delicious.
2. Estos libros son muy caros.	These books are really expensive.
3. Esta semana yo tengo trabajo.	This week I have work.
4. Este lunes yo tengo trabajo.	This Monday I have work.
5. ¿Esos dulces son muy dulces?	Are those candies very sweet?
6. Esas verduras están frescas.	Those vegetables are fresh.
7. Esos tacos son muy picantes.	Those tacos are too spicy.
8. Aquellos niños son mis hermanos.	Those boys over there are my brothers.
9. Aquellas niñas son mis hermanas.	Those girls over there are my sisters.
10. Aquella persona es mi padre.	That person over there is my father.
11. Aquel hombre es mi padre.	That man over there is my father.
12. Aquel animal es mi gata.	That animal over there is my cat.

In sentence 6, we use ***están*** (estar) since vegetable freshness isn't permanent. But in sentence 7, we use ***son*** (ser) because these tacos will always be spicy.

In sentence 10 "my father" is male; HOWEVER, the word ***persona*** is always *feminine* regardless of actual gender, so we must use ***aquella*** (feminine for 'that~ over there').

 *Más Detalles* **More Details** 

Está vs Esta

Está (with an accent mark) is a conjugation of ***estar*** (to be). ***Esta*** (without an accent mark) means "this". Their pronunciation is different. An accent mark shows where to stress a word. Words with accent marks follow the rules taught in lesson 2.

The rule is that when a word ends in a vowel, the default accent is on the second to the last syllable. So, ***esta*** is pronounced as if it were ***ésta*** (ES-ta).

Esta sopa está caliente.
This soup is hot.

15-6. Plurality for *quién* (who)

Quién is used to say "who" for a single person. For more than one person, use ***quiénes***.

SINGULAR (QUIÉN)	PLURAL (QUIÉNES)
A person is at your door. 1. ¿Quién eres tú? Who are you?	**Several people are at your door.** ¿Quiénes son ustedes? Who are you guys?
Your friend mentions Carlos. 2. ¿Quién es Carlos? Who is Carlos?	**You are looking at pictures.** ¿Quiénes son tus padres? Who are your parents?
You saw a person go into the kitchen. 3. ¿Quién está en la cocina? Who is in the kitchen?	**You hear voices in the kitchen.** ¿Quiénes están en la cocina? Who is in the kitchen? (many people)

Location uses ***estar*** since location can change.

15-7. Preposition word + question word order

When asking questions involving a preposition word like ***con*** (with), ***a*** (to), ***de*** (from), etc. the preposition word ALWAYS comes BEFORE the question word.

EXAMPLE SENTENCES	
1. ¿Con quién vas?	With whom are you going?
2. ¿A dónde vas?	To where are you going?
3. ¿De dónde eres?	From where are you?

This uses ***ser*** since a person's "origin" is permanent.

For practice, let's look at some questions and answers.

EXAMPLE Q&A

This can be ***quién*** or ***quiénes*** since we don't know how many people.

1. **¿Con quiénes trabajas ahora?** — **With whom are you working now?**
   Yo trabajo con Carlos y Juan. — I work with Carlos and Juan.
2. **¿A dónde vas mañana?** — **To where are you going tomorrow?**
   Voy a la casa de mi novia. — I'm going to my girlfriend's house.
3. **¿De dónde es tu padre?** — **Where is your father from?**
   Él es de Guatemala. — He's from Guatemala.
   (An *origin* is permanent so ***ser*** is used.)
4. **¿En qué días trabajas?** — **On what days do you work?**
   Los lunes y los jueves. — Mondays and Thursdays.

15-8. a + el contraction

When Spanish ***a*** (to) is followed by masculine gender companion word ***el***, it contracts to ***al***.

EXAMPLE SENTENCES

1. Voy al restaurante con mi amigo hoy.
   I'm going to the restaurant with my friend today.
2. Vamos al parque con nuestros perros.
   We are going to the park with our dogs.
3. Voy al baño.
   I'm going to the bathroom.

15-9. "Whose" in Spanish

To ask who owns an object in Spanish, we use ***de quién*** (literally "of whom").

EXAMPLE SENTENCES

Someone holds up a pair of socks.

1. ¿De quién son estos?
   Whose are these?

Someone holds up one shoe.

2. ¿De quién es este?
   Whose is this?

Someone holds up an apple.

3. ¿De quién es esta?
   Whose is this?

In English we use "whose" directly in front of the object. For example, we might ask "Whose apple is this?" However, in Spanish the "whose" word isn't used directly in front of the noun. Instead, Spanish sounds more like "Whose is this apple?"

EXAMPLE Q&A

1. De quién son estas calcetas? — Son de Carlos.
   Whose are these socks? / Whose socks are these? — They are Carlos's.
2. De quién es este zapato? — Es de mi mamá.
   Whose is this shoe? / Whose shoe is this? — It's my mom's.
3. De quién es esta manzana? — Es mía.
   Whose is this apple? / Whose apple is this? — It's mine.

15-10. What!? Even possessive words have gender and plurality?

You should be used to it by now, but the possession words ***mío*** (mine), ***tuyo*** (yours), ***suyo*** (his, hers, theirs) ***nuestro*** (ours) must match the gender and plurality of the owned item.

EXAMPLE Q&A

The possession words MUST change to match the gender of the thing owned.

1. **¿De quién es este dinero?** (masculine) — **Whose money is this?**
   - Es mío. — It's mine.
   - Es suyo. — It's hers / his / theirs / yours (formal)
   - Es tuyo. — It's yours.
   - Es nuestro. — It's ours.

2. **¿De quién es esta casa?** (feminine) — **Whose house is this?**
   - Es mía. — It's mine.
   - Es suya. — It's hers / his / theirs / yours (formal)
   - Es tuya. — It's yours.
   - Es nuestra. — It's ours.

Let's not forget plural form (when necessary), while also still paying attention to gender.

3. **¿De quién son estos libros?** — **Whose books are these?**
   - Son míos. — They're mine.
   - Son suyos. — It's hers / his / theirs / yours (formal)
   - Son tuyos. — They're yours.

4. **¿De quién son estas calcetas?** — **Whose socks are these?**
   - Son mías. — They're mine.
   - Son suyas. — It's hers / his / theirs / yours (formal)
   - Son tuyas. — They're yours.

Remember, when we are talking about the property of someone without the possession words "mine", "his", etc., we use ***de*** followed by the owner to show possession.

5. ¿De quién es aquella comida?	**Whose food is that over there?**
Es de Sofía.	It is Sofía's.
Es de mi hermana.	It is my sister's.
Es de la Sra. Gonzales.	It is Mrs. Gonzales's.
Es del Sr. Smith.	It is Mr. Smith's.

Titles like Sr. and Sra. require ***el*** or ***la***.

15 Practice and Review *Práctica y Repaso*

1. Question and Answer (Spanish → English)

Each question has multiple answers. Cover up the right side and try to translate.

1. ¿Mañana es lunes?	**Is tomorrow Monday?**
Sí, mañana es lunes.	Yes, tomorrow is Monday.
No, mañana es sábado.	No, tomorrow is Saturday.
No, hoy es lunes.	No, today is Monday.
2. ¿De quién es este auto?	**Whose is this car?**
Este auto es mío.	This car is mine.
Este auto es de mi amigo.	This car is my friend's.
Ese auto es de Daniela.	That is Daniela's car.
3. ¿Tú solo hablas español?	**Do you only speak Spanish?**
No, también hablo japonés.	No, I also speak Japanese.
Sí, pero estudio inglés ahora.	Yes, but I'm studying English now.
いいえ、日本語も話せます。	* No, I can also speak Japanese.
아니요, 한국어도 할 수 있어요.	* No, I can also speak Korean.

* *Japanese From Zero!* and *Korean From Zero!* also available at **FromZero.com**.

4. ¿Tú vas a la escuela mañana?	**Are you going to school tomorrow?**
Solo en la mañana.	Only in the morning.
Sí, también voy al trabajo en la noche.	Yes, I'll also go to work at night.
No, no tengo escuela mañana.	No, I don't have school tomorrow.
5. ¿De quién son estos libros?	**Whose are these books?**
Esos libros son míos.	Those books are mine.
Esos libros son de Laura.	Those books are Laura's.
Esos libros son de la escuela.	Those books are the school's.

2. Question and answer (English → Spanish)

Each question has multiple answers. Cover up the right side and try to translate.

Context: A person holding a bag of delivered food. (the contents are unknown)

1. Is this yours?	**¿Esto es tuyo?**
Yes, that is mine.	Sí, eso es mío.
No, that is yours.	No, eso es tuyo.
No, that is theirs.	No, eso es suyo.
2. Do you have time tomorrow?	**¿Tienes tiempo mañana?**
Yes, I have time tomorrow or Saturday.	Sí, tengo tiempo mañana o el sábado.
No, but I have time on Friday.	No, pero tengo tiempo el viernes.
Yes, but only in the morning.	Sí, pero solo en la mañana.
3. Where is your friend going?	**¿A dónde va tu amigo?**
He is going to the bathroom.	Él va al baño.
He's going to the store.	Va a la tienda.
I don't know.	No sé.

Context: A person is holding ***dos helados de chocolate*** (two chocolate ice creams) (m.)

4. Whose are these?	**¿De quién son estos?**
Those are Juan's.	Esos son de Juan.
Those are yours.	Esos son tuyos.
One is yours and one is María's.	Uno es tuyo y uno es de María.
5. Where are you going on Saturday?	**¿A dónde vas el sábado?**
On Saturday I'll go to Spain.	El sábado yo voy a España.
I'll go to the mall.	Voy al centro comercial.
I'll go to a new restaurant.	Voy a un restaurante nuevo.

3. Spanish to English Conversation

Try translating the entire conversation before looking at the translation below.

1. Conversation between a Spanish learner and a native speaker

- ¿Qué es "only" en español?
- En español "only" es "solo".
- Entonces, ¿"Yo solo tengo un hermano" es "I only have one brother"?
- ¡Sí! Correcto.
- ¿Es "correcto" "correct" en inglés?
- ¡Sí! Correcto.

What is "only" in Spanish?
In Spanish, "only" is "solo".
So, "Yo solo tengo un hermano" is "I only have one brother?"
Yes! Correct.
Is "correcto" "correct" in English?
Yes! Correct.

2. Conversation between two friends at a party with hundreds of people.

¿Quiénes son tus amigos?
Ellos son mis amigos. (pointing)
¿El hombre y la mujer a la derecha de la puerta?
Sí, ellos.

Who are your friends?
They are my friends.
The man and the woman to the right of the door?
Yes, they.

3. Conversation between classmates at school.

¿De quién es este libro?
¿No es tuyo?
No, el mío está en mi escritorio.
Entonces no sé.

Whose is this book?
It's not yours?
No, mine is on my desk.
Then I don't know.

● 4. English to Spanish conversation

Try translating the entire conversation before looking at the translation below.

1. Conversation between friends standing outside of their work's office building.

¿De quién es aquel auto?
Es mío.
¿Qué? Aquel auto es rojo. ¿Tu auto no es blanco?
Sí, pero es mi auto nuevo.
Entonces, ¿en dónde está tu auto blanco?
Está en mi casa dentro del garaje.

- Whose care is that over there?
- It's mine.
- What? That car over there is red. Isn't your car white?
- Yes, but it's my new car.
- Then, where is your white car?
- It's at my house in the garage.

2. Conversation on the phone with a friend who wants hang out.

- ¿En dónde estás ahora?
- Voy al centro comercial nuevo con mi mamá.
- ¿Tienes tiempo esta semana?
- Sí, el jueves o el fin de semana.
- Genial, entonces yo voy a tu casa el domingo.
- ¡Ok!

- Where are you now?
- I'm going to the mall with my mom.
- Do you have time this weekend?
- Yes, on Thursday or on the weekend.
- Cool, then I'll go to your house on Sunday.
- Ok!

3. Conversation between friends waiting at the bus stop.

- Tengo hambre. ¿Y tú?
- No tengo.
- ¿Tienes un dulce o algo?
- Tengo unas manzanas. ¿Quieres una?
- ¡Sí, por favor! Gracias.

- I'm a bit hungry. And you?
- I'm not.
- Do you have (a piece of) candy or something?
- I have some apples. You want one?
- Yes, please! Thank you.

15 Workbook 15: Lesson Activities

15 Vocabulary Drills *Ejercicios de Vocabulario*

1. Writing and Vocabulary

Write the Spanish for each of the pictures. Make sure to add accent marks when needed.

building, pants, strawberry, bed, ice cream, garage, meat, fish, shirt, pig

1.__________ 2.__________ 3.__________ 4.__________ 5.__________

6.__________ 7.__________ 8.__________ 9.__________ 10.__________

2. Gender Matching

Write the following words and circle the gender companion word for each one.
NOTE: All but one word is used.

este, esta, fin, viernes, semana, mía, clase, viejo, lunes, tuya, esto

1) ______________________
(mine) feminine

2) el / la ______________________
(week)

3) el / la ______________________
(Friday)

4) el / la ______________________
(class)

5) el / la ______________________
(end)

6) ______________________
(old) masculine / mixed group

7) el / la ______________________
(Monday)

8) ______________________
(yours) feminine

9) ______________________
(this) masculine

10) ______________________
(this) feminine

15 Usage Activities *Actividades de Uso*

● 3. Reading Comprehension

Translate the following on a separate piece of paper or type in an electronic device.

Hermano y hermana

Brothers and sisters might have rooms next to each other, but not everything is equal.

❶ Esta es mi habitación.

❷ Yo tengo una cama grande y no tengo una televisión.

❸ La habitación de mi hermana es pequeña.

❹ La cama de ella es muy pequeña, pero tiene una televisión grande.

❺ Yo también quiero una televisión grande, pero no tengo dinero.

❻ Entonces necesito un trabajo nuevo.

❼ Ahora mi trabajo es malo.

❽ Pero mi hermana tiene un buen trabajo.

● 4. Reading Comprehension Questions

Answer the following questions about the reading comprehension. Write full sentences with pronouns and verbs in Spanish.

1. ¿La cama de la hermana del niño es grande?

____

2. ¿Quién tiene una televisión?

____

3. ¿La habitación de quién es grande?

____

4. ¿El trabajo del hermano es bueno?

____

5. ¿Quién habla? ¿El hermano o la hermana?

____

6. ¿La hermana necesita un trabajo nuevo?

____

7. ¿La hermana tiene dos televisiones?

____

5. Spanish translation

Translate the following conversations into English.

1.
A: ¿El lunes tienes clases? B: No, esta semana no tengo, entonces voy a un restaurante nuevo. A: ¿Con quién? B: Voy con mi amiga Sofía.
A:
B:
A:
B:

6. English translation

Translate the following conversation into Spanish.

1.
A: Where are you going on the weekend? B: I'm going to Spain. A: Who are you going to Spain with? B: With my friend (a girl) and my aunt.
A:
B:
A:
B:

2.
A: Is this your shirt? B: No, it isn't mine. A: Then, whose is it? B: I don't know, but it's very small.
A:
B:
A:
B:

7. Verb conjugation drills

Fill in the blanks with the proper verb conjugations.

1. Ir (to go)			
Pronouns	**Present Tense**	**Pronouns**	**Present Tense**
yo		**nosotros**	
tú		**ustedes**	
él / ella / usted		**ellos / ellas**	

15 Answer Key *Clave de Respuestas*

1. Writing and Vocabulary (answers)

1. pez
fish

2. helado
ice create

3. camisa
shirt

4. edificio
building

5. cerdo
pig

6. garaje
garage

7. fresa
strawberry

8. pantalón
pants

9. carne
meat

10. cama
bed

2. Gender Matching (answers)

1) mía
2) la semana
3) el viernes
4) la clase
5) el fin
6) viejo
7) el lunes
8) tuya
9) este
10) esta

3. Reading Comprehension (translation)

❶ This is my room.
❷ I have a big bed and I don't have a television.
❸ My sister's room is small.
❹ Her bed is very small, but she has a large television.
❺ I also want a big television, but I don't have money.
❻ So, I need a new job.
❼ Now my job is bad.
❽ But my sister has a good job.

4. Reading Comprehension Questions (answers)

1. Is the boy's sister's bed big? — No, su cama es pequeña.
2. Who has a television. — La hermana tiene una televisión.
3. Who's room is big? — La habitación del hermano es grande.
4. Is the brother's work good? — No, el trabajo del hermano es malo.
5. Who's speaking. The brother or the sister? — El hermano.
6. Does the sister need a new job? — No, el hermano necesita un trabajo nuevo. No, su trabajo es bueno.
7. Does the sister have two TVs? — No, ella solo tiene una televisión.

5. Spanish translation (answers)

1. A: On Monday, do you have classes?
   B: No, I don't have (any) this week, so I'm going to a new restaurant.
   A: With whom?
   B: I'm going with my friend Sofía.

6. English translation (answers)

1. A: ¿A dónde vas el fin de semana?
   B: Yo voy a España.
   A: ¿Con quién vas a España?
   B: Con mi amiga y mi tía.

2. A: ¿Esta es tu camisa?
   B: No, no es mía.
   A: Entonces ¿de quién es?
   B: No sé, pero es muy pequeña.

7. Verb conjugation drills (answers)

1. Ir (to go)

Pronouns	Present Tense	Pronouns	Present Tense
yo	voy	nosotros	vamos
tú	vas	ustedes	van
él / ella / usted	va	ellos / ellas	van

Vocabulary Builder 9:
Groups O, P and Q

Group O Basic Hygiene Products

el papel de baño	toilet paper	**la pasta de dientes**	tooth paste
el champú	shampoo	**el cepillo de dientes**	tooth brush
el jabón	soap	**el desodorante**	deodorant

Group P Words at a Café

el huevo	egg	**el sándwich**	sandwich
el tocino	bacon	**el pan**	bread
el pan tostado	toast	**la mantequilla**	butter
la leche	milk	**el jamón**	ham

Group Q Personal Information Words

la nacionalidad	nationality	**el apellido**	last name
el número de teléfono	telephone number	**la dirección**	address

17 PAGES	8 USAGE SECTIONS	17 NEW WORDS

16 Lesson 16: Which?

16 New Words *Palabras Nuevas*

Nouns etc.

¿cuál?	which?	**el dólar**	dollar
¿cuánto?	how much?; how many?	**el cargador**	charger
la botella	bottle	**el efectivo**	cash
la esquina	corner	**la conveniencia**	convenience
un poco	a little; a bit	**todo**	everything
tal vez	maybe	**mucho**	a lot; much
la salsa	sauce		

Verbs

costar	to cost	**vender**	to sell
venir	to come		

16 New Expressions *Expresiones Nuevas*

Don't worry about the grammar here. Just learn the phrases for communication.

1. ¿De verdad? **Really?**

16 Culture Clip *Clip Cultural*

16-1. Corner stores VS convenience stores

In Spanish speaking countries, "corner stores" called ***tienda de la esquina*** or ***tiendita*** in Latin America, *or* ***ultramarinos*** in Spain, are small grocery shops that carry standard groceries, essential toiletries, cleaning supplies, and local products from the area. ***Tiendas de la esquina*** are family-owned, often manned by the owners themselves, and while they aren't usually open 24 hours like a chain-convenience store, "corner stores" have significantly lower prices. If you visit a Spanish speaking country, try shopping at a ***tienda de la esquina***; you'll get a better deal and you may find something interesting you wouldn't at a convenience store.

16 Word Usage *Uso de Palabras*

W-1 el dólar — dollar

You probably already figured out the plural of ***dólar*** is ***dólares***. If not, try giving the lesson on plurals a quick review. Notice the accent mark stays on ***dólares***.

EXAMPLE SENTENCES

1. Solo tengo cinco dólares. — I only have five dollars.
2. Necesito cien dólares. — I need 100 dollars.
3. ¿Tienes tres dólares? — Do you have three dollars?

Other Currencies

Area	Currency	Singular	Plural
Europe	Euro	euro	euros
South America	Peso	peso	pesos
United Kingdom	Pound	libra	libras
Japan	Yen	yen	yenes
China	Yuan	yuan	yuanes

Pronuounced "eh-ooh-ro"

Note: In Europe and South America, the currency used may vary in some countries.

W-2 tal vez — maybe; might

Tal vez is used just like English "maybe" or "might". You just put it in front of the phrase. You might also see it written as ***talvez*** without a space; both spellings are acceptable.

EXAMPLE SENTENCES

1. Tal vez George es estadounidense. — Maybe George is American.
2. Tal vez no voy a la escuela hoy. — I might not go to school today.
3. Tal vez como pizza mañana. — Maybe I'll eat pizza tomorrow.
4. Tal vez mi mamá viene el martes. — Maybe my mom is coming Tuesday.

EXAMPLE Q&A

1. **¿A cuánto está este libro?** — **How much is this book (at)?**
   Está a ciento cincuenta pesos. — It's (at) 150 pesos.
   No sé. Tal vez está caro. — I don't know. Maybe it's expensive.

W-2

cuánto — how much; how many

Cuánto means "how much" and its plural ***cuántos*** means "how many". ***Cuánto*** must also match the gender of the noun being counted.

EXAMPLES (MASULINE)

1. ¿cuánto dinero?	how much money?
2. ¿cuánto tiempo?	how much time?
3. ¿cuántos amigos?	how many friends?
4. ¿cuántos hijos?	how many children?

EXAMPLES (FEMININE)

5. ¿cuánta agua?	how much water?
6. ¿cuánta comida?	how much food?
7. ¿cuántas mascotas?	how many pets?
8. ¿cuántas hermanas?	how many sisters?

Now let's look at ***cuánto*** (how much; how many) in action.

EXAMPLE SENTENCES

1. ¿Cuánto tiempo tienes?	How much time do you have?
2. ¿Cuánto dinero necesitas?	How much money do you need?
3. ¿Cuánta comida tenemos en casa?	How much food do we have at home?
4. ¿Cuánta agua quieres?	How much water do you want?
5. ¿Cuántas botellas de agua tienes?	How many bottles of water do you have?
6. ¿Cuántos libros lees en una semana?	How many books do you read in a week?

 *Más Detalles* **More Details** 

How hungry are you?

As we learned previously, when asking "Are you hungry?" we say ***¿Tú tienes hambre?*** - meaning "Do you have hunger?" Because of this, we can ask, "How hungry are you?" or literally, "How much hunger do you have?" using ***cuánto***.

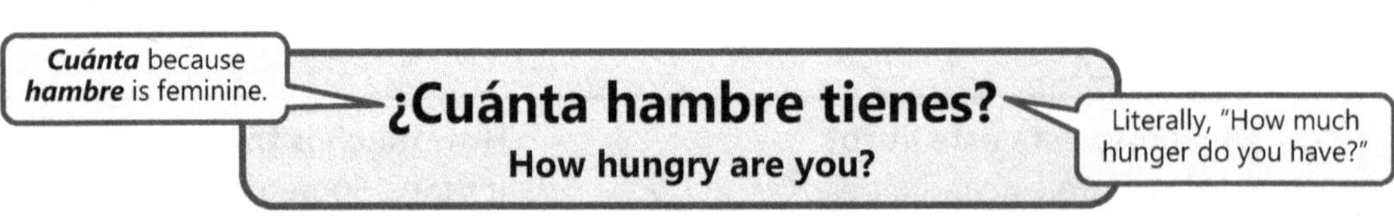

W-3

mucho	a lot; much; many
un poco	a bit; a little; a few; a little bit

Mucho (a lot) and ***un poco*** (a bit) can be used to show amounts or levels. They must match gender and plurality of the noun they are showing amounts or levels of.

EXAMPLES (MUCHO)

Singular	Plural
1. mucho dinero a lot of money; much money	3. muchos hermanos a lot of brothers; many brothers
2. mucha comida a lot of food; much food	4. muchas hermanas a lot of sisters; many sisters

NOTE: For ***un poco*** / ***una poca*** in singular form you must have ***de*** before the noun.

EXAMPLES (UN POCO)

de (of) is required.

Singular	Plural
5. un poco de dinero a bit of money	7. unos pocos amigos a few friends
6. una poca de comida a bit of food	8. unas pocas mascotas a few pets

Let's make sentences using the plural and gender specific versions of ***mucho*** and ***un poco***.

EXAMPLE SENTENCES

1. Tengo mucho tiempo.	I have a lot of time.
2. Ella tiene muchos novios.	She has many boyfriends.
3. Bebo mucha agua todos los días.	I drink a lot of water every day.
4. No comemos muchas verduras.	We don't eat many vegetables.
5. Hablo un poco de español.	I speak a bit of Spanish.
6. Ella solo tiene unos pocos amigos.	She only has a few friends.
7. Solo tengo una poca de agua.	I only have a little bit of water.

IMPORTANT NOTE When used with adjectives, ***un poco*** stays masculine and never changes from ***un poco*** no matter what the adjective's gender or plurality is.

EXAMPLE SENTENCES

Even though ***sopa*** and ***fría*** are feminine ***un poco*** remains masculine.

1. Mi sopa está un poco fría.	My soup is a bit cold.
2. Mis pies están un poco fríos.	My feet are a bit cold.

W-4 todo — everything

We previously learned that ***todos~*** means "all~" or "every~" when used in front of a noun.

EXAMPLES

todos los días every day	todas las mañanas every morning
todos mis amigos all my friends	todos los maestros all the teachers

Todo can be used on its own (without a noun) to mean "everything".

EXAMPLE SENTENCES

1. Todo es caro en este centro comercial.	Everything is expensive in this mall.
2. Quiero todo en esta tienda.	I want everything in this store.
3. Todo es delicioso en este restaurante.	Everything is delicious at this restaurant.
4. Tengo todo en mi casa.	I have everything at my house.

W-5 la salsa — sauce

Let's talk for a minute. Really??? Salsa is just "sauce"? I've lived my entire life not knowing this. That's all I wanted to say here... - George Trombley

EXAMPLE SENTENCES

1. Esta salsa es muy picante.	This sauce is very spicy.
2. ¿Quieres salsa verde o roja?	Do you want red or green sauce?

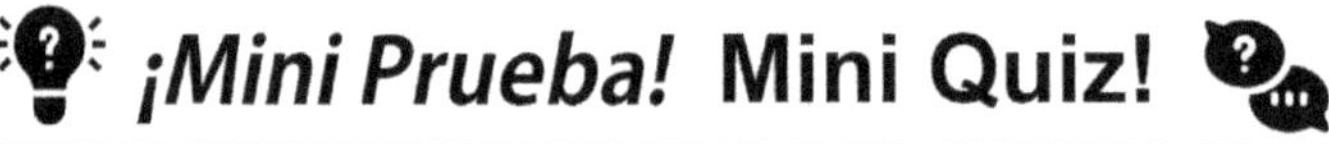

★ ★ ★ Cover the ➡ right side and test your ability to translate! ★ ★ ★

1. todas las mañanas	every morning
2. mucho tiempo	a lot of time
3. Solo tengo un poco de dinero.	I only have a bit of money.
4. ¿Cuántas mascotas tienes?	How many pets do you have?
5. Everything is a bit expensive.	Todo es un poco caro.

16 Verb Usage *Uso de Verbos*

V-1

vender	**to sell**		**regular**
Yo	***vendo*** (item).	I **sell** (item).	
Tú	***vendes*** (item).	You **sell** (item).	
Él / Ella / Usted	***vende*** (item).	He / She / You (polite) **sell(s)** (item).	
Nosotros	***vendemos*** (item).	We **sell** (item).	
Ustedes / Ellos / Ellas	***venden*** (item).	You guys **sell** (item).	

EXAMPLE SENTENCES

1. Mi mamá <u>vende</u> tacos en el mercado. — My mom <u>sells</u> tacos at the market.
2. Solo <u>vendemos</u> juegos en esta tienda. — We only <u>sell</u> games in this shop.
3. <u>¿Venden</u> café? — Do you guys <u>sell</u> coffee?
4. <u>Vendo</u> mi ropa vieja en el internet. — I <u>sell</u> my old clothes on the internet.
5. <u>¿Venden</u> en dólares? — Do you guys <u>sell</u> in dollars?

V-2

costar	**to cost**		**irregular**
Yo	***cuesto*** (price).	I **cost** (price).	
Tú	***cuestas*** (price).	You **cost** (price).	
Él / Ella / Usted	***cuesta*** (price).	He / She / You (polite) **cost(s)** (price).	
Nosotros	***costamos*** (price).	We **cost** (price).	
Ustedes	***cuestan*** (price).	You guys **cost** (price).	

While ***costar*** can be used to refer to the cost of a person or services they provide, it's more commonly used to talk about the <u>price of goods</u>. In this case, pronouns don't matter. The only concern is whether you have only one item vs having many.

Single Items

esto ***cuesta~*** (this **costs~**)
el auto ***cuesta~*** (the car **costs~**)

Multiple Items

estos ***cuestan~*** (these **cost~**)
los autos ***cuestan~*** (the cars **cost~**)

EXAMPLE SENTENCES

1. Esta camiseta <u>cuesta</u> cien dólares. — This T-shirt <u>costs</u> 100 dollars.
2. Estos zapatos <u>cuestan</u> setenta dólares. — These shoes <u>cost</u> 70 dollars.
3. Este cargador <u>cuesta</u> solo cincuenta pesos. — This charger <u>costs</u> only 50 pesos.
4. Estas fresas <u>cuestan</u> veinte pesos. — These strawberries <u>cost</u> 20 pesos.

V-3

venir	**to come**	**irregular**
Yo	***vengo*** to a (place).	I **come** to (place).
Tú	***vienes*** a (place).	You **come** to (place).
Él / Ella / Usted	***viene*** a (place).	He / She / You (polite) **come(s)** to (place).
Nosotros	***venimos*** a (place).	We **come** to (place).
Ustedes / Ellos / Ellas	***vienen*** a (place).	You guys **come** to (place).

Venir is irregular, it's conjugated similarly to ***tener*** (to have) with the exception of ***venimos***, which ends with ***imos*** instead of ***emos***.

EXAMPLE SENTENCES

1. Mi papá <u>viene</u> a mi casa todos los domingos.
   My dad <u>comes</u> to my house every Sunday.
2. ¿<u>Vienes</u> mañana?
   Are you <u>coming</u> tomorrow?
3. ¿De dónde <u>vienes</u>?
   From where are you <u>coming</u>?

 **¡Mini Prueba! Mini Quiz!** 

★ ★ ★ Cover the ➡ right side and test your ability to translate! ★ ★ ★

1. Venimos a México todos los años. — We come to Mexico every year.
2. ¿A dónde vas? — Where are you going?
3. Este auto cuesta diez mil dólares. — This car costs 10,000 dollars.
4. Todos mis amigos son estudiantes. — All my friends are students.
5. Mi gato está arriba de mi escritorio. — My cat is on top of my desk.
6. Where are you? — ¿Dónde estás?
7. Is this yours? — ¿Esto es tuyo?
8. Is this sauce spicy? — ¿Esta salsa es picante?

16 Grammar and Usage *Gramática y Uso*

● 16-2. How to use *cuál* (which; which one)

Cuál (which) can be used to ask someone to specify a certain item. ***Cuál*** also has a plural version, ***cuáles***, used with plural nouns.

EXAMPLE SENTENCES

Standing in front of a room full of puppies.

1. ¿Cuál perro es tuyo?	Which dog is yours?
2. ¿Cuáles perros son tuyos?	Which dogs are yours?
3. ¿Cuál es tu perro?	Which is your dog?
4. ¿Cuáles son tus perros?	Which ones are your dogs?

EXAMPLE Q&A

1. ¿Cuál libro es tuyo?	**Which book is yours?**
Mi libro es este.	My book is this one.
Mis libros son este y ese.	My books are this one and that one.
2. ¿Cuáles camisetas son baratas?	**Which t-shirst are inexpensive?**
Estas están solo a ochenta pesos.	These are just 80 pesos.
Lo siento. Todas las camisetas son caras.	I'm sorry. All the t-shirts are expensive.
3. ¿Cuál idioma es tu favorito?	**Which language is your favorite?**
Mi idioma favorito es el español.	My favorite language is Spanish.
No tengo un idioma favorito.	I don't have a favorite language.

EXAMPLE CONVERSATION

1. You are at a new restaurant in Tijuana with a Mexican friend.

¿Cuál no es picante?	Which one isn't spicy?
La salsa verde no es picante.	The green sauce isn't spicy.
¿Entonces, la salsa roja es picante?	So, the red sauce is spicy?
¡Sí! Es muy picante.	Yes! It's very spicy.

¡Mini Prueba! Mini Quiz!

★ ★ ★ Cover the ➡ right side and test your ability to translate! ★ ★ ★

1. ¿Cuál es tu nombre?	What's your name?
2. ¿Cuál salsa es dulce y picante?	Which sauce is sweet and spicy?
3. Which bed do you want?	¿Cuál cama quieres?
4. Which socks are yours?	¿Cuáles calcetas son tuyas?
5. Which languages are easy?	¿Cuáles idiomas son fáciles?

16-3. *Qué* (what) vs *Cuál* (which)

We know ***cuál*** means "which" and ***qué*** means "what". So why is "What's your name" ***¿Cuál es tu nombre?*** in Spanish? This is because in some cases ***cuál*** gets translated as "what".

First let's remember that when English uses "which", you always use ***cuál***.

EXAMPLE SENTENCES

Looking at a photo of many cars.

1. ¿Cuál es tu auto? — Which (one) is your car?
2. ¿Cuál auto quieres? — Which car do you want?
3. ¿Cuáles autos son de Japón? — Which cars are from Japan?

Now let's look at questions where ***cuál*** translates to "what" instead of "which".

EXAMPLE SENTENCES

1. ¿Cuál es tu comida favorita? — What is your favorite food?
2. ¿Cuál es la nacionalidad de Carlos? — What is Carlos's nationality?
3. ¿Cuál es su número? — What is his/her number?
4. ¿Cuál es tu dirección? — What is your address?

So why not use ***qué*** instead of ***cuál*** in the sentences above? It's because although ***qué*** and ***cuál*** can both mean "what", they are used in different situations in Spanish.

Cuál is asking for a single piece of information with no explanation.
Qué is asking for an explanation.

So, by changing the question word the meaning of the question changes.

EXAMPLE SENTENCES

1. ¿Cuál es tu nombre? — What is your name?

   Here we just want someone's name. The answer will be something like, "Moopy Deeder."

2. ¿Qué es tu nombre? — What is your name?

   Here we want information behind the name. The person assumes we know their name but want to know its origin. The answer for a strange name might be that her father was a science fiction writer and named her after one of his alien characters also named "Moopy Deeder."

3. ¿Cuál es tu comida favorita? — What is your favorite food?

   Here we just want the name of the favorite food. The answer may be "Seared Pork".

4. ¿Qué es tu comida favorita? — What is your favorite food?

   Here we want a description of the food. We already know what their favorite is, but now we want to know what's in it. The answer might be, "It's pork soaked in soy sauce, and then seared black"

16-4. The "one" pronoun

In English we say "the blue one" or plural the "the big ones". We can do this also in Spanish by using any gender companion word (***el***, ***la***, ***una***, ***uno***) directly in front of the adjective.

EXAMPLES

1. el rojo / la roja
   the red one
2. el grande / la grande
   the big one
3. una roja / uno rojo
   a red one
4. uno grande / una grande
   a big one

Uno, not ***un*** is always used creating the "one" pronoun.

EXAMPLE Q&A

1. ¿Cuál quieres?	**Which one do you want?**
Quiero el blanco.	I want the white one.
Quiero uno amarillo.	I want a yellow one.

We can also make plural versions using ***los***, ***las***, ***unos***, and ***unas***.

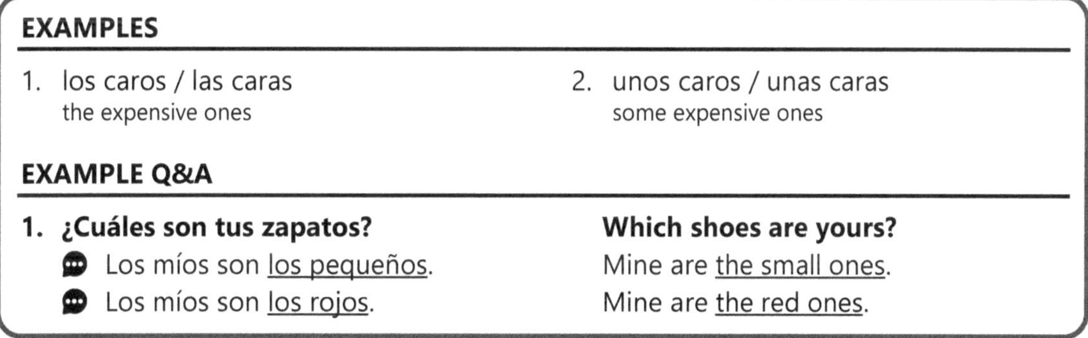

EXAMPLES

1. los caros / las caras
   the expensive ones
2. unos caros / unas caras
   some expensive ones

EXAMPLE Q&A

1. ¿Cuáles son tus zapatos?	**Which shoes are yours?**
Los míos son los pequeños.	Mine are the small ones.
Los míos son los rojos.	Mine are the red ones.

We can do the same thing with nouns being used as adjectives.

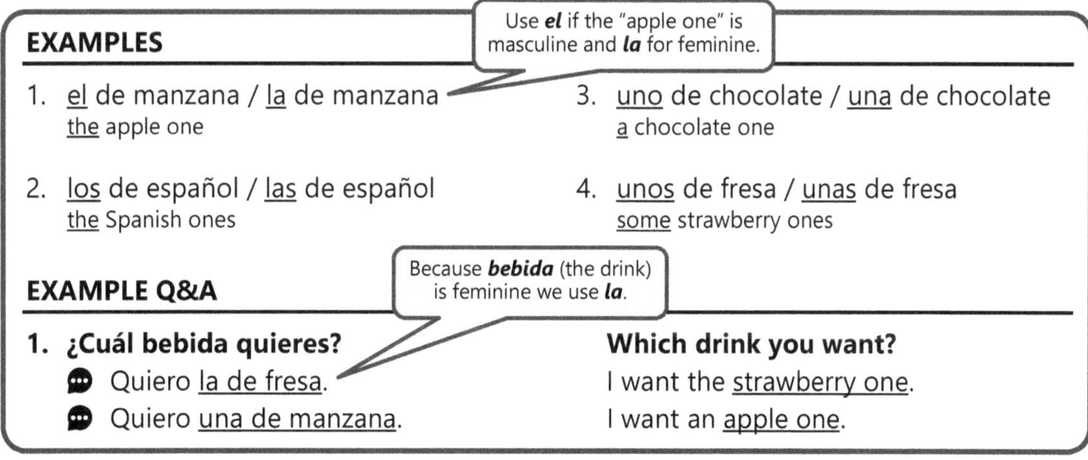

EXAMPLES

Use ***el*** if the "apple one" is masculine and ***la*** for feminine.

1. el de manzana / la de manzana
   the apple one
2. los de español / las de español
   the Spanish ones
3. uno de chocolate / una de chocolate
   a chocolate one
4. unos de fresa / unas de fresa
   some strawberry ones

EXAMPLE Q&A

Because ***bebida*** (the drink) is feminine we use ***la***.

1. ¿Cuál bebida quieres?	**Which drink you want?**
Quiero la de fresa.	I want the strawberry one.
Quiero una de manzana.	I want an apple one.

16-5. Asking how much something costs

There are two ways to ask how much something costs in Spanish. Here's the first:

¿Cuánto cuesta (item)?
How much does (item) cost?

When talking about costing money, even for feminine words, you must use masculine ***cuánto*** since ***dinero*** (money) the thing being used to buy, is masculine.

EXAMPLE Q&A

1. ¿Cuánto cuesta este libro?	**How much does this book cost?**
Cuesta cien pesos.	It costs 100 pesos.
Cuesta cinco dólares.	It costs 5 dollars.
2. ¿Cuánto cuestan estos libros?	**How much do these books cost?**
Cuestan quinientos pesos.	They cost 500 pesos.
Cuestan mil dólares.	They cost 1000 dollars.

Remember for multiple items ***costar*** must be in plural form.

16-6. Another way to say cost using *estar*

Now let's look at the second way to ask how much something costs. Here we don't need the verb ***costar*** (to cost) but instead use ***estar*** (to be).

¿A cuánto está (item)?

The ***a*** means "at", so the question asks, "How much is the item at?" ***Estar*** is used because price can change. To say an item's cost, we can say, ***Está a (price)*** meaning "It's at (price)".

EXAMPLE Q&A

1. ¿A cuánto está este libro?	**How much is this book (at)?**
Está a ciento setenta pesos.	It's (at) 170 pesos.
No sé. Tal vez está caro.	I don't know. Maybe it's expensive.
2. ¿A cuánto están las manzanas en México?	**How much are apples in Mexico?**
No sé pero muy baratas.	I don't know but very cheap.
Una manzana cuesta cuatro pesos.	One apple costs 4 pesos.
Una manzana a cuatro pesos.	One apple (at) 4 pesos.

cuatro pesos
por una manzana

16-7. Being good and bad at something

Previously we've used ***en*** for locations to say "in", "on", or "at". ***En*** can also be used to say someone is good or bad "at" a particular thing.

EXAMPLE SENTENCES (LEVEL 1)

1. Yo soy bueno en los idiomas.	I'm good at languages.
2. Yo soy malo en los idiomas.	I'm bad at languages.
3. Yo no soy bueno en el español.	I'm not good at Spanish.
4. Yo no soy malo en el español.	I'm not bad at Spanish.
5. Yo soy bueno en los deportes.	I'm good at sports.
6. Yo soy malo en los deportes.	I'm bad at sports.

Let's make more variety with the examples using a few more words that we already know.

EXAMPLE SENTENCES (LEVEL 2)

1. Yo soy un poco malo en los idiomas.	I'm a little bad at languages.
2. Yo solo soy bueno en el fútbol.	I'm only good at soccer.
3. Yo soy malo en todos los deportes.	I'm bad at all sports.
4. Yo no soy bueno en nada.	I'm not good at anything.
5. Él es malo en su trabajo.	He's bad at his job.

EXAMPLE Q&A (LEVEL 2)

1. ¿En qué eres bueno?	**What are you good at?**
Yo soy bueno en los juegos.	I'm good at games.
No sé. Tal vez en el español.	I don't know. Maybe at Spanish.
Yo soy bueno en todo.	I'm good at everything.

Let's go hardcore and make really big sentences. Theoretically you should be able to understand them since you know all the concepts.

EXAMPLE SENTENCES (LEVEL 3)

1. Yo no soy bueno en el español, pero yo soy bueno en otros idiomas.
   I'm not good at Spanish, but I'm good at other languages.
2. Él es bueno en los idiomas, pero él es muy malo en todos los deportes.
   He's good at languages, but he's really bad at all sports.
3. Tú eres muy inteligente, pero solo eres bueno en los juegos y malo en escuela.
   You're very smart, but you're only good at games and bad at school.

16-8. The other one - *el otro*

When saying "the other one", it would sound strange to say ***otro <u>uno</u>*** or ***otra <u>una</u>***. Instead, do not say ***uno*** or ***una*** but just say ***el otro*** or ***la otra***, depending on the gender.

EXAMPLE SENTENCES

1. Mi amiga tiene dos mascotas. Una es un gato pequeño, y <u>la otra</u> es un perro blanco.
   My friend has two pets. One is a small cat, and the other one is a white dog.
2. Yo tengo dos autos. Uno es Toyota, y <u>el otro</u> es un Honda.
   I have two cars. One is a Toyota, and the other one is a Honda.
3. Mi hermano tiene dos novias. Una es coreana, y <u>la otra</u> es mexicana.
   My brother has two girlfriends. One is Korean, and the other one is Mexican.

16 Practice and Review *Práctica y Repaso*

1. Question and Answer (Spanish → English)

Each question has multiple answers. Cover up the right side and try to translate.

1. ¿De dónde es María?	**Where is María from?**
No sé, tal vez de Argentina.	I don't know, maybe from Argentina.
María es de Estados Unidos.	María is from the United States.
De España, tal vez.	From Spain, maybe.
2. ¿Cuánto dinero tienes ahora?	**How much money do you have now?**
Tengo cien pesos.	I have one hundred pesos.
Tengo mil pesos.	I have one thousand pesos.
Tengo ciento veinte dolares.	I have one hundred twenty dollars.
3. ¿Cuál es tu comida favorita?	**What's your favorite food?**
Mi comida favorita son los tacos.	My favorite food *are* tacos.
Mi comida favorita es la pizza.	My favorite food is pizza.
Tal vez las manzanas.	Maybe apples.
4. ¿Disculpe, aquí venden tacos?	**Excuse me. Do you sell tacos here?**
¡Por supuesto! ¿Cuántos quieres?	Of course! How many do you want?
Sí, también tenemos tacos.	Yes, we also have tacos.
No, disculpa, solo pizza.	No, sorry, only pizza.
5. ¿A cuánto está el café mediano?	**How much is the medium coffee?**
Está a 25 pesos.	It's 25 pesos.
El café mediano cuesta un euro.	The medium coffee costs one euro.
Está a un dólar.	It´s one dollar.

2. Question and answer (English → Spanish)

Each question has multiple answers. Cover up the right side and try to translate.

1. **What's your nationality?** — **¿Cuál es tu nacionalidad?**
   - I'm Spanish. — Yo soy español.
   - I have two nationalities. — Yo tengo dos nacionalidades.
   - I'm from France, but I don't speak French. — Yo soy de Francia, pero no hablo francés.

2. **How much are the large pizzas?** — **¿Cuánto cuestan las pizzas grandes?**
   - Two hundred fifty pesos. — A doscientos cincuenta pesos.
   - Large pizzas are ten dollars. — Las pizzas grandes están a diez dólares.
   - We don't have large pizzas. — No tenemos pizzas grandes.

3. **Which one is your car?** — **¿Cuál es tu auto?**
   - My car is this red car. — Mi auto es este auto rojo.
   - My car is that one over there. — Mi auto es aquel.
   - My car isn't here. — Mi auto no está aquí.

4. **How much is the apple juice?** — **¿Cuánto cuesta el jugo de manzana?**
   - The apple juice is one euro. — El jugo de manzana está a un euro.
   - Sorry, we don't have apple juice. — Disculpe, no tenemos jugo de manzana.
   - Sorry, we only have orange juice. — Disculpe, solo tenemos jugo de naranja.

5. **Do you drink coffee?** — **¿Bebes café?**
   - Yes, I drink a lot of coffee. — Sí, bebo mucho café.
   - Sometimes a little in the mornings. — A veces un poco en las mañanas.
   - Yes, I drink coffee, but only a little. — Sí, bebo café, pero solo un poco.

3. Spanish to English Conversation

Try translating the entire conversation before looking at the translation below.

1. Conversation at a corner store.

Disculpe, ¿vende cepillos de dientes?
Sí, ¿cuántos necesitas?
¿Cuánto cuestan?
Cuestan diez pesos.
Quiero cinco, por favor.
Okay, son 50 pesos.
Gracias.

Excuse me, do you sell toothbrushes?
Yes, how many do you need?
How much are they?
They are ten pesos.
I want five, please.
Okay, it's 50 pesos.
Thank you.

2. Conversation at a boardgame shop between two hardcore fans of the game being played for a weekend tournament.

Hola, mi nombre es Jack. ¿Cuál es tu nombre?
Mi nombre es Sofía.
Mucho gusto, Sofía. Eres muy buena en este juego.
Gracias. Este es mi juego favorito.
¿¡De verdad!? ¡Este es mi juego favorito también! ¡¿Cuál es tu número de teléfono!?
Yo tengo novio...

Hello, my name is Jack. What's your name?
My name is Sofía.
Nice to meet you, Sofía. You're very good at this game.
Thanks. This is my favorite game.
Really!? This is my favorite game, too! What's your phone number?
I have a boyfriend...

4. English to Spanish Conversation

Try translating the entire conversation before looking at the translation below.

1. Conversation at a fast food restaurant.

How much are burgers?
They cost seventy pesos.
And how much are pizzas?
Pizzas are a hundred pesos
Ok, two pizzas, please.

¿Cuánto cuestan las hamburguesas?
Cuestan setenta pesos.
Y ¿cuánto cuestan las pizzas?
Las pizzas están a cien pesos.
Ok, dos pizzas, por favor.

2. Conversation between friends at a parking lot.

Which one is your car?
My car is that one over there.
The red one?
No, the blue one.

¿Cuál es tu auto?
Mi auto es aquel.
¿El rojo?
No, el azul.

3. Conversation between friends deciding what to drink at a new coffee shop.

What do you want?
I want a coffee. How much is the small coffee?
The small coffee is one dollar.
And how much is the large coffee?
It's 2 dollars.
It's very cheap! I want a big coffee. And you?
I want a large tea, but it's a little expensive.
How much is the large tea?
It's ten dollars.
Ten dollars!?

¿Qué quieres?
Hmm, yo quiero un café. ¿Cuánto cuesta el café chico?
El café chico cuesta un dólar.
¿Y cuánto cuesta el café grande?
Está a dos dólares.
¡Está muy barato! Yo quiero un café grande. ¿Y tú?
Yo quiero un té grande, pero está un poco caro.
¿Cuánto cuesta el té grande?
Cuesta diez dólares.
¿¡diez dólares!?

4. Conversation between a tourist and his friend waiting in a long line at a popular burger street food cart that only takes cash.

What is "solo efectivo"?
It is "cash only".
Do you have cash?
No, I only have credit cards.
Then, I'll go to the ATM.
Ok, that convenience store over there has one.

¿Qué es "solo efectivo"?
Es "cash only"
¿Tú tienes efectivo?
No, solo tengo tarjetas de crédito.
Entonces, voy al cajero automático.
Ok, aquella tienda de conveniencia tiene uno.

5. Conversation between people who met for the first time.

What's your nationality?
I'm from France, but my nationality is Mexican.
So, do you speak French?
No, I only speak Spanish and English.
Do your parents speak French?
Yes, they speak French and Spanish.

¿Cuál es tu nacionalidad?
Yo soy de Francia, pero mi nacionalidad es mexicana.
Entonces, ¿hablas francés?
No, solo hablo español e inglés.
¿Tus papás hablan francés?
Sí, ellos hablan francés y español.

16 Workbook 16: Lesson Activities

16 Vocabulary Drills *Ejercicios de Vocabulario*

1. Writing and Vocabulary

Write the Spanish for each of the pictures. Make sure to add accent marks when needed.

cash, bottle, charger, shirt, shampoo, soap, toothpaste, toilet paper, deodorant, toothbrush

1.__________ 2.__________ 3.__________ 4.__________ 5.__________

6.__________ 7.__________ 8.__________ 9.__________ 10.__________

2. Gender Matching

Write the following words and circle the gender companion word for each one.

nacionalidad, esquina, efectivo, conveniencia, cargador, botella, dólar, jabón, desodorante, champú

1) el / la ____________________
(corner)

2) el / la ____________________
(shampoo)

3) el / la ____________________
(cash)

4) el / la ____________________
(deodorant)

5) el / la ______________________
(nationality)

6) el / la ______________________
(soap)

7) el / la ______________________
(dollar)

8) el / la ______________________
(charger)

9) el / la ______________________
(bottle)

10) el / la ______________________
(convenience)

16 Usage Activities *Actividades de Uso*

● 3. Reading Comprehension

Translate the following on a separate piece of paper or type in an electronic device.

Midnight Snack

Felipe woke up late feeling really hungry. He needs to buy some things, but he is short on money so he must consider his options.

❶ Mi nombre es Felipe. Estoy en casa ahora y tengo mucha hambre.

❷ Quiero un café y un sándwich.

❸ Pero no tengo pan y necesito leche.

❹ El pan está a cincuenta pesos en la tienda de conveniencia.

❺ Y la leche cuesta veintisiete pesos.

❻ Yo no tengo mucho dinero.

❼ En la tienda de conveniencia todo está muy caro.

❽ Pero, en la tiendita el pan está barato. Cuesta solo treinta pesos.

❾ Y la leche cuesta solo quince pesos.

❿ Pero, en la tiendita no venden mi leche favorita.

⓫ Entonces, también voy a la tienda de conveniencia.

4. Reading Comprehension Questions

Answer the following questions about the reading comprehension.

1. ¿En la tiendita cuánto cuesta el pan?

____

2. ¿Cuánto dinero tiene Felipe?

____

3. ¿En dónde venden la leche favorita de Felipe?

____

4. ¿Qué necesita Felipe?

____

5. ¿La tienda de conveniencia es barata?

____

6. ¿Qué comida está a veintisiete pesos?

____

7. ¿En la tiendita el pan está a cuarenta pesos?

____

5. Spanish translation

Translate the following conversations into English.

1.
A: Tengo sed. ¿Venden jugo de manzana en la tienda de la esquina? B: Por supuesto. A: ¿Cuánto cuesta? B: No sé, tal vez quince pesos.

A:
B:
A:
B:

6. English Translation

Translate the following conversations into Spanish.

1.
A: How many shoes do you have? B: I don't know. I have a lot. A: Which ones are your favorites? B: My favorites are these.
A:
B:
A:
B:

2.
A: Are you hungry? B: Yes, a little bit. And you? A: I'm very hungry. B: Do you want pizza? I have pizza at my home. A: Yes, I want pizza. Thanks!
A:
B:
A:
B:
A:

7. Verb conjugation drills

Fill in the blanks with the proper verb conjugations.

1. Costar (to cost)	
Pronouns	**Present Tense**
yo	
tú	
él / ella / usted	
nosotros	
ustedes	
ellos / ellas	

2. Vender (to sell)	
Pronouns	**Present Tense**
yo	
tú	
él / ella / usted	
nosotros	
ustedes	
ellos / ellas	

16 Answer Key *Clave de Respuestas*

1. Writing and Vocabulary (answers)

1. botella
bottle

2. jabón
soap

3. cepillo de dientes
toothbrush

4. efectivo
cash

5. papel de baño
toilet paper

6. pasta de dientes
toothpaste

7. champú
shampoo

8. desodorante
deodorant

9. cargador
charger

10. camisa
shirt

2. Gender Matching (answers)

1) la esquina
2) el champú
3) el efectivo
4) el desodorante
5) la nacionalidad
6) el jabón
7) el dólar
8) el cargador
9) la botella
10) la conveniencia

3. Reading Comprehension Translation

❶ My name is Felipe. I'm at home and I'm very hungry.
❷ I want a coffee and a sandwich.
❸ But I don't have bread and I need milk.
❹ Bread is 50 pesos at the convenience store.
❺ And milk costs 27 pesos.
❻ I don't have much money.
❼ At the convenience store everything is very expensive.
❽ But, at the corner store bread is cheap. It only costs 30 pesos.
❾ And milk costs 15 pesos.
❿ But, at the corner store they don't sell my favorite milk.
⓫ So, also I will go to the convenience store.

4. Reading Comprehension Questions (answers)

1.	How much is bread at the corner store?	Cuesta treinta pesos. / Está a treinta pesos.
2.	How much money does Felipe have?	No sé. / No tiene mucho dinero.
3.	Where do they sell Felipe's favorite milk.	Venden la leche en la tienda de conveniencia.
4.	What does Felipe need?	Él necesita leche. / Él necesita pan y leche.
5.	Is the convenience store cheap?	No, todo está muy caro. / No, es caro.
6.	What food is 27 pesos?	La leche está a veintisiete pesos.
7.	At the corner store, is bread 40 pesos?	No, está a treinta pesos. No, cuesta treinta pesos.

5. Spanish translation (answers)

1. A: I'm thirsty. Do they sell apple juice at the corner store?
   B: Of course.
   A: How much does it cost?
   B: I don't know, maybe 15 pesos.

6. English Translation (answers)

1. A: ¿Cuántos zapatos tienes?
   B: No sé. Tengo muchos.
   A: ¿Cuáles son tus favoritos?
   B: Mis favoritos son estos.

2. A: ¿Tienes hambre?
   B: Sí, un poco. ¿Y tú?
   A: Yo tengo mucha hambre.
   B: ¿Quieres pizza? Tengo pizza en mi casa.
   A: Sí, quiero pizza. ¡Gracias!

7. Verb conjugation drills (answers)

1. costar (to cost)	
yo	cuesto
tú	cuestas
él / ella / usted	cuesta
nosotros	costamos
ustedes	cuestan
ellos / ellas	cuestan

2. vender (to sell)	
yo	vendo
tú	vendes
él / ella / usted	vende
nosotros	vendemos
ustedes	venden
ellos / ellas	venden

Vocabulary Builder 10:
Groups R and S

Group R Words at a Restaurant

la gaseosa	soda	**el arroz**	rice
el refresco	soda	**el bistec**	steak
la hamburguesa	burger	**la papa**	potato
el sabor	flavor	**la sal**	salt
la pimienta	pepper (black pepper)	**el azúcar**	sugar

Group S Music Words

la música	music	**el rock**	rock
el rap	rap	**el hip hop**	hip hop
el jazz	jazz	**el metal**	metal
la balada	ballad	**el blues**	blues

16 PAGES	8 USAGE SECTIONS	14 NEW WORDS

17 Lesson 17: Liking things

From the teacher...

The Spanish "like verbs" are unique and they act different from other verbs. There are quite a few new rules, so you might need to run through this lesson a few times.

17 New Words *Palabras Nuevas*

Nouns etc.

la cosa	thing	**la primavera**	spring
la tarjeta	card	**el verano**	summer
menos	less	**el otoño**	fall
más	more	**el invierno**	winter
el clima	weather	**la estación**	season
la vainilla	vanilla		

Verbs

gustar	to like	**encantar**	to really like; to love
agradar	to like		

17 Word Usage *Uso de Palabras*

W-1 la cosa — thing

La cosa (thing) never changes gender. Even if we know the "thing" is *masculine* the grammatical gender stays as *feminine*. Plurality must still match.

EXAMPLE SENTENCES

Holding a *libro* (book) in your hand. (masculine)

1. Esta cosa es muy cara. This thing is so expensive.

Holding *fresas* (strawberries) in your hand. (feminine)

2. Estas cosas son muy caras. These things are so expensive.

W-2	la tarjeta	card

Tarjeta (card) is used for all types of cards such business card, credit card etc. Based on context ***tarjeta*** alone will be understood as a business card or credit card etc.

EXAMPLE SENTENCES

At a business meeting

1. Esta es mi tarjeta.	This is my business card.

At a store

2. Solo tengo tarjetas.	I only have credit cards.

We can use ***de*** or adjectives to further clarify which card it is as needed.

EXAMPLES

1. tarjeta de presentación	business card
2. tarjeta de crédito	credit card
3. tarjeta de débito	debit card
4. tarjeta roja	red card (in sports)
5. tarjeta de puntos	point card

W-3	más	more
W-4	**menos**	**less**

These are used just like their English words. They are put in front of the word you want *more* or *less* of.

EXAMPLE SENTENCES

1. Necesito más dinero.	I need more money.
2. Quiero menos verduras.	I want less vegetables.
3. ¿Tienen más pan?	Do you have any more bread?
4. Quiero algo menos picante.	I want something less spicy.

NOTE: When ***más*** is used with adjectives it's like adding ***-er*** for some adjectives.

más picante (spicier; hotter) **más grande** (bigger) **más pequeño** (smaller)

W-5

el sabor	flavor

El sabor (flavor) isn't a hard word. However since flavors are nouns when you ask "What flavor?" you must include ***de*** before ***qué***.

EXAMPLE CONVERSATION

1. Conversation between a person with a sweet tooth and a shop worker.

Quiero helado por favor.	I want ice cream please.
¿De qué sabor?	What flavor?
De chocolate y de fresa.	Chocolate and strawberry.

2. Conversation between friends at a birthday party.

¿Qué sabor de helado quieres?	What flavor of ice cream do you want?
¿Tienes de vainilla?	Do you have vanilla?
No tenemos de vainilla.	We don't have vanilla.
Entonces, ¿tienes de chocolate?	Then, do you have chocolate?
Lo siento, no tenemos ese sabor.	Sorry, we don't have that flavor.
¿Qué? ¿Entonces de qué sabor tienes?	What? Then what flavor do you have?
Solo tenemos de fresa y de mango.	We only have strawberry and mango.

¿De qué sabor tienes?

~~chocolate~~ | fresa | ~~vainilla~~

17 Verb Usage *Uso de Verbos*

From the teacher...

There are two big differences in how Spanish "like" verbs work. Pay attention to the next few sections since understanding them gives you a strong foundation for similar verbs later.

17-1. Subject and object Pronouns (¡muy importante!)

In English we never say, "He likes she" or "She likes he." In cases where a pronoun is the object, we use object pronouns, "her", "him" etc. Spanish also has *object* pronouns.

For the "like" verbs in this lesson, we'll need to know the Spanish *object* pronouns.

Spanish Object Pronouns	
(subject pronouns)	(object pronouns)
yo	**me** (Pronounced, "meh.")
tú	**te**
él, ella, usted	**le**
nosotros	**nos**
ellos, ellas, ustedes	**les**

17-2. Pronoun usage with the "like" verbs

When saying you like a person, *object* pronouns are used. Before we discuss how conjugation changes, let's keep it simple and focus on just the pronoun changes.

1. ***Me*** gustar — Similar to: **Me** like~ — NEVER: ~~***Yo***~~ gustar
2. ***Te*** gustar — Similar to: **You** like~ — NEVER: ~~***Tú***~~ gustar
3. ***Le*** gustar — Similar to: **Him / Her** likes~ — NEVER: ~~***Él / Ella***~~ gustar
4. ***Nos*** gustar — Similar to: **Us** like~ — NEVER: ~~***Nosotros***~~ gustar
5. ***Les*** gustar — Similar to: **They** like~ — NEVER: ~~***Ellos/ellas***~~ gustar

We purposely didn't conjugate ***gustar*** above since the conjugation rules are different for the "like" verbs. But don't worry, the rules are simple.

17-3. Liking things in Spanish

The "like" verbs are different from verbs we learned so far. First, they use the object pronouns ***me***, ***te***, ***le*** etc. And second, they must conjugate based on WHAT is liked.

EXAMPLE SENTENCES

1. Me gusta el Español.	I like Spanish.
2. Me gusta la pizza.	I like pizza.
3. Me gustan los gatos.	I like cats.
4. Me gustan tus ojos.	I like your eyes.

In examples 1 and 2 the thing being liked is *singular* so ***gusta*** is used. And in 3 and 4 the liked item is plural so ***gustan*** is used. The object being liked sets the conjugation.

17-4. Liking people in Spanish

Gustar also only becomes ***gusta*** or ***gustan*** for liking people most of the time.

EXAMPLE SENTENCES

1. Me gusta él.	I like him.
2. Me gusta ella.	I like her.
3. Me gusta Daniela.	I like Daniela.
4. Me gustan ustedes.	I like you guys.
5. Me gustan ellos.	I like them.
6. Me gustan Dianiela y Sofía.	I like Daniela and Sofía.

Even though these examples are liking people, the verb is still changed to ***gusta*** for singular items and ***gustan*** for plural. Now let's change *who* is doing the liking.

EXAMPLE SENTENCES

1. Le gusta él.	She likes him.
2. Le gusta ella.	He likes her.
3. Nos gusta la pizza.	We like pizza.
4. Te gustan los gatos.	You like cats.
5. Les gustan mis zapatos.	They like my shoes.
6. Te gustan los luchadores mexicanos.	You like Mexican wrestlers.

As you can see, it doesn't matter WHO likes the object when changing gustar. You only need to know the number of objects to know whether to use ***gusta*** or ***gustan***.

So far it's easy, use ***gusta*** for singular and ***gustan***, for plural. In the next section we will see when ***gustar*** must change into other forms.

17-5. Most commonly used "like" conjugations

Gustar (to like) conjugates to ***gusta*** and ***gustan***, maybe 97% of the time. However, in the following cases gustar must conjugate differently based on "who" is being liked.

Gusto MUST be used when the object is ***yo*** (I, me).
¿Te gusto yo? **Do you like me?**

Gustas MUST be used when the object is ***tú*** (you).
Me gustas tú. **I like you.**

Gustamos MUST be used when the object is ***nosotros*** (us).
Les gustamos nosotros. **They like us.**

With all that logic behind us, NOW we can finally put it all in one chart!

V-1

gustar		to like	regular (special usage)
(*) gusto	yo.	**(*) like(s)** (me).	
(*) gustas	tú.	**(*) like(s)** (you).	
(*) gustamos	nosotromos.	**(*) like(s)** (us).	
(*) gusta	él / ella / usted.	**(*) like(s)** (him / her / you (polite) / item).	
(*) gustan	ellos / ellas.	**(*) like(s)** (you guys / them / items).	
(*) The indirect pronoun showing WHO is doing the liking. (***Me***, ***Te***, ***Les*** etc.)			

EXAMPLE SENTENCES

1. Me gustan los gatos. — I like cats.
2. Le gusta la maestra. — He/she likes the teacher.
3. Nos gustan los idiomas. — We like languages.
4. Le gustas tú. — He/she likes you.
5. Nos gusta tu familia. — We like your family.

To make negatives, such as, "I don't like" you just add ***no*** in front of ***me gusta*** etc.

1. No me gusta la tarea. — I don't like homework.
2. ¿No te gustan mis zapatos? — You don't like my shoes?
3. ¡No me gustas tú! — I don't like you!

V-2

agradar		to like (as a person)	regular (special usage)
(*) agrado	yo.	**(*) like(s)** (me).	
(*) agradas	tú.	**(*) like(s)** (you).	
(*) agradamos	nosotromos.	**(*) like(s)** (us).	
(*) agrada	él / ella / usted.	**(*) like(s)** (him / her / you (polite) / item).	
(*) agradan	ellos / ellas.	**(*) like(s)** (you guys / them / items).	
(*) The indirect pronoun showing WHO is doing the liking. (***Me***, ***Te***, ***Les*** etc.)			

For people, ***agradar*** is when you like someone, but not romantically. Only ***gustar*** is used for "like" romantically. For objects, ***agradar*** is less *like* than ***gustar*** similar to "kind of like."

EXAMPLE SENTENCES

1. Me gusta tu hermana. — I like your sister. (as a possible girlfriend)
2. Me agrada tu hermana. — I like your sister. (as a person)

NOTE: Try not to accidentally tell your friend you "like" their sister.

3. ¿Te agradan mis zapatos? — Do you like my shoes?
4. Le agradan los autos rojos. — He/She likes red cars.
5. Nos agrada este restaurante. — We like this restaurant.

V-3

encantar		to really like; like a lot; love; adore	regular (special usage)
(*) encanto	yo.	**(*) really like(s)** (me).	
(*) encantas	tú.	**(*) really like(s)** (you).	
(*) encantamos	nosotromos.	**(*) really like(s)** (us).	
(*) encanta	él / ella / usted.	**(*) really like(s)** (him / her / you (polite) / item).	
(*) encantan	ellos / ellas.	**(*) really like(s)** (you guys / them / items).	
(*) The indirect pronoun showing WHO is doing the liking. (***Me***, ***Te***, ***Les*** etc.)			

Encantar means you REALLY LIKE something in the same way we "love" something in English. And although ***encantar*** can mean romantic love it can also just be "really like".

EXAMPLE SENTENCES

1. Le encantan los gatos negros. — He/She loves black cats.
2. Me encanta el chocolate. — I love chocolate.
3. Nos encantan los estadounidenses aquí. — We love Americans here.

We can also ask questions using ***gustar*** and answer with ***encantar***.

EXAMPLE Q&A

1. **¿Te gusta la comida picante?**	**Do you like spicy food?**
Sí! Me encanta la comida picante.	Yes, I love spicy food.
No, no me gustan las cosas picantes.	No, I don't like spicy things.
2. **¿Qué cosas te gustan?**	**What things do you like?**
Me gusta la música.	I like music.
Me encantan las películas.	I love movies.

Le gusta Maria.
Le gusta Jorge.

Le gustan los tacos grandes.

 *Más Detalles* **More Details** 

Which conjugation for two types?
If someone says, they like ***tú y los gatos*** (you and cats) do we use ***gustas*** for the ***tú*** or ***gustan*** for ***los gatos***? OR do we use ***gustan*** since there are multiple objects?

Actually we choose conjugation depending on the first item in the list.

1. I like YOU and cats.	Me gustas tú y los gatos.
2. I like CATS and you.	Me gustan los gatos y tú.

What about two objects connected by "and" of the same type?
Let's so someone says they love all the seasons. Since "all the seasons" is plural we must use ***encantan*** (or other plural like verb).

Me encantan todas las estaciones.
I love all the seasons.

But what if they only like spring and summer? In this case, just like the previous section, we use ***encanta*** (or other singular like verb) because the first item in the list is singular.

Me encanta la primavera y el verano.
I love spring and summer.

NOTE: Even native speakers will sometimes mix these conjugations up so don't worry too much! Remember language isn't an art to master, but it's a tool to communicate!

17 Memorization Techniques *Técnicas de memorización*

17-6. Which "like" verb for which situation

When I was learning Spanish I struggled to know which "like" verb to use. So, in this section I wanted to show you how I learned to distinguish them.

First you need to consider whether the thing being liked is a person or an object.
We can use the A-G-E method to remember the level of like. Let's start with objects.

The A-G-E method (with objects)

Starting with the lowest level of "like" we have ***Agradar***, then we have "normal like", ***Gustar***, and finally ***Encantar*** when an object is "really liked" or "loved."

EXAMPLE SENTENCES (FOR OBJECTS)

1. Me **A**grada este libro. ♥ I like this book.
2. Me **G**usta este libro. ♥♥ I like this book.
3. Me **E**ncanta este libro. ♥♥♥ I really like this book.

NOTE: Animals, bugs, plants, or any living things that aren't people are treated as objects.

The A-G-E method (with people)

The lowest level of like, ***Agradar***, is used when you just like someone as a person. ***Gustar*** is used when there are definitely romantic feelings, and ***Encantar*** the highest level of like, shows even higher possible romantic feelings.

She wants to know if he likes her as a friend. She thinks it's possible he might like her romantically. She wonders if maybe he "really likes" her. She also wants him to like her more than ***gustar***.

EXAMPLE SENTENCES (FOR PEOPLE)

1. Yo le **A**grado.  He likes me. (as a person)
2. Yo le **G**usto.  He likes me romantically.
3. Yo le **E**ncanto.  He really likes me (loves me).

17 Grammar and Usage *Gramática y Uso*

17-7. Dropping the pronoun for the "like" verbs

Unlike other verbs where we can drop the pronoun, such as with ***yo como*** becoming just ***como*** to mean "I eat", the "like" verbs always require the pronouns.

EXAMPLE SENTENCES

1. Me gusta la comida mexicana.	I like Mexican food.
2. ¡Le encanta el invierno!	He/she loves winter!
3. Nos agradan personas de Barcelona.	We like people from Barcelona.

HOWEVER, when the verb is specific to the pronoun, having the pronoun can feel redundant. So, it's natural to drop it in Spanish in these cases.

EXAMPLE SENTENCES

1. ¿Te gusto?	Do you like me?
2. Me encantas.	I really like you.
3. Me agradas.	I like you. (as a person)
4. Les encantamos.	They really like us.

Having ***yo*** here we be redundant.

We can also keep the pronoun but change the sentence order. The meaning is the same.

5. Tú me encantas.	You, I really like.
6. Tú me agradas.	You, I like. (as a person)
7. Nosotros les encantamos.	Us, they really like.

gustar

17-8. The person marker "*a*"

We know how to say, "I like" "he likes" etc. using pronouns. But, in order to say a specific person likes something, such as "Jorge" or "your brother" etc, we need a person marker.

We've learned that ***a*** is the destination marker. It goes before locations such as in ***a México*** (to Mexico). The person marker is also ***a*** and is used in front of the person doing the liking.

EXAMPLE SENTENCES

"***A***" marks the person doing the liking.

6. A Jorge le gustan los libros. — George likes books.
7. A mi hermano le gustan los libros. — My brother likes books.
8. A mi madre le gustan los libros. — My mother likes books.

A (name)	***le (gustar)***	***(thing)***
A María	***le gusta***	***el dinero.***
A Carlos	***le gustan***	***los libros.***
A José	***le gusta***	***esta foto.***

With ***le gusta*** (he/she likes) we aren't sure if the person doing the liking is a "he", or a "she" but using the person marker ***a***, we can specify the pronoun.

EXAMPLE SENTENCES

9. A ella le gustan los libros. — She likes books.
10. A el le gustan los libros. — He likes books.

The same can be said for ***les gusta*** (you guys like/they like). Using the person marker ***a***, we can specify whether we mean, "you guys" or "they".

EXAMPLE SENTENCES

11. A ustedes les gustan los libros. — You guys like books.
12. A ellos les gustan los libros. — They / those guys like books.
13. A ellas les gustan los libros. — They / those girls like books.

BE WARNED!

Sometimes when people learn a new rule, such as using "***a***" to mark the person who likes, they forget the other rules learned. So don't forget that when the thing we like is ***yo***, ***tú***, or ***nosotros*** the verb must also change to match. (even when the pronoun is dropped)

EXAMPLE SENTENCES

1. A Carlos le gustas tú.	Carlos likes you.
2. A la hermana de Jorge le encanto yo.	George's sister really likes me.
3. ¿A tu mamá no le agradamos?	Does your mother not like us?

AND FINALLY!

We've previously learned when the location marker "***a***" (to) is followed by masculine gendered location, A + EL becomes AL. The same happens with person marker "***a***".

EXAMPLE SENTENCES (A + EL)

1. Yo voy al baño ahora.	I'll go to the bathroom now.
2. Al gato le gustas tú.	The cat likes you.
3. Al gato no le gusto yo.	The doesn't like me.
4. ¿Al amigo de María le gusto yo?	Does Maria's friend like me?

17-9. Turning verbs into nouns to power up your Spanish

Knowing how to use a verb as a noun as in "to work" or "working" can evolve your Spanish. It allows us to say things like "I like to work" or "Cooking is hard."

EXAMPLES

1. trabajar	to work; working
2. cocinar	to cook, cooking
3. hablar	to speak; speaking

EXAMPLE SENTENCES

1. Me gusta trabajar.	I like to work.
2. No me gusta cocinar.	I don't like to cook.
3. Hablar español es fácil.	Speaking Spanish is easy.

Using this concept we can make even more detailed sentences.

4. Me gusta trabajar en la biblioteca	I like working in the library.
5. A mi papá le encanta comer naranjas.	My father really likes to eat oranges.
6. A Jorge le gusta ir a Corea.	George likes to go to Korea.
7. No me gusta cocinar en las mañanas.	I don't like cooking in the mornings.
8. Vender autos en invierno es difícil.	Selling cars in the winter is difficult.

17 Practice and Review *Práctica y Repaso*

1. Question and Answer (Spanish → English)

Each question has multiple answers. Cover up the right side and try to translate.

1. ¿Cuánto dinero tienes ahora?	**How much money do you have now?**
Solo tengo veinte dolares.	I only have twenty dollars.
No tengo dinero.	I don't have money.
Solo tengo tarjetas de crédito.	I only have credit cards.
Tengo ciento veinte euros.	I have a hundred and twenty euros.
2. ¿En dónde te gusta comer?	**Where do you like to eat?**
En mi casa.	At my house.
Me gusta comer en mi cama.	I like to eat in my bed.
En restaurantes baratos.	At inexpesive restaurants.
Solo no me gusta comer afuera.	I just don't like to eat out(side).
3. ¿Qué es esta cosa en español?	**What is this thing in Spanish?**
Esto es una tarjeta de crédito.	This is a credit card.
Eso es pan tostado.	That is toast.
Esto es pasta de dientes.	This is toothpaste.
Eso es un cajero automático.	That's an ATM.
4. ¿Te gustan los gatos?	**Do you like cats?**
Sí, ¡me encantan los gatos!	Yes, I love cats!
No, solo me gustan los perros.	No, I only like dogs.
No, pero tu gato me agrada.	No, but I like your cat.
Sí, pero no tengo uno.	Yes, but I don't have one.
5. ¿Qué te gusta?	**What do you like?**
Me gustan los libros.	I like books.
Me gusta el chocolate.	I like chocolate.
Me gustan los juegos.	I like games.
Me gusta el fútbol.	I like soccer.

2. Question and Answer (English→ Spanish)

Each question has multiple answers. Cover up the right side and try to translate.

1. **What do you like to eat?** — **¿Qué te gusta comer?**
   - I like to eat chocolate. — Me gusta comer chocolate.
   - I like to eat fruits and vegetables. — Me gusta comer frutas y verduras.
   - I love to eat tacos. — Me encanta comer tacos.
   - I like oranges. — Me gustan las naranjas.

2. **Does your mom like your boyfriend?** — **¿A tu mamá le agrada tu novio?**
   - Yes, she likes him a little bit. — Sí, le agrada un poco.
   - Yes, my mom loves my boyfriend. — Sí, a mi mamá le encanta mi novio.
   - I don't have a boyfriend. — Yo no tengo un novio.
   - What boyfriend? — ¿Qué novio?

3. **I like you. Do you like me?** — **Me gustas. ¿Yo te gusto?**
   - Yes, I like you too. — Sí, tu también me gustas.
   - No, I'm sorry. — No, lo siento.
   - No, I like your friend. — No, me gusta tu amiga.
   - I like you (as a person), but I don't like you (romantically). — Me agradas, pero no me gustas.

4. **Do you like studying languages?** — **¿Te gusta estudiar idiomas?**
   - Not much. — No mucho.
   - Yes, I study Spanish and Chinese. — Sí, estudio español y chino.
   - Yes, I study every day. — Sí, estudio todos los días.

5. **Does Carlos like Maria?** — **¿A Carlos le gusta María?**
   - No, Maria likes Carlos. — No, a María le gusta Carlos.
   - Yes, and Maria likes Carlos too. — Sí, y a María le gusta Carlos también.
   - No, Carlos likes Sofia. — No, a Carlos le gusta Sofía.
   - Yes, Carlos really likes María. — Sí, a Carlos le encanta María.

3. Spanish to English Conversation

Try translating the entire conversation before looking at the translation below.

1. Conversation between friends.

¿Te gusta el helado?	Do you like ice cream?
Si me gusta, pero no mucho.	Yes I like it, but not a lot.
¿Cuál es tu helado favorito?	What's your favorite ice cream?
El de chocolate, ¿y el tuyo?	Chocolate (flavor), And yours?
Mi favorito es el de mango,	My favorite is mango,
¡me encanta el helado de mango!	I love mango ice cream!

2. Conversation between friends eating at a restaurant.

¿Te gusta la comida picante?	Do you like spicy food?
Sí, me agrada, pero no como mucha.	Yes, I like it, but I don't eat a lot.
No me gusta mucho, pero esta sopa me encanta, es deliciosa.	I don't like it a lot, but I love this soup, it's delicious.
Sí, esta sopa es muy buena.	Yeah, this soup is very good.

3. Conversation between people at a language meetup.

¿En dónde vives?	Where do you live?
Vivo en Argentina.	I live in Argentina.
¿Te gusta vivir en Argentina?	Do you like living in Argentina?
Sí, las personas son amables y me gusta mucho la comida de Argentina.	Yes, people are kind and I really like Argentinian food.

4. Conversation between friends at a coffee shop where the drinks were delivered while they were both in the bathroom.

¿De quién es este café?	Whose is that coffee?
¿Está caliente o frío?	Is it cold or hot?
Está frío.	It's cold.
Entonces es tuyo, no me gusta el café frío.	Then is yours, I don't like cold coffee.

4. English to Spanish conversation

Try translating the entire conversation before looking at the translation below.

1. Conversation between friends.

What's your favorite food?	¿Cuál es tu comida favorita?
Strawberries, I love to eat strawberries. What's your favorite food?	Las fresas. Me encanta comer fresas. ¿Cuál es tu comida favorita?
I don't know. I have many.	No sé, tengo muchas.
Then, Do you have a favorite drink?	Entonces, ¿tienes una bebida favorita?
Yes! I love orange juice.	Sí, ¡me encanta el jugo de naranja!

2. Conversation between two elementary school kids. (one in an alien mask)

Does your mom cook?	¿Tu mamá cocina?
No, she doesn't like to cook.	No, no le gusta cocinar.
Then, What do you eat?	Entonces, ¿Qué comes?
I eat at restaurants.	Como en restaurantes.
Everyday?	¿Todos los días?
No, sometimes my dad cooks.	No, a veces mi papá cocina.

3. Conversation between a tourist and a street vendor on a hot day at the beach.

Hello, excuse me, Do you have ice cream?	Hola, disculpe, ¿tiene helado?
Sorry, I only have sodas and juices	Lo siento, solo tengo refrescos y jugos.
Then, a cold juice please.	Entonces, un jugo frío por favor.
What flavor?	¿De qué sabor?
Apple please. How much is it?	De manzana por favor. ¿Cuánto es?
It's twenty pesos	Son veinte pesos.

5. Conversation between two friends at a shopping mal.

¡Me encanta ese vestido!	I love that dress.
A mi también ¿Cuánto cuesta?	Me too. How much is it?
¡Cuesta trescientos pesos!	It's three hundred pesos!
¡Está muy barato!	It's really inexpensive!

17 Workbook 17: Lesson Activities

17 Vocabulary Drills *Ejercicios de Vocabulario*

1. Writing and Vocabulary

Write the Spanish for each of the pictures. Make sure to add accent marks when needed.

hamburguer, soda, spring, salt, winter, pepper, fall, sugar, steak, summer

1.__________ 2.__________ 3.__________ 4.__________ 5.__________

6.__________ 7.__________ 8.__________ 9.__________ 10.__________

2. Gender Matching

Write the following words and circle the gender companion word for each one.

gaseosa, refresco, papa, sabor, pimienta, clima, estación, invierno, primavera, cosa

1) el ____________________
(soda) (masculine version)

2) la ____________________
(soda) (feminine version)

3) el / la ____________________
(thing)

4) el / la ____________________
(winter)

5) el / la ____________________
(potato)

6) el / la ____________________
(pepper)

7) el / la ____________________
(flavor)

8) el / la ____________________
(season)

9) el / la ____________________
(spring)

10) el / la ____________________
(weather)

17 Usage Activities *Actividades de Uso*

● 3. Reading Comprehension

Translate the following on a separate piece of paper or type in an electronic device.

Family Likes

Antonio thinks we care about his family and what they like. But hey at least you can practice your Spanish!

❶ Mi nombre es Antonio. Me encantan los animales.

❷ Tengo un perro, un gato y dos hámsteres.

❸ A mi hermana no le gustan los animales, pero le gusta leer novelas.

❹ Las novelas de drama son sus favoritas.

❺ A mi mamá no le gusta leer, pero le gusta el café.

❻ No le gusta el café negro, y le encanta el café con azúcar.

❼ Mi papa no bebe café. No le gusta.

❽ Solo le gustan el refresco.

❾ Pero no le gustan los refrescos con azúcar.

❿ A todos en mi familia les gusta la comida mexicana.

⓫ Hoy vamos a un restaurante nuevo y comemos comida deliciosa.

4. Reading Comprehension Questions

Answer the following questions about the reading comprehension. Write full sentences with pronouns and verbs.

1. ¿A quién le gusta el café?

____

2. ¿De qué novelas le gustan a la hermana?

____

3. ¿Cuántos animales tiene Antonio?

____

4. ¿Quién tiene dos autos?

____

5. ¿A quién no le gusta el azúcar?

____

6. ¿A quién en familia de Antonio le gusta la comida mexicana?

____

7. ¿Qué no le gusta a la mamá de Antonio?

____

8. ¿Cuántos autos tiene el papá de Antonio?

____

9. ¿Qué animales le gustan a la hermana de Antonio?

____

5. Spanish translation

Translate the following conversations into English.

1.
A: ¿Tienes novia? B: No tengo novia, pero me gusta María. A: Lo siento, María tiene novio. B: ¿Quién es el novio de María? A: Yo soy el novio de María. B: Oh...
A:
B:
A:
B:
A:
B:

6. English Translation

Translate the following conversations into Spanish.

1.
A: Do you like Mexican food? B: Yes, I like quesadillas and I LOVE tacos. A: I LOVE tacos too, and I also kind of like burritos. B: I don't like burritos.
A:
B:
A:
B:

7. Verb conjugation drills

Fill in the blanks with the proper verb conjugations.

1. Agradar (to like as a person)	
Pronouns	**Present Tense**
Yo	
Tú	
Él / ella / usted	
nosotros	
ustedes	
ellos / ellas	

1. Gustar (to like)	
Pronouns	**Present Tense**
Yo	
Tú	
Él / ella / usted	
nosotros	
ustedes	
ellos / ellas	

3. Encantar (to really like; to love)	
Pronouns	**Present Tense**
Yo	
Tú	
Él / ella / usted	
nosotros	
ustedes	
ellos / ellas	

17 Answer Key *Clave de Respuestas*

1. Writing and Vocabulary (answers)

1. azúcar
sugar

2. invierno
winter

3. hamburguesa
hamburger

4. pimienta
pepper

5. otoño
autumn; fall

6. sal
salt

7. primavera
spring

8. verano
summer

9. bistec
steak

10. refresco
soda

2. Gender Matching (answers)

1) el refresco
2) la gaseosa
3) la cosa
4) el invierno
5) la papa
6) el pimiento
7) el sabor
8) la estación
9) la primavera
10) el clima

3. Reading Comprehension Translation

❶ My name is Antonio. I love animals.
❷ I have a dog, a cat, and two hamsters.
❸ My sister doesn't like animals, but she likes to read novels.
❹ Drama novels are her favorite.
❺ My mother doesn't like to read, but she likes coffee.
❻ She doesn't like black coffee, and she loves coffee with sugar.
❼ My dad doesn't drink coffee. He doesn't like it.
❽ He only likes soda.
❾ But he doesn't like sodas with sugar.
❿ Everyone in my family likes Mexican food.
⓫ Today we're going to a new restaurant and we will eat delicious food.

4. Reading Comprehension Questions (answers)

1.	Who likes coffee.	La mamá de Antonio.
2.	What novel (type) does the sister like?	Le gustan las noevlas de drama.
3.	How many animals does Antonio have?	Cuatro animales.
4.	Who has two cars?	No sé. (we don't know!)
5.	Who doesn't like coffee with sugar?	Mamá de Antonio.
6.	Who in Antonio's family likes Mexican food.	A todos en su familia les gusta.
7.	What doesn't Antonio's mother like?	No le gusta leer.
8.	How many cars does Antonio's father have?	No sé.
9.	What animals does Antonio's sister like?	No le gustan los animales.

5. Spanish translation (answers)

1. A: Do you have a girlfriend?
   B: I don't have a girlfriend, but I like Maria.
   A: Sorry, Maria has a boyfriend.
   B: Who is Maria's boyfriend?
   A: I am Maria's boyfriend.
   B: Oh...

6. English Translation (answers)

1. A: ¿Te gusta la comida de México?
   B: Si, me gustan las quesadillas y me encantan los tacos.
   A: Me encantan los tacos también, y me agradan los burritos.
   B: No me gustan los burritos.

7. Verb conjugation drills (answers)

1. agradar (to like as a person)	
yo	agrado
tú	agradas
él / ella / usted	agrada
nosotros	agradamos
ustedes	agradan
ellos / ellas	agradan

2. gustar (to like)	
yo	gusto
tú	gustas
él / ella / usted	gusta
nosotros	gustamos
ustedes	gustan
ellos / ellas	gustan

3. encantar (to really like)	
yo	encanto
tú	encantas
él / ella / usted	encanta
nosotros	encantamos
ustedes	encantan
ellos / ellas	encantan

17 PAGES	6 USAGE SECTIONS	27 NEW WORDS

18 Lesson 18: Time to tell time

18 New Words *Palabras Nuevas*

Nouns etc.

¿cuándo?	when?	**y cuarto**	quarter past
¿qué hora?	what time?	**y media**	half past
la hora	hour; time	**el mediodía**	noon
~en punto	~o'clock	**la tarde**	afternoon
siempre	always	**la noche**	night
a veces	sometimes	**la madrugada**	middle of the night
nunca	never	**la fiesta**	party
el desayuno	breakfast	**la cena**	dinner
solo	alone	**el espagueti**	spaghetti

Prepositions

a	at (a time)	**desde**	from
hasta	until		

Adverbs

normalmente	normally	**usualmente**	usually

Verbs

dormir	to sleep	**despertar**	to wake up
desayunar	to eat breakfast	**cenar**	to eat dinner

18 Memorization Techniques *Técnicas de memorización*

18-1. How to remember *esta* vs *está*

Esta means "this" and ***está*** means "is / are". The only difference is the accent on ***está***. Here are a couple of ways that MIGHT help you remember which is which.

Technique #1 - Think of the accent mark as the "star" from estar.

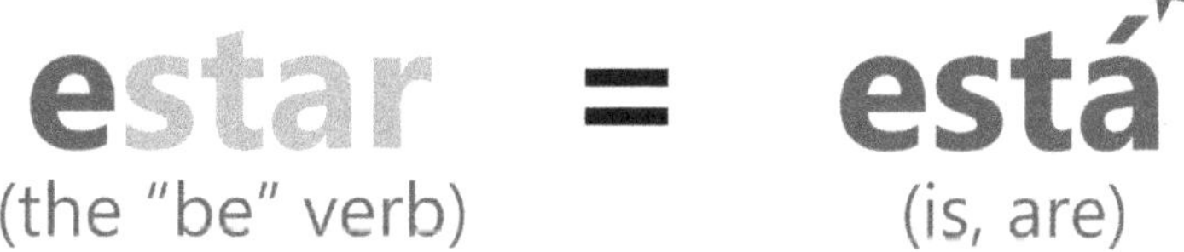

Technique #2 - Memorize this sentence.

esta persona **está** en México
(this) (is)

18 Word Usage *Uso de Palabras*

W-1

siempre	**always**
a veces	**sometimes**
nunca	**never**

Nunca (never), ***a veces*** (sometimes), ***siempre*** (always) are normally put directly in front of the verb.

EXAMPLE SENTENCES

1. Mi mamá siempre cocina los viernes.
   My mom always cooks on Fridays.
2. Mi mamá a veces cocina los miércoles.
   My mom sometimes cooks on Wednesdays.
3. Mi mamá nunca cocina los domingos.
   My mom never cooks on Sundays.
4. Yo siempre estudio en la mañana.
   I always study in the morning.
5. Yo a veces estudio en la biblioteca.
   I sometimes study at the library.
6. Yo nunca estudio en la escuela.
   I never study at school.

W-2 ~en punto — ~o'clock

"O'clock" in Spanish is ***en punto***. To say 2 o'clock and later the pattern is ***las*** + # + ***en punto***. ***Las*** is used since ***la hora*** (time) is feminine. 1 o'clock is singular, ***la una en punto***.

Basic Time in Spanish			
la una en punto	one o'clock	las siete en punto	seven o'clock
las dos en punto	two o'clock	las ocho en punto	eight o'clock
las tres en punto	three o'clock	las nueve en punto	nine o'clock
las cuatro en punto	four o'clock	las diez en punto	ten o'clock
las cinco en punto	five o'clock	las once en punto	eleven o'clock
las seis en punto	six o'clock	las doce en punto	twelve o'clock

After we learn the preposition word ***a*** (at), in the very next section we can make examples.

W-3 a — at; to; until

We already learned that when ***a*** is used with a location it translates as "to".

EXAMPLE SENTENCES

1. Voy a México hoy. — I'll go to Mexico today.
2. Leo a mi hijo todos los días. — I read to my son every day.
3. Escribo a mi madre todas las semanas. — I write to my mother every week.
4. ¿Vienes a mi casa hoy? — Are you coming to my house today?

When ***a*** is paired with a time, it translates to "at".

EXAMPLE SENTENCES

1. Como a las seis en punto. — I eat at 6 o'clock.
2. Trabajo a las ocho en punto. — I work at 8 o'clock.
3. Voy a las once en punto. — I go at 11 o'clock.

We use ***de*** (from) and ***a*** to say, "from (location) to (location)" or "from (time) to (time)". In "from-to" statements, ***a*** can translate to "to" and "until".

EXAMPLE SENTENCES

Here ***a*** translates as "to".

1. Voy de San Francisco a Tijuana.
   I'm going from San Francisco to Tijuana.
2. Trabajo de las nueve en punto a las cinco en punto.
   I work from 9 o'clock to / until 5 o'clock.

We can use ***a*** (to; at) more than once in a sentence, once for *time* and once for *location*.

EXAMPLE SENTENCES

1. Yo voy a la escuela a las siete en punto.
   I go to school at 7 o'clock.
2. Yo voy al trabajo a la una en punto.
   I go to work at 1 o'clock.

Don't forget ***a + el*** becomes just ***al***.

W-4

desde	**from**
hasta	**until; to**

In addition to ***de*** (from) ***a*** (to; until), there is also ***desde*** (from) and ***hasta*** (to; until).

1. ***Desde*** and ***hasta*** are used when stressing a certain or targeted time or place.
2. ***Desde*** and ***hasta*** are used when specifying the origin or final time / destination.

Consider the following using just ***de*** and ***desde***.

EXAMPLE SENTENCES

1. In this sentence there isn't a *specific* time, but a repeated time on every Monday.

I work Mondays from 8 o'clock.
Trabajo los lunes de las ocho en punto.

2. In this sentence, your work is from one specific time on *only* this Monday.

I work this Monday from 8 o'clock.
Trabajo este lunes desde las ocho en punto.

3. Here, the first time is non-specific, but the second time is specific to next Monday.

I always work Mondays from 8 o'clock. But this Monday I work from 10 o'clock.
Siempre trabajo los lunes de las ocho en punto. Pero este lunes trabajo desde las diez en punto.

In the case of ***a*** and ***hasta***, ***a*** only means "to; until" when combined with ***de*** (from). Without ***de*** it can only mean "at".

Here, ***a*** couldn't be used as "until", since there is no ***de*** (from).

EXAMPLE SENTENCES

1. I work Mondays until 8 o'clock.
   Trabajo los lunes hasta las ocho en punto.

Just like in English, ***en punto*** (o'clock) can be dropped.

2. I work this Monday until 8 o'clock.
   Trabajo este lunes hasta las ocho en punto.

We can use ***a*** as "until" since there is a ***de*** (from).

3. I work Mondays until eight. But Thursdays I work until ten.
   Trabajo los lunes hasta las ocho. Pero los jueves trabajo hasta las diez.
4. I work Mondays from three until eight. But Thursdays I work from five until ten.
   Trabajo los lunes de las tres a las ocho. Pero los jueves trabajo desde las cinco hasta las diez.
5. Esta semana trabajo desde el lunes hasta el jueves.
   This week I work from Monday to Thursday.
6. Tengo trabajo desde la una en punto.
   I have work from 1 o'clock.
7. Estudio español desde las diez hasta las doce.
   I study Spanish from ten until twelve.

Más Detalles More Details

Can't I just always use *desde* and *hasta* to keep it easy?
It's not a bad idea, however, other people will use ***de*** and ***a***, so you need to understand their usage. As you have more interactions with Spanish speakers you will naturally learn when ***desde*** and ***hasta*** works better than ***de*** and ***a*** and vice-versa.

In writing, such as novels, news articles, etc., ***desde*** and ***hasta*** are more commonly used. But amongst friends and in casual conversation, ***a*** and ***de*** are commonly used.

W-5	**solo**	**alone; by myself**

We learned previously that ***solo*** means "only" or "just". It also means "alone". Notice that the position of ***solo*** in the sentence changes its meaning in English.

EXAMPLE SENTENCES

1. Yo solo estudio español. — I only study Spanish.
2. Yo estudio español solo. — I study Spanish alone.

You can even have two versions of solo in one sentence.

3. Yo solo estudio español solo. — I only study Spanish alone.

18 Verb Usage *Uso de Verbos*

V-1

dormir	**to sleep**	**irregular**
Yo ***duermo***	I **sleep**	
Tú ***duermes***	You **sleep**	
Él / Ella / Usted ***duerme***	He / She / You (polite) **sleep**	
Nosotros ***dormimos***	We **sleep**	
Ustedes ***duermen***	You guys **sleep**	

EXAMPLE SENTENCES

1. Mis padres duermen a las ocho en punto. — My parents sleep at 8 o'clock.
2. A veces duermo con mi perro. — Sometimes I sleep with my dog.
3. Duermo a las once en punto hoy. — I'll sleep at 11 o'clock today.
4. Mi hijo nunca duerme en su cuarto. — My son never sleeps in his room.
5. ¿En dónde duermes? ¿En un hotel? — Where do you sleep? In a hotel?

V-2

despertar	**to wake up**	**irregular**
Yo ***despierto***	I **wake** *up*	
Tú ***despiertas***	You **wake** *up*	
Él / Ella / Usted ***despierta***	He / She / You (polite) **wakes** up	
Nosotros ***despertamos***	We **wake** *up*	
Ustedes ***despiertan***	You guys **wake** *up*	

EXAMPLE SENTENCES

1. Yo siempre despierto a las siete en punto.
   I always wake up at 7 o'clock.
2. ¿Tú despiertas feliz todos los días?
   Do you wake up happy every day?
3. Nosotros despertamos a las ocho en punto los miércoles.
   We wake up at 8 o'clock on Wednesdays.

V-3

desayunar	**to eat breakfast**	regular
Yo	***Desayuno***	I *eat breakfast*
Tú	***desayunas***	You *eat breakfast*
Él / Ella / Usted	***desayuna***	He / She / You (polite) *eat breakfast*
Nosotros	***desayunamos***	We *eat breakfast*
Ustedes	***desayunan***	You guys *eat breakfast*

EXAMPLE SENTENCES

1. Nosotros nunca desayunamos.
   We never eat breakfast.

2. Hoy nosotros desayunamos en mi restaurante favorito.
   Today we will eat breakfast at my favorite restaurant.

3. ¿Ustedes desayunan huevos en España?
   Do you guys eat eggs for breakfast in Spain?

   We can put a food immediately after ***desayunar***.

4. Mi hermana desayuna frutas todas las mañanas.
   My sister eats fruits for breakfast every morning.

V-4

cenar	**to eat dinner**	regular
Yo	***ceno***	I **eat dinner**
Tú	***cenas***	You ***eat*** **dinner**
Él / Ella / Usted	***cena***	He / She / You (polite) **eat dinner**
Nosotros	***cenamos***	We **eat dinner**
Ustedes	***cenan***	You guys **eat dinner**

EXAMPLE SENTENCES

1. Ceno con mi mamá todos los domingos.
   I eat dinner with my mom every Sunday.

2. ¿A veces tú cenas con tus padres?
   Do you sometimes eat dinner with your parents?

3. Él cena con su novia esta noche.
   He will eat dinner with his girlfriend tonight.

18 Grammar and Usage *Gramática y Uso*

18-2. More specific time in Spanish

We already know how to say "o'clock" times in Spanish with ***en punto*** or just the numbers ***las dos***, ***las tres,*** etc. For more specific times, we can add the number of minutes after the hour. It's optional to have ***con*** (with) or ***y*** (and) in between.

las tres con doce
las tres y doce
las tres doce

3:12 PM

DIGITAL CLOCKS FROM ZERO!

(hour) **con** (minutes)
(hour) **y** (minutes)
(hour) (minutes)

EXAMPLES

las cuatro con quince	4:15	las ocho treinta	8:30
las diez y cinco	10:05	las nueve cuarenta y cinco	9:45

When saying something is at a certain time, ***ser*** is used.

EXAMPLE SENTENCES

1. Mi clase es a las diez veinte.
   My class is at 10:20.
2. Tengo trabajo desde las siete con cinco.
   I have work from 7:05.
3. Yo ceno con mi amigo a las seis treinta.
   I will eat dinner with my friend at 6:30.
4. Siempre tengo hambre a las doce y diez.
   I'm always hungry at 12:10.
5. A veces bebo té a las dos.
   Sometimes I drink tea at 2 o'clock.

One o'clock is the exception to the rule. It's the only non-plural time, ***la una en punto***.

6. Mañana mi clase es a la una en punto.
   Tomorrow my class is at 1 o'clock.
7. Tengo trabajo desde la una en punto.
   I have work from 1 o'clock.
8. Tengo trabajo hasta la una en punto.
   I have work until 1 o'clock.

Use ***desde*** for "from" a time.

● 18-3. Asking and answering "What time is it?"

Spanish has singular and plural ways to ask "What time is it?"

If you think literally, your head might explode, but both phrases above translate to "What time is it?" and both are used equally. This is just a quirk of Spanish since time can be plural. It also doesn't matter which one is asked, you can still answer with any time.

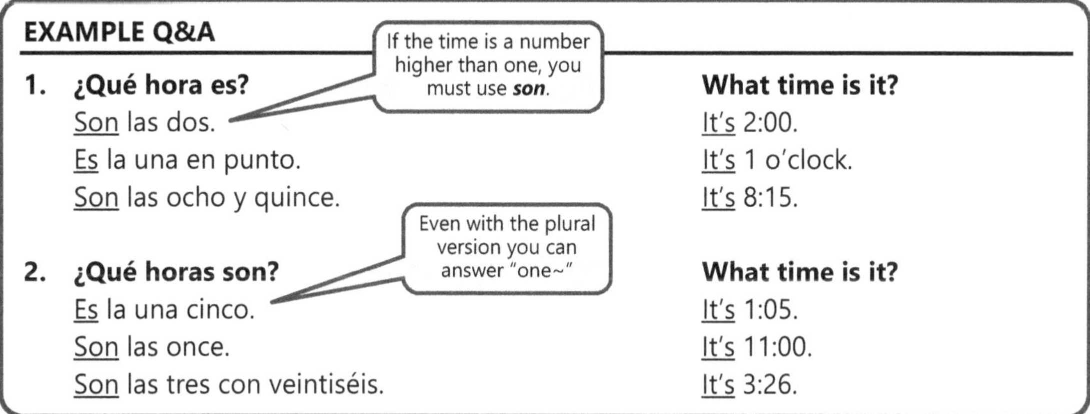

EXAMPLE Q&A

	Spanish	English
1.	**¿Qué hora es?**	**What time is it?**
	Son las dos.	It's 2:00.
	Es la una en punto.	It's 1 o'clock.
	Son las ocho y quince.	It's 8:15.
2.	**¿Qué horas son?**	**What time is it?**
	Es la una cinco.	It's 1:05.
	Son las once.	It's 11:00.
	Son las tres con veintiséis.	It's 3:26.

When not asking about time in general, but what time an event is, the plurality changes based on the item being asked about and not the time itself. You must also add the ***a*** (at)

EXAMPLE Q&A

1.	**¿A qué hora es tu clase?**	**At what time is your class?**
	Es a las dos.	It's at two.
	Es a la una.	It's at one.
2.	**¿A qué horas son tus clases?**	**At what times are your classes?**
	Son a las tres y las cinco.	They're at three and five.
	Una es a las tres y otra es a las cinco.	One is at three and the other is at five.

 *Más Detalles* **More Details** 

Don't make this time mistake!

It's a common mistake for even natives to ask ***¿A qué horas son?*** when asking time; but an ***a*** is never needed for just asking the time, it should be ***¿Qué horas son?***

18-4. More detailed ways to say time

Using the words from this lesson, we can say more nuanced times. For example, using ***y media*** we can say "half past" a time.

EXAMPLE Q&A (Y MEDIA)

1. **¿Qué horas son?**	**What time is it?**
Son las dos y media.	It's half past two.
Es a la una y media.	It's half past one.

We can do the same with ***y cuarto*** (quarter past).

EXAMPLE Q&A (Y CUARTO)

Q1. ¿A qué hora trabajas?
- Trabajo a las tres y cuarto.
- No trabajo hoy, pero tengo escuela a la una y media.

What time do you work?
- I work at quarter past three.
- I don't work today, but I have school at half past one.

We can specify the times of day by using ***la mañana*** (morning), ***la tarde*** (afternoon), ***la noche*** (night), and ***la madrugada*** (middle of the night).

Usage of these words is based on how *dark* or *light* it is outside.

dawn to noon

TIME + de la mañana
TIME in the morning

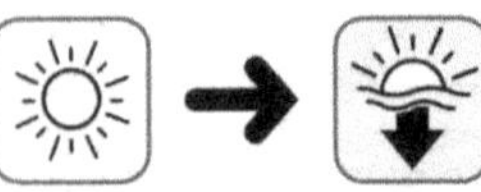
noon to dusk

TIME + de la tarde
TIME in the afternoon

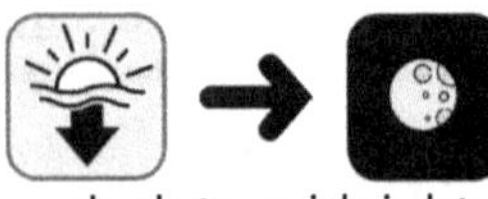
dusk to midnight

TIME + de la noche
TIME at night

midnight to dawn

TIME + de la madrugada
TIME in the middle of the night

EXAMPLE SENTENCES

1. Son las nueve de la noche.
   It's 9 at night.
2. Mis perros siempre despiertan a las tres de la madrugada.
   My dogs always wake up at three in the middle of the night.
3. Mañana voy al trabajo a las diez de la mañana.
   Tomorrow I go to work at 10 in the morning.
4. A veces cenamos a las cuatro de la tarde.
   Sometimes we have dinner at 4 in the afternoon.

This would be strange because dinner is normally later in the day.

EXAMPLE CONVERSATION

1. Conversation between a neighbor and a child.

¿A qué hora vas a la escuela?
Voy a las cinco de la mañana.
¿Entonces a qué hora vas a tu casa?
A veces al mediodía, pero hoy voy a las nueve de la noche.

What time do you go school?
I go at five in the morning.
So, what time do you go home?
Sometimes at noon, but today I'll go at nine at night.

18-5. When are we going to teach "when"?

Cuando means "when" in Spanish. Just like English, ***cuando*** can be used to ask "When are you going?" or to state a certain circumstance "When I was young..."

When ***cuando*** is used as a question word, or when it's used to refer to a specific time even outside of a question, an accent mark goes over ***a***.

EXAMPLE SENTENCES ('WHEN' AS A QUESTION)

1. ¿Cuándo vas a la escuela? — When do you go to school?
2. ¿Cuándo quieres beber café? — When do you want to drink coffee?
3. No sé cuándo es la fiesta. — I don't know when the party is.

When used to state a "circumstance", ***cuando*** never has an accent mark.

EXAMPLE SENTENCES ('WHEN' AS A CIRCUMSTANCE)

1. Cuando voy a la escuela, siempre voy con mi amigo Jorge.
   When I go to school, I always go with my friend Jorge.
2. Cuando mi mamá no cocina, yo solo como pizza.
   When my mom doesn't cook, I only eat pizza.

 *Más Detalles* **More Details** 

A bit more about cuando

We learned ***cuándo*** has an accent mark when asking "when" something happens but not with *circumstances*. However, in *casual* usage, especially online, accent marks are often omitted to save typing time. Since ***cuando*** and ***cuándo*** both mean "when", understanding shouldn't be a problem, but it's always better to use proper spelling.

Previously ***solo*** (only; alone) had an accent mark when it meant "only" as in ***sólo***. However, the *Royal Spanish Academy*, which maintains Spanish language worldwide, officially changed the rule so that, ***solo*** never has an accent mark, regardless of usage. Perhaps, eventually ***cuando*** might also undergo the same rule change.

18-6. A bit more on "from" and "to"

In this lesson we learned two ways to say "from" and "to". Because ***de*** (from) and ***a*** (to) are a bit more informal than ***desde*** (from) and ***hasta*** (to), ***de*** and ***a*** usage is a bit more flexible.

Flexibility with times

In English we say "from 9 to 5" instead of "from 9 o'clock to 5 o'clock". In Spanish, when using ***de*** (from) and ***a*** (to), we can simplify things more, dropping ***en punto*** and even ***las***.

EXAMPLE SENTENCES

1. Hoy trabajo de nueve a cinco. — Today I work from 9 to 5.
2. Mi clase es de dos a tres. — My class is from 2 to 3.

However, if using ***desde*** and ***hasta***, we are not be able to drop the ***las*** from the times.

EXAMPLE SENTENCES

1. Hoy trabajo desde las nueve hasta las cinco. — Today I work from 9 to 5.
2. Mi clase es desde las dos hasta las tres. — My class is from 2 to 3.

Flexibility with weekdays

Similar to time, with ***de*** (from) and ***a*** (to) we can drop the ***el*** / ***los*** when using weekdays.

EXAMPLE SENTENCES

1. Trabajo de domingo a martes. — I work from Sunday to Tuesday.
2. Mis clases son de lunes a viernes. — My classes are from Monday to Friday.

18 Practice and Review *Práctica y Repaso*

● 1. Question and Answer (Spanish → English)

Each question has multiple answers. Cover up the right side and try to translate.

1. **¿A qué hora trabajas?** — **What time do you work at?**
   - Trabajo a las seis de la mañana. — I work at six in the morning.
   - Trabajo a las siete y media. — I work at seven thirty.
   - No tengo trabajo. Yo soy estudiante. — I don't have a job. I'm a student.
   - Hoy a las ocho y mañana a la una. — Today at 8 and tomorrow at 1.

2. **¿Qué te gusta desayunar?** — **What do you like to eat for breakfast?**
   - No desayuno. Solo bebo café. — I don't eat breakfast. I just drink coffee.
   - Siempre desayuno fruta. — I always eat fruit for breakfast.
   - Yo nunca desayuno. — I never eat breakfast.
   - Me gusta desayunar huevos. — I like to eat eggs for breakfast.

3. **¿A qué hora es la cena?** — **What time is dinner?**
   - La cena es a las siete de la noche. — Dinner is at 7 at night.
   - Hoy la cena es a las diez. — Today dinner is at ten.
   - A las ocho en punto. — At eight o' clock.
   - No sé, tal vez a las nueve. — I don't know, maybe at nine.

4. **¿Vas mucho al cine?** — **Do you go to the movie theater a lot?**
   - No mucho, solo a veces. — Not much, only sometimes.
   - Sí, voy todos los fines de semana. — Yes, I go every weekend.
   - No, no me gusta ir al cine. — No, I don't like going to the movie theater.
   - Sí, voy todos los sábados. — Yes, I go every Saturday.

5. **¿Cuándo es tu clase de español?** — **When is your Spanish class?**
   - Mi clase de español es los lunes a las once. — My Spanish class is Mondays at eleven.
   - Mi clase es hoy al medio día. — My class is today at noon.
   - Mi clase es mañana a las tres en punto. — My class is tomorrow at three o'clock.

● 2. Question and answer (English → Spanish)

Each question has multiple answers. Cover up the right side and try to translate.

1. **What time is it?** — **¿Qué hora es?**
   - It's two thirty five. — Son las dos treinta y cinco.
   - It's seven fifty three. — Son las siete cincuenta y tres.
   - It's quarter past ten. — Son las diez y cuarto.

2. **What time is the class at?** — **¿A qué hora es la clase?**
   - The class is at 2:30. — La clase es a las dos y media.
   - The class is in ten minutes. — La clase es en diez minutos.
   - Do we have class today? — ¿Tenemos clase hoy?

3. **What time is breakfast usually?** — **¿A qué hora es el desayuno usualmente?**
   - Breakfast is at eight in the morning. — El desayuno es a las ocho de la mañana.
   - Breakfast is from six to ten. — El desayuno es de seis a diez.
   - It's from seven to twelve usually. — Es de siete a doce usualmente.

4. **When is the party?** — **¿Cuándo es la fiesta?**
   - The party is tomorrow. — La fiesta es mañana.
   - The party is at five in the afternoon. — La fiesta es a las cinco de la tarde.
   - The party is at seven in the evening. — La fiesta es a las siete de la noche.

5. **Do you guys like to cook?** — **¿Les gusta cocinar?**
   - Yes, we love to cook. — Sí, nos encanta cocinar.
   - No, we only cook sometimes. — No, solo cocinamos a veces.
   - Yes, but we don't have time, so we always eat out. — Sí, pero no tenemos tiempo, entonces siempre comemos afuera.

3. Spanish to English Conversation

Try translating the entire conversation before looking at the translation below.

1. Conversation between students.

Cuando tienes escuela ¿a qué hora duermes normalmente?
Normalmente a las once de la noche.
¿Y cuándo no tienes escuela?
Cuando no tengo escuela, también duermo a las once.

When you have school, what time do you sleep at normally?
Normally at 11 at night.
And when you don't have school?
When I don't have school, I also sleep at 11.

2. Conversation between friends deciding what to eat.

¿Qué quieres comer?
Tengo mucha hambre, pero no tengo mucho dinero.
Entonces, ¿quieres cocinar algo?
Sí, pero no tengo nada en mi refrigerador.

What do you want to eat?
I want to eat a burger, but I don't have a lot of money.
Then, co you want to cook something?
Yes, but I don't have anything in my fridge.

3. Conversation between a mother and her son.

¿A qué hora es tu examen mañana?
Mañana no tengo examen.
¿Cuándo es tu examen entonces?
Mi examen es el viernes.

What time is your test tomorrow?
I don't have a test tomorrow.
When is your test then?
My test is on Friday.

4. Conversation between strangers on the street.

Disculpe, ¿qué hora es?
Son las tres y media.
¡Muchas gracias! Adiós.
De nada. Adiós.

Excuse me, what time is it?
It's 3:30.
Thanks a lot! Good bye.
You're welcome. Good bye.

4. English to Spanish conversation

Try translating the entire conversation before looking at the translation below.

1. Conversation between friends discussing their jobs

Where do you work?
I work at a clothing store in the mall.
Do you like working there?
Yes, everyone is very kind.

¿En dónde trabajas?
Trabajo en una tienda de ropa en el centro comercial.
¿Te gusta trabajar ahí?
Sí, todos son muy amables.

2. Conversation between friends discussing their class schedule.

From what time to what time are your classes.
My classes are from seven to three.
Everyday?
Yes, from Monday to Friday. And you?
I have classes from nine to one, Monday to Thursday.
You don't have classes on Friday!?

¿Desde qué hora hasta qué hora son tus clases?
Mis clases son de siete a tres.
¿Todos los días?
Sí, de lunes a viernes. ¿Y tú?
Tengo clases de nueve a una, de lunes a jueves.
¿¡No tienes clases los viernes!?

3. Conversation over the phone with a friend runnning late to a party.

Hello. Are you coming to my party?
Yes, I'm going now.
From where are you coming?
I'm going from my parent's house. I'll be at your house at 5:30.
Ok, see you later.

Hola, ¿vienes a mi fiesta?
Sí, voy ahora.
¿De dónde vienes?
Voy de la casa de mis papás. Estoy en tu casa a las cinco y media.
Ok, nos vemos.

4. Conversation between friends walking on the street deciding what to eat.

What do you eat when your family is not home?
I usually eat spaghetti at that Italian restaurant over there.
Isn't it a bit expensive?
Yes, but it's delicious.
You only eat spaghetti.
No! I sometimes also eat something from the corner store.

¿Qué comes cuando tu familia no está en casa?
Usualmente como espagueti en aquel restaurante italiano.
¿No es un poco caro?
Sí, pero es delicioso.
¿Solo comes espagueti?
¡No! A veces también como algo de la tiendita.

18 Workbook 18: Lesson Activities

18 Vocabulary Drills *Ejercicios de Vocabulario*

1. Writing and Vocabulary

Write the Spanish for each of the pictures. Make sure to add accent marks when needed.

right, fish, night, breakfast, party, spaghetti, alone, t-shirt, left, sugar

1.__________ 2.__________ 3.__________ 4.__________ 5.__________

6.__________ 7.__________ 8.__________ 9.__________ 10.__________

2. Gender Matching

Write the following words and circle the gender companion word for each one.

mañana, espagueti, cena, desayuno, hora, tarde, noche, madrugada, fiesta, mediodía

1) el / la ____________________
(night)

2) el / la ____________________
(middle of the night)

3) el / la ____________________
(breakfast)

4) el / la ____________________
(dinner)

5) el / la ______________________
(hour / time)

6) el / la ______________________
(afternoon)

7) el / la ______________________
(party)

8) el / la ______________________
(noon)

9) el / la ______________________
(spaghetti)

10) el / la ______________________
(morning)

18 Usage Activities *Actividades de Uso*

3. Dealing with Time

Write the Spanish for each time including the time of day similar to the example.

6:20 PM **Example:** Las seis y veinte de la tarde.

12:17 AM 1) ______________________

5:15 AM 2) ______________________

10:03 PM 3) ______________________

3:00 PM 4) ______________________

8:30 AM 5) ______________________

2:10 AM 6) ______________________

4. Fix the sentence

The sentences below are wrong. Make only one change to correct them and then translate.

1. ¿Tú bebo café?

   Corrected Sentence: ______________________________

   Corrected Translation: ______________________________

2. Mi trabajo es a las una.

   Corrected Sentence: ______________________________

   Corrected Translation: ______________________________

3. Me gusto los perros.

   Corrected Sentence: ______________________________

   Corrected Translation: ______________________________

4. Mi amigo desayunas con su mamá todos los lunes.

   Corrected Sentence: ______________________________

   Corrected Translation: ______________________________

5. ¿Qué hora duermes?

   Corrected Sentence: ______________________________

   Corrected Translation: ______________________________

6. Trabajo de ocho y media desde cinco y cincuenta.

   Corrected Sentence: ______________________________

   Corrected Translation: ______________________________

5. Reading comprehension

Translate the following on a separate piece of paper or type in an electronic device.

The Weekend

Let's look into the schedules of Carlos and his girlfriend. Let's see who has a better schedule.

1. En este día de la semana, trabajo solo dos horas desde las cinco de la mañana.
2. Me gusta este trabajo. Pero no me gusta trabajar en las mañanas.
3. Mi novia también trabaja desde las cinco de la mañana.
4. A ella le gusta trabajar en las mañanas.
5. Pero, ella trabaja de lunes a miércoles. Solo tres días.
6. Y yo trabajo de lunes a viernes.
7. Mañana es sábado, entonces no tenemos trabajo.
8. En la mañana, vamos al cine.
9. Y en la noche cenamos en mi restaurante favorito con su familia.
10. ¡Me encanta el fin de semana!

6. Reading comprehension questions

Answer the following reading comprehension questions. Write full Spanish sentences.

1. ¿Con quién cena Carlos el sábado?

   ____

2. ¿Qué día es hoy?

   ____

3. ¿A dónde van Carlos y su novia el sábado en la mañana?

   ____

4. ¿A quién le gusta trabajar en las mañanas?

   ____

5. ¿De qué día a qué día trabaja la novia de Carlos?

____

6. ¿A dónde van Carlos y su novia el sábado en la noche?

____

7. ¿De qué hora a que hora trabaja Carlos los viernes?

____

8. ¿Desde qué hora tiene trabajo Carlos los domingos?

____

9. ¿Quién trabaja en el cine?

____

7. Spanish translation

Translate the following conversations into English.

1.
A: ¿Cuándo tienes clases? B: Tengo clases mañana. ¿Y tú? A: Yo también tengo clases de las siete de la mañana a las tres de la tarde. B: Yo solo tengo de siete a diez de la mañana.
A:
B:
A:
B:

8. English Translation

Translate the following conversations into Spanish.

1.
A: Excuse me, what time is it? B: It's 3:45. A: Thanks, see you! B: You're welcome, bye.
A:
B:
A:
B:

9. Verb conjugation drills

Fill in the blanks with the proper verb conjugations.

1. Dormir (to sleep)	
Pronouns	**Present Tense**
yo	
tú	
él / ella / usted	
nosotros	
ustedes	
ellos / ellas	

2. Despertar (to wake up)	
Pronouns	**Present Tense**
yo	
tú	
él / ella / usted	
nosotros	
ustedes	
ellos / ellas	

3. Desayunar (to eat breakfast)

Pronouns	Present Tense
yo	
tú	
él / ella / usted	
nosotros	
ustedes	
ellos / ellas	

4. Cenar (to eat dinner)

Pronouns	Present Tense
yo	
tú	
él / ella / usted	
nosotros	
ustedes	
ellos / ellas	

18 Answer Key *Clave de Respuestas*

1. Writing and Vocabulary (answers)

1. espagueti
spaghetti

2. izquierda
left

3. fiesta
party

4. camiseta
T-shirt

5. solo
alone

6. pez
fish

7. noche
night

8. azúcar
sugar

9. desayuno
breakfast

10. derecha
right

2. Gender Matching (answers)

1) la noche
2) la madrugada
3) el desayuno
4) la cena
5) la hora
6) la tarde
7) la fiesta
8) el mediodía
9) el espagueti
10) la mañana

3. Dealing with Time (answers)

( ) is optional

1) Las doce (y) diecisiete de la mañana.
2) Las cinco (y) quince de la mañana.
3) Las diez (y) tres de la noche.
4) Las tres de la tarde.
5) Las ocho y media de la mañana.
6) Las dos (y) diez de la madrugada.

4. Fix the sentence (answers)

1. ¿Tú beb**es** café? / Do you drink coffee?
2. Mi trabajo es a **la** una. / My work is at 1 (o'clock).
3. Me gust**an** los perros. / I like dogs.
4. Mi amigo desayun**a** con su mamá todos los lunes. / My friend eats with his mom every Monday.
5. ¿**A** qué hora duermes? / At what time do you sleep?
6. Trabajo de ocho y media **a** cinco y cincuenta. / I work from 8:30 to 5:15.

5.Reading comprehension (answers)

❶ On this day of the week I only work two hours from five in the morning.
❷ I like this job. But I don't like to work mornings.
❸ My girlfriend also works from five in the morning.
❹ She likes working mornings.
❺ But, she works from Monday to Wednesday. Only three days.

❻ And I work from Monday to Friday.
❼ Tomorrow is Saturday, so we don't have work.
❽ In the morning, we'll go to the movie theater.
❾ And in the evening we'll eat dinner at my favorite restaurant with her family.
❿ I love the weekend!

6. Reading comprehension questions (answers)

1. Who is Carlos eating dinner with on Saturday. Con su novia y la familia de su novia.
2. What day is today? Hoy es viernes.
3. Where are Carlos and his girlfriend going Saturday morning? Ellos van al cine.
4. Who likes to work in the mornings? A la novia de Carlos.
5. From what day to what day does Carlos's girlfriend work? De lunes a miércoles.
6. Where are Carlos and his girlfriend going Saturday night? Al restaurante favorito de Carlos.
7. From what time to what time does Carlos work on Friday? De cinco a siete.
8. What time does Carlos have work on Sundays? Él no tiene trabajo los domingos.
9. Who works at the movies? No sé. (this isn't stated in the selection)

7. Spanish translation (answers)

1. A: When do you have classes?
   B: I have classes tomorrow. And you?
   A: I also have classes from 7 in the morning to 3 in the afternoon.
   B. I only have classes from 7 to 10 in the morning.

8. English Translation (answers)

1. A: Disculpe, ¿qué hora es?
   B: Son las tres (y) cuarenta y cinco.
   A: Gracias, nos vemos.
   B: De nada, adiós.

9. Verb conjugation drills (answers)

1. dormir (to sleep)	
yo	duermo
tú	duermes
él / ella / usted	duerme
nosotros	dormimos
ustedes	duermen
ellos / ellas	duermen

2. despertar (to wake)	
yo	despierto
tú	despiertas
él / ella / usted	despierta
nosotros	despertamos
ustedes	despiertan
ellos / ellas	despiertan

3. desayunar (to eat breakfast)	
yo	desayuno
tú	desayunas
él / ella / usted	desayuna
nosotros	desayunamos
ustedes	desayunan
ellos / ellas	desayunan

4. cenar (to eat dinner)	
yo	ceno
tú	cenas
él / ella / usted	cena
nosotros	cenamos
ustedes	cenan
ellos / ellas	cenan

YOU DID IT!!!!!!!!!!!!!!!!

We are so happy for you!

(Don’t stop!)

GLOSSARY

English-Spanish

A

above | arriba 146
address | la dirección 213
afternoon | la tarde 262
age | la edad 55
all~ | todos 99
alone | solo 262
also | también 125
always | siempre 262
American | estadounidense 82
animal | el animal 169
another | el otro 125
anything | algo 125
anything | nada 125
apple | la manzana 65
Argentina | Argentina 82
Argentinian | argentino 82
at (a time) | a 262
ATM | el cajero automático 138
aunt | la tía 98
Australia | Australia 82
Australian | australiano 82

B

bacon | el tocino 213
bad | malo 170
ballad | la balada 238
banana | el plátano 65
bank | el banco 138
bathroom | el baño 124
bean | el frijol 65
bear | el oso 59
beautiful | bonito 170
bed | la cama 146
bedroom | el cuarto 124
bedroom | la habitación 124
below | abajo, debajo 146
between | entre 146
beverage | la bebida 125
big | grande 125
bit | un poco 214
black | negro 169
blue | azúl 146
blues | el blues 238
book | el libro 66
bookshop | la librería 124
bottle | la botella 214
boy | el niño 60
boy's name | Juan 83
boy's name | Luis 83
bra | el brasier 98
Brazil | Brasil 82
Brazilian | brasileño 82
bread | el pan 213
bread | el pan 65
breakfast | el desayuno 262
bride | la novia 99
briefs | el calzón 98
brother | el hermano 98
brown | café 169
building | el edificio 138
burger | la hamburguesa 238
bus | el autobús 99
but | pero 125
butter | la mantequilla 213

C

cafeteria | la cafetería 169
Canada | Canadá 65
candy (piece of) | el dulce 125
cantaloupe | el melón 55
card | la tarjeta 239
cash | el efectivo 214
cat | el gato 60
charger | el cargador 214
cheap | barato 170
child | el niño 60
Chile | Chile 82
Chilean | chileno 82
China | China 82
Chinese | chino 82
chocolate | el chocolate 169
church | la iglesia 124
city center | el centro 124
city | la ciudad 55
class | la clase 193
clothes | la ropa 99
coffee | el café 65
cold | frío 170
coldness | el frío 83
Colombia | Colombia 82
Colombian | colombiano 82
color | el color 169
come (to) | venir 214
computer | la computadora 170
convenience | la conveniencia 214
cook (to) | cocinar 99
cool | genial 170
corner | la esquina 214
cost (to) | costar 214
cousin (female) | la prima 98
cousin (male) | el primo 98
creature | la criatura 60
crocodile | el cocodrilo 59

D

dad | el papá 98
daughter | la hija 98
day | el día 99
delicious | delicioso 170
delivery person | el repartidor 59
deodorant | el desodorante 213
difficult | difícil 125
dining room | el comedor 124
dinner | la cena 262
doctor | el doctor 59
dog | el perro 60
dollar | el dólar 214
door | la puerta 99
downtown | el centro 124
drama | el drama 169
dress | el vestido 55
drink (to) | beber 66
drink | la bebida 125
driver (uber, bus etc.) | el chofer 59
drugstore | la farmacia 138
dumb | tonto 170

E

ear | la oreja 54
easy | fácil 125
eat (to) | comer 66
eat breakfast (to) | desayunar 262
eat dinner (to) | cenar 262
egg | el huevo 213
end | el fin 193
engineer | el ingeniero 59
England | Inglaterra 65
English (language) | el inglés 66
English | inglés 82
everything | todo 214
every~ | todos 99
excellent | excelente 125
expensive | caro 170
eye | el ojo 54

F

fall | el otoño 239
fast | veloz 125
father | el padre 98
favorite | favorito 193
finger | el dedo 54
fish | el pez 59
flavor | el sabor 238
flower | la flor 55
food, meal | la comida 66
foot | el pie 54
France | Francia 82
French | francés 82
fresh | fresco 193
Friday | el viernes 193
friend | el amigo 83
from | de 193
from | desde 262
fruit | la fruta 65

G

game | el juego 125
garage | el garaje 124
garden | el jardín 124
German | alemán 82
Germany | Alemania 82
giraffe | la jirafa 59
girl | la niña 60
girlfriend | la novia 99
girl' name | Sofía 83

room (hotel, etc.) | la habitación 124
room | el cuarto 124

S

sad | triste 146
salesperson | el vendedor 59
salt | la sal 238
sandwich | el sándwich 213
Saturday | el sábado 193
sauce | la salsa 214
school | la escuela 124
season | la estación 239
sell (to) | vender 214
seller | el vendedor 59
shampoo | el champú 213
she | ella 66
shirt | la camisa 98
shoe | el zapato 98
short | bajo 170
sister | la hermana 98
skirt | la falda 98
sleep (to) | dormir 262
sleepiness | el sueño 83
small | chico 146
small | pequeño 146
smart phone | el celular 170
smart | inteligente 125
soap | el jabón 213
sock | la calceta 98
soda | el refresco 238
soda | la gaseosa 238
something | algo 125
sometimes | a veces 262
son | el hijo 98
spaghetti | el espagueti 262
Spain | España 65
Spanish (language) | el español 66
Spanish | español 82
speak (to) | hablar 66
spicy | picante 193
spring | la primavera 239
station | la estación 124
steak | el bistec 238
stomach | el estómago 54
stop (bus stop, etc) | la parada 124
store | la tienda 99
strawberry | la fresa 170
strong | fuerte 125
study (to) | estudiar 66
sugar | el azúcar 238
summer | el verano 239
supermarket | el supermercado 138
sweet | dulce 125

T

t-shirt | la camiseta 98
tall | alto 170
taxi driver | el taxista 59
tea | el té 65
teacher | el maestro 60
telephone number | el número de teléfono 213
telephone | el teléfono 170
that (one) over there | aquello 193
that (one) | eso 193
theirs | suyo 193
their~ | su 99
there | ahí 170
they (feminine) | ellas 99
they (masculine) | ellos 99
thing | la cosa 239
thirst | la sed 83
this (one) | esto 193
Thursday | el jueves 193
tiger | el tigre 59
time | el tiempo 83
time | la hora 262
to come | venir 214
to cook | cocinar 99
to cost | costar 214
to drink | beber 66
to eat breakfast | desayunar 262
to eat dinner | cenar 262
to eat | comer 66
to go | ir 193
to have | tener 83
to like | agradar 239
to like | gustar 239
to live | vivir 66
to love | encantar 239
to need | necesitar 125
to open | abrir 99
to read | leer 99
to really like | encantar 239
to sell | vender 214
to sleep | dormir 262
to speak | hablar 66
to study | estudiar 66
to wake up | despertar 262
to want | querer 125
to work | trabajar 170
to write | escribir 66
to | a 193
to, (as in "to the right") | a 146
toast | el pan tostado 213
today | hoy 193
toilet paper | el papel de baño 213
tomorrow | el mañana 99
too | también 125
tooth brush | el cepillo de dientes 213
tooth paste | la pasta de dientes 213
too~ | muy 170
tree | el árbol 55
truck driver | el camionero 59
Tuesday | el martes 193

U

ugly | feo 170
uncle | el tío 98
under | abajo, debajo 146
United States | Estados Unidos 65
until | hasta 262
upstairs | arriba 146
usually | usualmente 262

V

vanilla | la vainilla 239
vegetable | la verdura 65
very~ | muy 170
volcano | el volcán 99

W

wake up (to) | despertar 262
want (to) | querer 125
warm | caliente 170
water | el agua 65
we (feminine) | nosotras 99
we (masculine) | nosotros 99
weak | débil 125
weather | el clima 239
Wednesday | el miércoles 193
week | la semana 193
well then | entonces 125
well | entonces 125
what time? | ¿qué hora? 262
what? | ¿qué? 125
when? | ¿cuándo? 262
where? | ¿dónde? 146
which? | ¿cuál? 214
white | blanco 169
who? | ¿quién? 193
window | la ventana 99
winter | el invierno 239
with | con 193
woman | la mujer 146
work (to) | trabajar 170
work | el trabajo 99
worker | el trabajador 60
wrestler | el luchador 60
write (to) | escribir 66

Y

yard | el jardín 124
yellow | amarillo 169
yes | sí 66
you (respectful) | usted 99
you guys | ustedes 99
you | tú 66
yours | tuyo 193
your~ | tu 99
y'all | ustedes 99

GLOSSARY

Spanish-English

normalmente | normally 262
número de teléfono (el) | telephone number 213

A

a | at (a time) 262
a | to 193
a | to, (as in "to the right") 146
a veces | sometimes 262
abajo, debajo | below; under 146
abogado (el) | lawyer 59
abrir | to open 99
adentro | inside 146
afuera | out; outside 146
agradar | to like 239
agua (el) | water 65
ahora (el) | now 125
ahí | there 170
Alemania | Germany 82
alemán | German 82
algo | something; anything 125
allí | over there 170
alto | tall 170
amable | kind 146
amarillo | yellow 169
amigo (el) | friend 83
animal (el) | animal 169
apellido (el) | last name 213
aquello | that (one) over there 193
aquí | here 170
Argentina | Argentina 82
argentino | Argentinian 82
arriba | above; upstairs 146
arroz (el) | rice 238
Australia | Australia 82
australiano | Australian 82
autobús (el) | bus 99
azúcar (el) | sugar 238
azúl | blue 146

B

bajo | short 170
balada (la) | ballad 238
banco (el) | bank 138
barato | cheap; inexpensive 170
baño (el) | bathroom; restroom 124
beber | to drink 66
bebida (la) | drink; beverage 125
biblioteca (la) | library 124
bistec (el) | steak 238
blanco | white 169
blues (el) | blues 238
boca (la) | mouth 54
bonito | beautiful 170
botella (la) | bottle 214
brasier (el) | bra 98
Brasil | Brazil 82
brasileño | Brazilian 82
bueno | good 170
búho (el) | owl 59

C

cabeza (la) | head 54
cafetería (la) | cafeteria 169
café (el) | coffee 65
café | brown 169
cajero automático (el) | ATM 138
calceta (la) | sock 98
caliente | hot; warm 170
calor (el) | heat 83
calzón (el) | briefs; panties 98
cama (la) | bed 146
camionero (el) | truck driver 59
camisa (la) | shirt 98
camiseta (la) | t-shirt 98
Canadá | Canada 65
canguro (el) | kangaroo 59
cargador (el) | charger 214
carne (la) | meat 65
caro | expensive 170
casa (la) | house; home 99
celular (el) | smart phone 170
cena (la) | dinner 262
cenar | to eat dinner 262
centro (el) | downtown; city center 124
centro comercial (el) | mall 138
cepillo de dientes (el) | tooth brush 213
cerdo (el) | pig 59
champú (el) | shampoo 213
chaqueta (la) | jacket 98
chico | small 146
Chile | Chile 82
chileno | Chilean 82
China | China 82
chino | Chinese 82
chocolate (el) | chocolate 169
chofer (el) | driver (uber, bus etc.) 59
cine (el) | movie theather 138
ciudad (la) | city 55
clase (la) | class 193
clima (el) | weather 239
cocina (la) | kitchen 124
cocinar | to cook 99
cocodrilo (el) | crocodile 59
Colombia | Colombia 82
colombiano | Colombian 82
color (el) | color 169
comedor (el) | dining room 124
comer | to eat 66
comida (la) | food, meal 66
computadora (la) | computer 170
con | with 193
conejo (el) | rabbit 59
conveniencia (la) | convenience 214
Corea | Korea 82
coreano | Korean 82
cosa (la) | thing 239
costar | to cost 214
criatura (la) | creature 60
cuarto (el) | room; bedroom 124
cárcel (la) | jail 124

D

de | from 193
de | of 146
dedo (el) | finger 54
delicioso | delicious 170
derecha | right 146
desayunar | to eat breakfast 262
desayuno (el) | breakfast 262
desde | from 262
desodorante (el) | deodorant 213
despertar | to wake up 262
difícil | difficult; hard 125
dinero (el) | money 83
dios (el) | god 99
dirección (la) | address 213
doctor (el) | doctor 59
dormir | to sleep 262
drama (el) | drama 169
dulce (el) | candy (piece of) 125
dulce | sweet 125
débil | weak 125
día (el) | day 99
dólar (el) | dollar 214

E

edad (la) | age 55
edificio (el) | building 138
efectivo (el) | cash 214
ella | she 66
ellas | they (feminine) 99
ellos | they (masculine) 99
en | in 66
en punto | ~o'clock 262
encantar | to really like; to love 239
entonces | well; well then 125
entre | between 146
escribir | to write 66
escuela (la) | school 124
eso | that (one) 193
espagueti (el) | spaghetti 262
España | Spain 65
español (el) | Spanish (language) 66
español | Spanish 82
esquina (la) | corner 214
estacionamiento (el) | parking lot 138
estación (la) | season 239
estación (la) | station 124
Estados Unidos | United States 65
estadounidense | American 82
estar | to be (is, am, are) 146
esto | this (one) 193

estudiar | to study 66
estómago (el) | stomach 54
excelente | excellent 125

F

falda (la) | skirt 98
farmacia (la) | drugstore 138
favorito | favorite 193
feliz | happy 146
feo | ugly 170
fiesta (la) | party 262
fin (el) | the end 193
flor (la) | flower 55
Francia | France 82
francés | French 82
fresa (la) | strawberry 170
fresco | fresh 193
frijol (el) | bean 65
fruta (la) | fruit 65
frío (el) | coldness 83
frío | cold 170
fuerte | strong 125
fácil | easy 125

G

garaje (el) | garage 124
gaseosa (la) | soda 238
gato (el) | cat 60
genial | cool; nice 170
grande | big; great 125
gustar | to like 239

H

habitación (la) | bedroom; room (hotel, etc.) 124
hablar | to speak 66
hambre (el) | hunger 83
hamburguesa (la) | burger 238
hasta | until 262
helado (el) | ice cream 66
hermana (la) | sister 98
hermano (el) | brother 98
hija (la) | daughter 98
hijo (el) | son 98
hip hop (el) | hip hop 238
hombre (el) | man 146
hora (la) | hour; time 262
horror (el) | horror 169
hotel (el) | hotel 169
hoy | today 193
huevo (el) | egg 213
hámster (el) | hamster 59

I

idioma (el) | language 125
iglesia (la) | church 124
ingeniero (el) | engineer 59
Inglaterra | England 65
inglés (el) | English (language) 66
inglés | English 82
inteligente | smart; intelligent 125
interesante | interesting 125
internet (el) | internet 169
interés (el) | interest 99
invierno (el) | winter 239
ir | to go 193
Italia | Italy 82
italiano | Italian 82
izquierda | left 146

J

jabón (el) | soap 213
jamón (el) | ham 213
japonés | Japanese 82
Japón | Japan 65
jardín (el) | garden; yard 124
jazz (el) | jazz 238
jirafa (la) | giraffe 59
Juan | (boy's name) 83
juego (el) | game 125
jueves (el) | Thursday 193
jugo (el) | juice 65

L

leche (la) | milk 213
leer | to read 99
librería (la) | bookshop 124
libro (el) | book 66
luchador (el) | wrestler 60
Luis | (boy's name) 83
lunes (el) | Monday 193
luz (la) | light 99

M

madre (la) | mother 98
madrugada (la) | middle of the night 262
maestro (el) | teacher 60
malo | bad 170
mamá (la) | mom 98
manga (el) | Japanese comics 99
mano (la) | hand 54
mantequilla (la) | butter 213
manzana (la) | apple 65
martes (el) | Tuesday 193
María | (girl's name) 83
mascota (la) | pet 83
mañana (el) | tomorrow 99
mañana (la) | morning 99
mediano | medium 146
mediodía (el) | noon 262
melón (el) | melon; cantaloupe 55
menos | less 239
mercado (el) | market 138
metal (el) | metal 238
mexicano | Mexican 193
mexicano | Mexican 82
mi | my~ 99
miércoles (el) | Wednesday 193
montaña (la) | mountain 55
mucho | a lot; much 214
mujer (la) | woman 146
muy | very~; too~ 170
más | more 239
México | Mexico 65
mío | mine 193
música (la) | music 238

N

nacionalidad (la) | nationality 213
nada | nothing; anything 125
naranja | orange 169
naranja (la) | orange (the fruit) 170
nariz (la) | nose 54
necesitar | to need 125
negro | black 169
neozelandés | New Zealand 82
niña (la) | girl 60
niño (el) | child; boy 60
no | no, not 66
noche (la) | night 170
noche (la) | night 262
nosotras | we (feminine) 99
nosotros | we (masculine) 99
novela (la) | novel 66
novia (la) | girlfriend; bride 99
Nueva Zelanda | New Zealand 82
nuevo | new 193
nuez (la) | nut 99
nunca | never 262
número (el) | number 55

O

ojo (el) | eye 54
oreja (la) | ear 54
oso (el) | bear 59
otoño (el) | fall 239
otro (el) | other; another 125

P

padre (el) | father 98
pan (el) | bread 213
pan (el) | bread 65
pan tostado (el) | toast 213
pantalón (el) | pant 98
papa (la) | potato 238
papde baño (el) | toilet paper 213
papá (el) | dad 98
parada (la) | stop (bus stop, etc) 124
parque (el) | park 124
pasta (la) | pasta 169
pasta de dientes (la) | tooth paste 213
película (la) | movie 170
pepperoni (el) | pepperoni 169
pequeño | small 146
pero | but 125
perro (el) | dog 60
pez (el) | fish 59
picante | spicy; hot 193

Other From Zero! Books

www.ingramcontent.com/pod-product-compliance
Lightning Source LLC
LaVergne TN
LVHW081315110826
845149LV00006B/1514
* 9 7 8 1 9 5 9 9 4 9 0 9 1 *